ASPECTS OF THE
THEORY OF SYNTAX

ASPECTS OF THE THEORY OF SYNTAX

Noam Chomsky

THE MIT PRESS

Massachusetts Institute of Technology
Cambridge, Massachusetts

ACKNOWLEDGMENT

This is Special Technical Report Number 11 of the Research Laboratory of Electronics of the Massachusetts Institute of Technology.

The Research Laboratory of Electronics is an interdepartmental laboratory in which faculty members and graduate students from numerous academic departments conduct research.

The research reported in this document was made possible in part by support extended the Massachusetts Institute of Technology, Research Laboratory of Electronics, by the JOINT SERVICES ELECTRONICS PROGRAMS (U.S. Army, U.S. Navy, and U.S. Air Force) under Contract No. DA36-039-AMC-03200(E); additional support was received from the U.S. Air Force (Electronic Systems Division under Contract AF19(628)-2487), the National Science Foundation (Grant GP-2495), the National Institutes of Health (Grant MH-04737-04), and The National Aeronautics and Space Administration (Grant NsG-496).

Eighteenth printing, 1994

Library of Congress Catalog Card Number: 65-19080
Printed in the United States of America

Preface

The idea that a language is based on a system of rules determining the interpretation of its infinitely many sentences is by no means novel. Well over a century ago, it was expressed with reasonable clarity by Wilhelm von Humboldt in his famous but rarely studied introduction to general linguistics (Humboldt, 1836). His view that a language "makes infinite use of finite means" and that its grammar must describe the processes that make this possible is, furthermore, an outgrowth of a persistent concern, within rationalistic philosophy of language and mind, with this "creative" aspect of language use (for discussion, see Chomsky, 1964, forthcoming). What is more, it seems that even Panini's grammar can be interpreted as a fragment of such a "generative grammar," in essentially the contemporary sense of this term.

Nevertheless, within modern linguistics, it is chiefly within the last few years that fairly substantial attempts have been made to construct explicit generative grammars for particular languages and to explore their consequences. No great surprise should be occasioned by the extensive discussion and debate concerning the proper formulation of the theory of generative grammar and the correct description of the languages that have been most intensively studied. The tentative character of any conclusions that can now be advanced concerning linguistic theory, or, for that matter, English grammar, should certainly be obvious to anyone working in this area. (It is sufficient to

consider the vast range of linguistic phenomena that have re-
sisted insightful formulation in any terms.) Still, it seems that
certain fairly substantial conclusions are emerging and receiving
continually increased support. In particular, the central role of
grammatical transformations in any empirically adequate generative grammar seems to me to be established quite firmly,
though there remain many questions as to the proper form
of the theory of transformational grammar.

This monograph is an exploratory study of various problems
that have arisen in the course of work on transformational grammar, which is presupposed throughout as a general framework
for the discussion. What is at issue here is precisely how this
theory should be formulated. This study deals, then, with questions that are at the border of research in transformational grammar. For some, definite answers will be proposed; but more
often the discussion will merely raise issues and consider possible approaches to them without reaching any definite conclusion. In Chapter 3, I shall sketch briefly what seems to me, in the
light of this discussion, the most promising direction for the
theory of generative grammar to take. But I should like to reiterate that this can be only a highly tentative proposal.

The monograph is organized in the following way. Chapter 1
sketches background assumptions. It contains little that is new,
but aims only to summarize and to clarify certain points that
are essential and that in some instances have been repeatedly
misunderstood. Chapters 2 and 3 deal with a variety of defects
in earlier versions of the theory of transformational grammar.
The position discussed is that of Chomsky (1957), Lees (1960a),
and many others. These writers take the syntactic component
of a transformational grammar to consist of a phrase structure
grammar as its *base*, and a system of transformations that map
structures generated by the base into actual sentences. This position is restated briefly at the beginning of Chapter 3. Chapter 2
is concerned with the base of the syntactic component, and with
difficulties that arise from the assumption that it is, strictly
speaking, a phrase structure grammar. Chapter 3 suggests a revision of the transformational component and its relation to base

structures. The notion of "grammatical transformation" itself is taken over without change (though with some simplifications). In Chapter 4, various residual problems are raised, and discussed briefly and quite inconclusively.

I should like to acknowledge with gratitude the very helpful comments of many friends and colleagues who have taken the trouble to read earlier versions of this manuscript. In particular, I am indebted to Morris Halle and Paul Postal, who have suggested many valuable improvements, as well as to Jerrold Katz, James McCawley, George Miller, and G. H. Matthews; and to many students whose reactions and ideas when this material has been presented have led to quite substantial modifications.

The writing of this book was completed while I was at Harvard University, Center for Cognitive Studies, supported in part by Grant No. MH 05120-04 and -05 from the National Institutes of Health to Harvard University, and in part by a fellowship of the American Council of Learned Societies.

NOAM CHOMSKY

Cambridge, Massachusetts
October 1964

Contents

ix

ASPECTS OF THE
THEORY OF SYNTAX

I

Methodological Preliminaries

§ 1. GENERATIVE GRAMMARS AS THEORIES OF LINGUISTIC COMPETENCE

THIS study will touch on a variety of topics in syntactic theory and English syntax, a few in some detail, several quite superficially, and none exhaustively. It will be concerned with the syntactic component of a generative grammar, that is, with the rules that specify the well-formed strings of minimal syntactically functioning units (*formatives*) and assign structural information of various kinds both to these strings and to strings that deviate from well-formedness in certain respects.

The general framework within which this investigation will proceed has been presented in many places, and some familiarity with the theoretical and descriptive studies listed in the bibliography is presupposed. In this chapter, I shall survey briefly some of the main background assumptions, making no serious attempt here to justify them but only to sketch them clearly.

Linguistic theory is concerned primarily with an ideal speaker-listener, in a completely homogeneous speech-community, who knows its language perfectly and is unaffected by such grammatically irrelevant conditions as memory limitations, distractions, shifts of attention and interest, and errors (random or characteristic) in applying his knowledge of the language in actual performance. This seems to me to have been the position of the founders of modern general linguistics, and no cogent reason for modifying it has been offered. To study actual linguistic performance, we must consider the interaction of a variety of factors, of which the underlying competence of the speaker-hearer is only one. In this respect, study of language is no different from empirical investigation of other complex phenomena.

We thus make a fundamental distinction between *competence* (the speaker-hearer's knowledge of his language) and *performance* (the actual use of language in concrete situations). Only under the idealization set forth in the preceding paragraph is performance a direct reflection of competence. In actual fact, it obviously could not directly reflect competence. A record of natural speech will show numerous false starts, deviations from rules, changes of plan in mid-course, and so on. The problem for the linguist, as well as for the child learning the language, is to determine from the data of performance the underlying system of rules that has been mastered by the speaker-hearer and that he puts to use in actual performance. Hence, in the technical sense, linguistic theory is mentalistic, since it is concerned with discovering a mental reality underlying actual behavior.[1] Observed use of language or hypothesized dispositions to respond, habits, and so on, may provide evidence as to the nature of this mental reality, but surely cannot constitute the actual subject matter of linguistics, if this is to be a serious discipline. The distinction I am noting here is related to the *langue-parole* distinction of Saussure; but it is necessary to reject his concept of *langue* as merely a systematic inventory of items and to return rather to the Humboldtian conception of underlying competence as a system of generative processes. For discussion, see Chomsky (1964).

A grammar of a language purports to be a description of the ideal speaker-hearer's intrinsic competence. If the grammar is, furthermore, perfectly explicit — in other words, if it does not rely on the intelligence of the understanding reader but rather provides an explicit analysis of his contribution — we may (somewhat redundantly) call it a *generative grammar*.

A fully adequate grammar must assign to each of an infinite range of sentences a structural description indicating how this sentence is understood by the ideal speaker-hearer. This is the traditional problem of descriptive linguistics, and traditional grammars give a wealth of information concerning structural descriptions of sentences. However, valuable as they obviously are, traditional grammars are deficient in that they leave unexpressed many of the basic regularities of the language with which they are concerned. This fact is particularly clear on the level of syntax, where no traditional or structuralist grammar goes beyond classification of particular examples to the stage of formulation of generative rules on any significant scale. An analysis of the best existing grammars will quickly reveal that this is a defect of principle, not just a matter of empirical detail or logical preciseness. Nevertheless, it seems obvious that the attempt to explore this largely uncharted territory can most profitably begin with a study of the kind of structural information presented by traditional grammars and the kind of linguistic processes that have been exhibited, however informally, in these grammars.[2]

The limitations of traditional and structuralist grammars should be clearly appreciated. Although such grammars may contain full and explicit lists of exceptions and irregularities, they provide only examples and hints concerning the regular and productive syntactic processes. Traditional linguistic theory was not unaware of this fact. For example, James Beattie (1788) remarks that

> Languages, therefore, resemble men in this respect, that, though each has peculiarities, whereby it is distinguished from every other, yet all have certain qualities in common. The peculiarities of individual tongues are explained in their respective grammars and dictionaries. Those things, that all languages have in common, or that are necessary to every language, are treated of in a science, which some have called *Universal* or *Philosophical* grammar.

Somewhat earlier, Du Marsais defines universal and particular grammar in the following way (1729; quoted in Sahlin, 1928, pp. 29–30):

> Il y a dans la grammaire des observations qui conviènnent à toutes les langues; ces observations forment ce qu'on appelle la grammaire

générale: telles sont les remarques que l'on a faites sur les sons articulés, sur les lettres qui sont les signes de ces sons; sur la nature des mots, et sur les différentes manières dont ils doivent être ou arrangés ou terminés pour faire un sens. Outre ces observations générales, il y en a qui ne sont propres qu'à une langue particulière; et c'est ce qui forme les grammaires particulières de chaque langue.

Within traditional linguistic theory, furthermore, it was clearly understood that one of the qualities that all languages have in common is their "creative" aspect. Thus an essential property of language is that it provides the means for expressing indefinitely many thoughts and for reacting appropriately in an indefinite range of new situations (for references, cf. Chomsky, 1964, forthcoming). The grammar of a particular language, then, is to be supplemented by a universal grammar that accommodates the creative aspect of language use and expresses the deep-seated regularities which, being universal, are omitted from the grammar itself. Therefore it is quite proper for a grammar to discuss only exceptions and irregularities in any detail. It is only when supplemented by a universal grammar that the grammar of a language provides a full account of the speaker-hearer's competence.

Modern linguistics, however, has not explicitly recognized the necessity for supplementing a "particular grammar" of a language by a universal grammar if it is to achieve descriptive adequacy. It has, in fact, characteristically rejected the study of universal grammar as misguided; and, as noted before, it has not attempted to deal with the creative aspect of language use. It thus suggests no way to overcome the fundamental descriptive inadequacy of structuralist grammars.

Another reason for the failure of traditional grammars, particular or universal, to attempt a precise statement of regular processes of sentence formation and sentence interpretation lay in the widely held belief that there is a "natural order of thoughts" that is mirrored by the order of words. Hence, the rules of sentence formation do not really belong to grammar but to some other subject in which the "order of thoughts" is studied. Thus in the *Grammaire générale et raisonnée* (Lancelot *et al.*, 1660) it is asserted that, aside from figurative speech, the sequence of words follows an "ordre naturel," which conforms "à l'expression naturelle de nos pensées." Consequently, few grammatical rules need be formulated beyond the rules of ellipsis, inversion, and so on, which determine the figurative use of language. The same view appears in many forms and variants. To mention just one additional example, in an interesting essay devoted largely to the question of how the simultaneous and sequential array of ideas is reflected in the order of words, Diderot concludes that French is unique among languages in the degree to which the order of words corresponds to the natural order of thoughts and ideas (Diderot, 1751). Thus "quel que soit l'ordre des termes dans une langue ancienne ou moderne, l'esprit de l'écrivain a suivi l'ordre didactique de la syntaxe française" (p. 390); "Nous disons les choses en français, comme l'esprit est forcé de les considérer en quelque langue qu'on écrive" (p. 371). With admirable consistency he goes on to conclude that "notre langue *pédestre* a sur les autres l'avantage de l'utile sur l'agréable" (p. 372); thus French is appropriate for the sciences, whereas Greek, Latin, Italian, and English "sont plus avantageuses pour les lettres." Moreover,

le bons sens choisirait la langue française; mais . . . l'imagination et les passions donneront la préférence aux langues anciennes et à celles de nos voisins . . . il faut parler français dans la société et dans les écoles de philosophie; et grec, latin, anglais, dans les chaires et sur les théâtres; . . . notre langue sera celle de la vérité, si jamais elle revient sur la terre; et . . . la grecque, la latine et les autres seront les langues de la fable et du mensonge. Le français est fait pour instruire, éclairer et convaincre; le grec, le latin, l'italien, l'anglais, pour persuader, émouvoir et tromper: parlez grec, latin, italien au peuple; mais parlez français au sage. (pp. 371-372)

In any event, insofar as the order of words is determined by factors independent of language, it is not necessary to describe it in a particular or universal grammar, and we therefore have principled grounds for excluding an explicit formulation of syntactic processes from grammar. It is worth noting that this naïve view of language structure persists to modern times in various forms, for example, in Saussure's image of a sequence of expressions corresponding to an amorphous sequence of concepts or in the common characterization of language use as merely a matter of use of words and phrases (for example, Ryle, 1953).

But the fundamental reason for this inadequacy of traditional grammars is a more technical one. Although it was well understood that linguistic processes are in some sense "creative," the technical devices for expressing a system of recursive processes were simply not available until much more recently. In fact, a real understanding of how a language can (in Humboldt's words) "make infinite use of finite means" has developed only within the last thirty years, in the course of studies in the foundations of mathematics. Now that these insights are readily available it is possible to return to the problems that were raised, but not solved, in traditional linguistic theory, and to attempt an explicit formulation of the "creative" processes of language. There is, in short, no longer a technical barrier to the full-scale study of generative grammars.

Returning to the main theme, by a generative grammar I mean simply a system of rules that in some explicit and well-defined way assigns structural descriptions to sentences. Obviously, every speaker of a language has mastered and internalized a generative grammar that expresses his knowledge of his language. This is not to say that he is aware of the rules of the grammar or even that he can become aware of them, or that his statements about his intuitive knowledge of the language are necessarily accurate. Any interesting generative grammar will be dealing, for the most part, with mental processes that are far beyond the level of actual or even potential consciousness; furthermore, it is quite apparent that a speaker's reports and viewpoints about his behavior and his competence may be in error. Thus a generative grammar attempts to specify what the speaker actually knows, not what he may report about his knowledge. Similarly, a theory of visual perception would attempt to account for what a person actually sees and the mechanisms that determine this rather than his statements about what he sees and why, though these statements may provide useful, in fact, compelling evidence for such a theory.

To avoid what has been a continuing misunderstanding, it is perhaps worth while to reiterate that a generative grammar is not a model for a speaker or a hearer. It attempts to characterize in the most neutral possible terms the knowledge of the language that provides the basis for actual use of language by a speaker-hearer. When we speak of a grammar as generating a sentence with a certain structural description, we mean simply that the grammar assigns this structural description to the sentence. When we say that a sentence has a certain derivation with respect to a particular generative grammar, we say nothing about how the speaker or hearer might proceed, in some practical or efficient way, to construct such a derivation. These questions belong to the theory of language use — the theory of performance. No doubt, a reasonable model of language use will incorporate, as a basic component, the generative grammar that expresses the speaker-hearer's knowledge of the language; but this generative grammar does not, in itself, prescribe the character or functioning of a perceptual model or a model of speech production. For various attempts to clarify this point, see Chomsky (1957), Gleason (1961), Miller and Chomsky (1963), and many other publications.

Confusion over this matter has been sufficiently persistent to suggest that a terminological change might be in order. Nevertheless, I think that the term "generative grammar" is completely appropriate, and have therefore continued to use it. The term "generate" is familiar in the sense intended here in logic, particularly in Post's theory of combinatorial systems. Furthermore, "generate" seems to be the most appropriate translation for Humboldt's term *erzeugen*, which he frequently uses, it seems, in essentially the sense here intended. Since this use of the term "generate" is well established both in logic and in the tradition of linguistic theory, I can see no reason for a revision of terminology.

§ 2. *TOWARD A THEORY OF PERFORMANCE*

There seems to be little reason to question the traditional view that investigation of performance will proceed only so far as understanding of underlying competence permits. Furthermore, recent work on performance seems to give new support to this assumption. To my knowledge, the only concrete results that have been achieved and the only clear suggestions that have been put forth concerning the theory of performance, outside of phonetics, have come from studies of performance models that incorporate generative grammars of specific kinds — that is, from studies that have been based on assumptions about underlying competence.[3] In particular, there are some suggestive observations concerning limitations on performance imposed by organization of memory and bounds on memory, and concerning the exploitation of grammatical devices to form deviant sentences of various types. The latter question is one to which we shall return in Chapters 2 and 4. To clarify further the distinction between competence and performance, it may be useful to summarize briefly some of the suggestions and results that have appeared in the last few years in the study of performance models with limitations of memory, time, and access.

For the purposes of this discussion, let us use the term "acceptable" to refer to utterances that are perfectly natural and immediately comprehensible without paper-and-pencil analysis, and in no way bizarre or outlandish. Obviously, acceptability will be a matter of degree, along various dimensions. One could go on to propose various operational tests to specify the notion more precisely (for example, rapidity, correctness, and uniformity of recall and recognition, normalcy of intonation).[4] For present purposes, it is unnecessary to delimit it more carefully. To illustrate, the sentences of (1) are somewhat more acceptable, in the intended sense, than those of (2):

(1) (i) I called up the man who wrote the book that you told me about

    (ii) quite a few of the students who you met who come from New York are friends of mine

(iii) John, Bill, Tom, and several of their friends visited us last night

(2) (i) I called the man who wrote the book that you told me about up

(ii) the man who the boy who the students recognized pointed out is a friend of mine

The more acceptable sentences are those that are more likely to be produced, more easily understood, less clumsy, and in some sense more natural.[5] The unacceptable sentences one would tend to avoid and replace by more acceptable variants, wherever possible, in actual discourse.

The notion "acceptable" is not to be confused with "grammatical." Acceptability is a concept that belongs to the study of performance, whereas grammaticalness belongs to the study of competence. The sentences of (2) are low on the scale of acceptability but high on the scale of grammaticalness, in the technical sense of this term. That is, the generative rules of the language assign an interpretation to them in exactly the way in which they assign an interpretation to the somewhat more acceptable sentences of (1). Like acceptability, grammaticalness is, no doubt, a matter of degree (cf. Chomsky, 1955, 1957, 1961), but the scales of grammaticalness and acceptability do not coincide. Grammaticalness is only one of many factors that interact to determine acceptability. Correspondingly, although one might propose various operational tests for acceptability, it is unlikely that a necessary and sufficient operational criterion might be invented for the much more abstract and far more important notion of grammaticalness. The unacceptable grammatical sentences often cannot be used, for reasons having to do, not with grammar, but rather with memory limitations, intonational and stylistic factors, "iconic" elements of discourse (for example, a tendency to place logical subject and object early rather than late; cf. note 32, Chapter 2, and note 9, Chapter 3), and so on. Note that it would be quite impossible to characterize the unacceptable sentences in grammatical terms. For example, we cannot formulate particular rules of the grammar in such a way as to exclude them. Nor, obviously, can we exclude them by limiting the number of reapplications of grammatical rules in the generation of a sentence, since unacceptability can just as well arise from application of distinct rules, each being applied only once. In fact, it is clear that we can characterize unacceptable sentences only in terms of some "global" property of derivations and the structures they define — a property that is attributable, not to a particular rule, but rather to the way in which the rules interrelate in a derivation.

This observation suggests that the study of performance could profitably begin with an investigation of the acceptability of the simplest formal structures in grammatical sentences. The most obvious formal property of utterances is their bracketing into constituents of various types, that is, the "tree structure" associated with them. Among such structures we can distinguish various kinds — for example, those to which we give the following conventional technical names, for the purposes of this discussion:

(3) (i) nested constructions
   (ii) self-embedded constructions
   (iii) multiple-branching constructions
   (iv) left-branching constructions
   (v) right-branching constructions

The phrases A and B form a nested construction if A falls totally within B, with some nonnull element to its left within B and some nonnull element to its right within B. Thus the phrase "the man who wrote the book that you told me about" is nested in the phrase "called the man who wrote the book that you told me about up," in (2i). The phrase A is self-embedded in B if A is nested in B and, furthermore, A is a phrase of the same type as B. Thus "who the students recognized" is self-embedded in "who the boy who the students recognized pointed out," in (2ii), since both are relative clauses. Thus nesting has to do with bracketing, and self-embedding with labeling of brackets as well. A multiple-branching construction is one with no internal structure. In (1iii), the Subject Noun Phrase is multiple-branch-

ing, since "John," "Bill," "Tom," and "several of their friends"
are its immediate constituents, and have no further association
among themselves. In terms of bracketing, a multiple-branching
construction has the form $[[A][B]\cdots[M]]$. A left-branching structure is of the form $[[[\cdots]\cdots]\cdots]$ — for example, in English, such
indefinitely iterable structures as $[[[[John]'s\ brother]'s\ father]'s$
$uncle]$ or $[[[the\ man\ who\ you\ met]\ from\ Boston]\ who\ was\ on\ the$
$train]$, or (1ii), which combines several kinds of left-branching.
Right-branching structures are those with the opposite property — for example, the Direct-Object of (1i) or $[this\ is\ [the\ cat$
$that\ caught\ [the\ rat\ that\ stole\ the\ cheese]]]$.

The effect of these superficial aspects of sentence structure on
performance has been a topic of study since almost the very
inception of recent work on generative grammar, and there are
some suggestive observations concerning their role in determining acceptability (that is, their role in limiting performance).
Summarizing this work briefly, the following observations seem
plausible:

(4) (i) repeated nesting contributes to unacceptability
   (ii) self-embedding contributes still more radically to unac-
        ceptability
  (iii) multiple-branching constructions are optimal in accepta-
        bility
   (iv) nesting of a long and complex element reduces accepta-
        bility
    (v) there are no clear examples of unacceptability involving
        only left-branching or only right-branching, although these
        constructions are unnatural in other ways — thus, for
        example, in reading the right-branching construction
        "this is the cat that caught the rat that stole the cheese,"
        the intonation breaks are ordinarily inserted in the wrong
        places (that is, after "cat" and "rat," instead of where the
        main brackets appear)

In some measure, these phenomena are easily explained. Thus
it is known (cf. Chomsky, 1959a; and for discussion, Chomsky,
1961, and Miller and Chomsky, 1963) that an optimal perceptual

device, even with a bounded memory, can accept unbounded left-branching and right-branching structures, though nested (hence ultimately self-embedded) structures go beyond its memory capacity. Thus case (4i) is simply a consequence of finiteness of memory, and the unacceptability of such examples as (2ii) raises no problem.

If (4ii) is correct,[6] then we have evidence for a conclusion about organization of memory that goes beyond the triviality that it must be finite in size. An optimal finite perceptual device of the type discussed in Chomsky (1959a) need have no more difficulty with self-embedding than with other kinds of nesting (see Bar-Hillel, Kasher, and Shamir, 1963, for a discussion of this point). To account for the greater unacceptability of self-embedding (assuming this to be a fact), we must add other conditions on the perceptual device beyond mere limitation of memory. We might assume, for example, that the perceptual device has a stock of analytic procedures available to it, one corresponding to each kind of phrase, and that it is organized in such a way that it is unable (or finds it difficult) to utilize a procedure φ while it is in the course of executing φ. This is not a necessary feature of a perceptual model, but it is a rather plausible one, and it would account for (4ii). See, in this connection, Miller and Isard (1964).

The high acceptability of multiple-branching, as in case (4iii), is easily explained on the rather plausible assumption that the ratio of number of phrases to number of formatives (the node-to-terminal node ratio, in a tree-diagram of a sentence) is a rough measure of the amount of computation that has to be performed in analysis. Thus multiple coordination would be the simplest kind of construction for an analytic device — it would impose the least strain on memory.[7] For discussion, see Miller and Chomsky (1963).

Case (4iv) suggests decay of memory, perhaps, but raises unsolved problems (see Chomsky, 1961, note 19).

Case (4v) follows from the result about optimal perceptual models mentioned earlier. But it is unclear why left- and right-branching structures should become unnatural after a certain point, if they actually do.[8]

One might ask whether attention to less superficial aspects of grammatical structure than those of (3) could lead to somewhat deeper conclusions about performance models. This seems entirely possible. For example, in Miller and Chomsky (1963) some syntactic and perceptual considerations are adduced in support of a suggestion (which is, to be sure, highly speculative) as to the somewhat more detailed organization of a perceptual device. In general, it seems that the study of performance models incorporating generative grammars may be a fruitful study; furthermore, it is difficult to imagine any other basis on which a theory of performance might develop.

There has been a fair amount of criticism of work in generative grammar on the grounds that it slights study of performance in favor of study of underlying competence. The facts, however, seem to be that the only studies of performance, outside of phonetics (but see note 3), are those carried out as a by-product of work in generative grammar. In particular, the study of memory limitations just summarized and the study of deviation from rules, as a stylistic device, to which we return in Chapters 2 and 4, have developed in this way. Furthermore, it seems that these lines of investigation can provide some insight into performance. Consequently, this criticism is unwarranted, and, furthermore, completely misdirected. It is the descriptivist limitation-in-principle to classification and organization of data, to "extracting patterns" from a corpus of observed speech, to describing "speech habits" or "habit structures," insofar as these may exist, etc., that precludes the development of a theory of actual performance.

§ 3. THE ORGANIZATION OF A GENERATIVE GRAMMAR

Returning now to the question of competence and the generative grammars that purport to describe it, we stress again that knowledge of a language involves the implicit ability to understand indefinitely many sentences.[9] Hence, a generative grammar must be a system of rules that can iterate to generate an in-

definitely large number of structures. This system of rules can
be analyzed into the three major components of a generative
grammar: the syntactic, phonological, and semantic components.[10]

The syntactic component specifies an infinite set of abstract
formal objects, each of which incorporates all information
relevant to a single interpretation of a particular sentence.[11]
Since I shall be concerned here only with the syntactic component, I shall use the term "sentence" to refer to strings of
formatives rather than to strings of phones. It will be recalled that
a string of formatives specifies a string of phones uniquely (up
to free variation), but not conversely.

The phonological component of a grammar determines the
phonetic form of a sentence generated by the syntactic rules.
That is, it relates a structure generated by the syntactic component to a phonetically represented signal. The semantic component determines the semantic interpretation of a sentence.
That is, it relates a structure generated by the syntactic component to a certain semantic representation. Both the phonological and semantic components are therefore purely interpretive. Each utilizes information provided by the syntactic
component concerning formatives, their inherent properties, and
their interrelations in a given sentence. Consequently, the syntactic component of a grammar must specify, for each sentence,
a *deep structure* that determines its semantic interpretation and
a *surface structure* that determines its phonetic interpretation.
The first of these is interpreted by the semantic component; the
second, by the phonological component.[12]

It might be supposed that surface structure and deep structure
will always be identical. In fact, one might briefly characterize
the syntactic theories that have arisen in modern structural
(taxonomic) linguistics as based on the assumption that deep and
surface structures are actually the same (cf. Postal, 1964a, Chomsky,
1964). The central idea of transformational grammar is that they
are, in general, distinct and that the surface structure is determined by repeated application of certain formal operations
called "grammatical transformations" to objects of a more

elementary sort. If this is true (as I assume, henceforth), then the syntactic component must generate deep and surface structures, for each sentence, and must interrelate them. This idea has been clarified substantially in recent work, in ways that will be described later. In Chapter 3, I shall present a specific and, in part, new proposal as to precisely how it should be formulated. For the moment, it is sufficient to observe that although the Immediate Constituent analysis (labeled bracketing) of an actual string of formatives may be adequate as an account of surface structure, it is certainly not adequate as an account of deep structure. My concern in this book is primarily with deep structure and, in particular, with the elementary objects of which deep structure is constituted.

To clarify exposition, I shall use the following terminology, with occasional revisions as the discussion proceeds.

The *base* of the syntactic component is a system of rules that generate a highly restricted (perhaps finite) set of *basic strings,* each with an associated structural description called a *base Phrase-marker.* These base Phrase-markers are the elementary units of which deep structures are constituted. I shall assume that no ambiguity is introduced by rules of the base. This assumption seems to me correct, but has no important consequences for what follows here, though it simplifies exposition. Underlying each sentence of the language there is a sequence of base Phrase-markers, each generated by the base of the syntactic component. I shall refer to this sequence as the *basis* of the sentence that it underlies.

In addition to its base, the syntactic component of a generative grammar contains a *transformational* subcomponent. This is concerned with generating a sentence, with its surface structure, from its basis. Some familiarity with the operation and effects of transformational rules is henceforth presupposed.

Since the base generates only a restricted set of base Phrase-markers, most sentences will have a sequence of such objects as an underlying basis. Among the sentences with a single base Phrase-marker as basis, we can delimit a proper subset called "kernel sentences." These are sentences of a particularly simple sort that involve a minimum of transformational apparatus in their generation. The notion "kernel sentence" has, I think, an important intuitive significance, but since kernel sentences play no distinctive role in generation or interpretation of sentences, I shall say nothing more about them here. One must be careful not to confuse kernel sentences with the basic strings that under-lie them. The basic strings and base Phrase-markers do, it seems, play a distinctive and crucial role in language use.

Since transformations will not be considered here in detail, no careful distinction will be made, in the case of a sentence with a single element in its basis, between the basic string underlying this sentence and the sentence itself. In other words, at many points in the exposition I shall make the tacit simplifying (and contrary-to-fact) assumption that the underlying basic string *is* the sentence, in this case, and that the base Phrase-marker is the surface structure as well as the deep structure. I shall try to select examples in such a way as to minimize possible confusion, but the simplifying assumption should be borne in mind through-out.

§ 4. *JUSTIFICATION OF GRAMMARS*

Before entering directly into an investigation of the syntactic component of a generative grammar, it is important to give some thought to several methodological questions of justification and adequacy.

There is, first of all, the question of how one is to obtain information about the speaker-hearer's competence, about his knowledge of the language. Like most facts of interest and importance, this is neither presented for direct observation nor extractable from data by inductive procedures of any known sort. Clearly, the actual data of linguistic performance will provide much evidence for determining the correctness of hypotheses about underlying linguistic structure, along with introspective reports (by the native speaker, or the linguist who has learned the language). This is the position that is universally adopted in practice, although there are methodological discussions that seem to imply a reluctance to use observed perform-ance or introspective reports as evidence for some underlying reality.

In brief, it is unfortunately the case that no adequate for-malizable techniques are known for obtaining reliable informa-tion concerning the facts of linguistic structure (nor is this particularly surprising). There are, in other words, very few reliable experimental or data-processing procedures for obtaining significant information concerning the linguistic intuition of the native speaker. It is important to bear in mind that when an operational procedure is proposed, it must be tested for adequacy (exactly as a theory of linguistic intuition — a grammar — must be tested for adequacy) by measuring it against the standard provided by the tacit knowledge that it attempts to specify and describe. Thus a proposed operational test for, say, segmenta-tion into words, must meet the empirical condition of conform-ing, in a mass of crucial and clear cases, to the linguistic intuition of the native speaker concerning such elements. Otherwise, it is without value. The same, obviously, is true in the case of any proposed operational procedure or any proposed grammatical description. If operational procedures were available that met this test, we might be justified in relying on their results in unclear and difficult cases. This remains a hope for the future rather than a present reality, however. This is the objective situa-tion of present-day linguistic work; allusions to presumably well-known "procedures of elicitation" or "objective methods" simply obscure the actual situation in which linguistic work must, for the present, proceed. Furthermore, there is no reason to expect that reliable operational criteria for the deeper and more important theoretical notions of linguistics (such as "gram-maticalness" and "paraphrase") will ever be forthcoming.

Even though few reliable operational procedures have been developed, the theoretical (that is, grammatical) investigation of the knowledge of the native speaker can proceed perfectly well. The critical problem for grammatical theory today is not a paucity of evidence but rather the inadequacy of present theories of language to account for masses of evidence that are hardly open to serious question. The problem for the grammarian is to construct a description and, where possible, an explanation for the enormous mass of unquestionable data concerning the linguistic intuition of the native speaker (often, himself); the problem for one concerned with operational procedures is to develop tests that give the correct results and make relevant distinctions. Neither the study of grammar nor the attempt to develop useful tests is hampered by lack of evidence with which to check results, for the present. We may hope that these efforts will converge, but they must obviously converge on the tacit knowledge of the native speaker if they are to be of any significance.

One may ask whether the necessity for present-day linguistics to give such priority to introspective evidence and to the linguistic intuition of the native speaker excludes it from the domain of science. The answer to this essentially terminological question seems to have no bearing at all on any serious issue. At most, it determines how we shall denote the kind of research that can be effectively carried out in the present state of our technique and understanding. However, this terminological question actually does relate to a different issue of some interest, namely the question whether the important feature of the successful sciences has been their search for insight or their concern for objectivity. The social and behavioral sciences provide ample evidence that objectivity can be pursued with little consequent gain in insight and understanding. On the other hand, a good case can be made for the view that the natural sciences have, by and large, sought objectivity primarily insofar as it is a tool for gaining insight (for providing phenomena that can suggest or test deeper explanatory hypotheses).

In any event, at a given stage of investigation, one whose concern is for insight and understanding (rather than for objectivity as a goal in itself) must ask whether or to what extent a wider range and more exact description of phenomena is relevant to solving the problems that he faces. In linguistics, it seems to me that sharpening of the data by more objective tests is a matter of small importance for the problems at hand. One who disagrees with this estimate of the present situation in linguistics can justify his belief in the current importance of more objective operational tests by showing how they can lead to new and deeper understanding of linguistic structure. Perhaps the day will come when the kinds of data that we now can obtain in abundance will be insufficient to resolve deeper questions concerning the structure of language. However, many questions that can realistically and significantly be formulated today do not demand evidence of a kind that is unavailable or unattainable without significant improvements in objectivity of experimental technique.

Although there is no way to avoid the traditional assumption that the speaker-hearer's linguistic intuition is the ultimate standard that determines the accuracy of any proposed grammar, linguistic theory, or operational test, it must be emphasized, once again, that this tacit knowledge may very well not be immediately available to the user of the language. To eliminate what has seemed to some an air of paradox in this remark, let me illustrate with a few examples.

If a sentence such as "flying planes can be dangerous" is presented in an appropriately constructed context, the listener will interpret it immediately in a unique way, and will fail to detect the ambiguity. In fact, he may reject the second interpretation, when this is pointed out to him, as forced or unnatural (independently of which interpretation he originally selected under contextual pressure). Nevertheless, his intuitive knowledge of the language is clearly such that both of the interpretations (corresponding to "flying planes are dangerous" and "flying planes is dangerous") are assigned to the sentence by the grammar he has internalized in some form.

In the case just mentioned, the ambiguity may be fairly transparent. But consider such a sentence as

(5) I had a book stolen

Few hearers may be aware of the fact that their internalized grammar in fact provides at least three structural descriptions for this sentence. Nevertheless, this fact can be brought to consciousness by consideration of slight elaborations of sentence

(5), for example: (i) "I had a book stolen from my car when I stupidly left the window open," that is, "someone stole a book from my car"; (ii) "I had a book stolen from his library by a professional thief who I hired to do the job," that is, "I had someone steal a book"; (iii) "I almost had a book stolen, but they caught me leaving the library with it," that is, "I had almost succeeded in stealing a book." In bringing to consciousness the triple ambiguity of (5) in this way, we present no new information to the hearer and teach him nothing new about his language but simply arrange matters in such a way that his linguistic intuition, previously obscured, becomes evident to him.

As a final illustration, consider the sentences

(6) I persuaded John to leave

(7) I expected John to leave

The first impression of the hearer may be that these sentences receive the same structural analysis. Even fairly careful thought may fail to show him that his internalized grammar assigns very different syntactic descriptions to these sentences. In fact, so far as I have been able to discover, no English grammar has pointed out the fundamental distinction between these two constructions (in particular, my own sketches of English grammar in Chomsky, 1955, 1962a, failed to note this). However, it is clear that the sentences (6) and (7) are not parallel in structure. The difference can be brought out by consideration of the sentences

(8) (i) I persuaded a specialist to examine John
    (ii) I persuaded John to be examined by a specialist

(9) (i) I expected a specialist to examine John
    (ii) I expected John to be examined by a specialist

The sentences (9i) and (9ii) are "cognitively synonymous": one is true if and only if the other is true. But no variety of even weak paraphrase holds between (8i) and (8ii). Thus (8i) can be true or false quite independently of the truth or falsity of (8ii). Whatever difference of connotation or "topic" or emphasis one may find between (9i) and (9ii) is just the difference that exists between the active sentence "a specialist will examine John" and its passive counterpart "John will be examined by a specialist." This is not at all the case with respect to (8), however. In fact, the underlying deep structure for (6) and (8ii) must show that "John" is the Direct-Object of the Verb Phrase as well as the grammatical Subject of the embedded sentence. Furthermore, in (8ii) "John" is the logical Direct-Object of the embedded sentence, whereas in (8i) the phrase "a specialist" is the Direct-Object of the Verb Phrase and the logical Subject of the embedded sentence. In (7), (9i), and (9ii), however, the Noun Phrases "John," "a specialist," and "John," respectively, have no grammatical functions other than those that are internal to the embedded sentence; in particular, "John" is the logical Direct-Object and "a specialist" the logical Subject in the embedded sentences of (9). Thus the underlying deep structures for (8i), (8ii), (9i), and (9ii) are, respectively, the following:[13]

(10) (i) Noun Phrase — Verb — Noun Phrase — Sentence
      (*I — persuaded — a specialist — a specialist will examine John*)
    (ii) Noun Phrase — Verb — Noun Phrase — Sentence
      (*I — persuaded — John — a specialist will examine John*)

(11) (i) Noun Phrase — Verb — Sentence
      (*I — expected — a specialist will examine John*)
    (ii) Noun Phrase — Verb — Sentence
      (*I — expected — a specialist will examine John*)

In the case of (10ii) and (11ii), the passive transformation will apply to the embedded sentence, and in all four cases other operations will give the final surface forms of (8) and (9). The important point in the present connection is that (8i) differs from (8ii) in underlying structure, although (9i) and (9ii) are essentially the same in underlying structure. This accounts for the difference in meaning. Notice, in support of this difference in analysis, that we can have "I persuaded John that (of the fact that) Sentence," but not "I expected John that (of the fact that) Sentence."

The example (6)–(7) serves to illustrate two important points. First, it shows how unrevealing surface structure may be as to underlying deep structure. Thus (6) and (7) are the same in surface structure, but very different in the deep structure that underlies them and determines their semantic interpretations. Second, it illustrates the elusiveness of the speaker's tacit knowledge. Until such examples as (8) and (9) are adduced, it may not be in the least clear to a speaker of English that the grammar that he has internalized in fact assigns very different syntactic analyses to the superficially analogous sentences (6) and (7).

In short, we must be careful not to overlook the fact that surface similarities may hide underlying distinctions of a fundamental nature, and that it may be necessary to guide and draw out the speaker's intuition in perhaps fairly subtle ways before we can determine what is the actual character of his knowledge of his language or of anything else. Neither point is new (the former is a commonplace of traditional linguistic theory and analytic philosophy; the latter is as old as Plato's *Meno*); both are too often overlooked.

A grammar can be regarded as a theory of a language; it is *descriptively adequate* to the extent that it correctly describes the intrinsic competence of the idealized native speaker. The structural descriptions assigned to sentences by the grammar, the distinctions that it makes between well-formed and deviant, and so on, must, for descriptive adequacy, correspond to the linguistic intuition of the native speaker (whether or not he may be immediately aware of this) in a substantial and significant class of crucial cases.

A linguistic theory must contain a definition of "grammar," that is, a specification of the class of potential grammars. We may, correspondingly, say that *a linguistic theory is descriptively adequate* if it makes a descriptively adequate grammar available for each natural language.

Although even descriptive adequacy on a large scale is by no means easy to approach, it is crucial for the productive development of linguistic theory that much higher goals than this be pursued. To facilitate the clear formulation of deeper questions, it is useful to consider the abstract problem of constructing an "acquisition model" for language, that is, a theory of language learning or grammar construction. Clearly, a child who has learned a language has developed an internal representation of a system of rules that determine how sentences are to be formed, used, and understood. Using the term "grammar" with a systematic ambiguity (to refer, first, to the native speaker's internally represented "theory of his language" and, second, to the linguist's account of this), we can say that the child has developed and internally represented a generative grammar, in the sense described. He has done this on the basis of observation of what we may call *primary linguistic data*. This must include examples of linguistic performance that are taken to be well-formed sentences, and may include also examples designated as nonsentences, and no doubt much other information of the sort that is required for language learning, whatever this may be (see pp. 31–32). On the basis of such data, the child constructs a grammar — that is, a theory of the language of which the well-formed sentences of the primary linguistic data constitute a small sample.[14] To learn a language, then, the child must have a method for devising an appropriate grammar, given primary linguistic data. As a precondition for language learning, he must possess, first, a linguistic theory that specifies the form of the grammar of a possible human language, and, second, a strategy for selecting a grammar of the appropriate form that is compatible with the primary linguistic data. As a long-range task for general linguistics, we might set the problem of developing an account of this innate linguistic theory that provides the basis for language learning. (Note that we are again using the term "theory" — in this case "theory of language" rather than "theory of a particular language" — with a systematic ambiguity, to refer both to the child's innate predisposition to learn a language of a certain type and to the linguist's account of this.)

To the extent that a linguistic theory succeeds in selecting a descriptively adequate grammar on the basis of primary linguistic data, we can say that it meets the condition of *explanatory adequacy*. That is, to this extent, it offers an explanation for the intuition of the native speaker on the basis of an empirical hypothesis concerning the innate predisposition of the child to develop a certain kind of theory to deal with the evidence presented to him. Any such hypothesis can be falsified (all too easily, in actual fact) by showing that it fails to provide a descriptively adequate grammar for primary linguistic data from some other language — evidently the child is not predisposed to learn one language rather than another. It is supported when it does provide an adequate explanation for some aspect of linguistic structure, an account of the way in which such knowledge might have been obtained.

Clearly, it would be utopian to expect to achieve explanatory adequacy on a large scale in the present state of linguistics. Nevertheless, considerations of explanatory adequacy are often critical for advancing linguistic theory. Gross coverage of a large mass of data can often be attained by conflicting theories; for precisely this reason it is not, in itself, an achievement of any particular theoretical interest or importance. As in any other field, the important problem in linguistics is to discover a complex of data that differentiates between conflicting conceptions of linguistic structure in that one of these conflicting theories can describe these data only by *ad hoc* means whereas the other can explain it on the basis of some empirical assumption about the form of language. Such small-scale studies of explanatory adequacy have, in fact, provided most of the evidence that has any serious bearing on the nature of linguistic structure. Thus whether we are comparing radically different theories of grammar or trying to determine the correctness of some particular aspect of one such theory, it is questions of explanatory adequacy that must, quite often, bear the burden of justification. This remark is in no way inconsistent with the fact that explanatory adequacy on a large scale is out of reach, for the present. It simply brings out the highly tentative character of any attempt to justify an empirical claim about linguistic structure.

To summarize briefly, there are two respects in which one can speak of "justifying a generative grammar." On one level (that of descriptive adequacy), the grammar is justified to the extent that it correctly describes its object, namely the linguistic intuition — the tacit competence — of the native speaker. In this sense, the grammar is justified on *external* grounds, on grounds of correspondence to linguistic fact. On a much deeper and hence much more rarely attainable level (that of explanatory adequacy), a grammar is justified to the extent that it is a *principled* descriptively adequate system, in that the linguistic theory with which it is associated selects this grammar over others, given primary linguistic data with which all are compatible. In this sense, the grammar is justified on *internal* grounds, on grounds of its relation to a linguistic theory that constitutes an explanatory hypothesis about the form of language as such. The problem of internal justification — of explanatory adequacy — is essentially the problem of constructing a theory of language acquisition, an account of the specific innate abilities that make this achievement possible.

§ 5. *FORMAL AND SUBSTANTIVE UNIVERSALS*

A theory of linguistic structure that aims for explanatory adequacy incorporates an account of linguistic universals, and it attributes tacit knowledge of these universals to the child. It proposes, then, that the child approaches the data with the presumption that they are drawn from a language of a certain antecedently well-defined type, his problem being to determine which of the (humanly) possible languages is that of the community in which he is placed. Language learning would be impossible unless this were the case. The important question is: What are the initial assumptions concerning the nature of language that the child brings to language learning, and how detailed and specific is the innate schema (the general definition of "grammar") that gradually becomes more explicit and differentiated as the child learns the language? For the present we cannot come at all close to making a hypothesis about innate schemata that is rich, detailed, and specific enough to account for the fact of language acquisition. Consequently, the main

task of linguistic theory must be to develop an account of
linguistic universals that, on the one hand, will not be falsified
by the actual diversity of languages and, on the other, will be
sufficiently rich and explicit to account for the rapidity and
uniformity of language learning, and the remarkable complexity and range of the generative grammars that are the
product of language learning.

The study of linguistic universals is the study of the properties of any generative grammar for a natural language. Particular assumptions about linguistic universals may pertain to
either the syntactic, semantic, or phonological component, or to
interrelations among the three components.

It is useful to classify linguistic universals as *formal* or *substantive*. A theory of substantive universals claims that items of a
particular kind in any language must be drawn from a fixed class
of items. For example, Jakobson's theory of distinctive features
can be interpreted as making an assertion about substantive
universals with respect to the phonological component of a
generative grammar. It asserts that each output of this component
consists of elements that are characterized in terms of some small
number of fixed, universal, phonetic features (perhaps on the
order of fifteen or twenty), each of which has a substantive
acoustic-articulatory characterization independent of any particular language. Traditional universal grammar was also a theory
of substantive universals, in this sense. It not only put forth
interesting views as to the nature of universal phonetics, but also
advanced the position that certain fixed syntactic categories
(Noun, Verb, etc.) can be found in the syntactic representations
of the sentences of any language, and that these provide the
general underlying syntactic structure of each language. A
theory of substantive semantic universals might hold for example, that certain designative functions must be carried out in
a specified way in each language. Thus it might assert that each
language will contain terms that designate persons or lexical
items referring to certain specific kinds of objects, feelings, behavior, and so on.

It is also possible, however, to search for universal properties of a more abstract sort. Consider a claim that the grammar of every language meets certain specified formal conditions. The truth of this hypothesis would not in itself imply that any particular rule must appear in all or even in any two grammars. The property of having a grammar meeting a certain abstract condition might be called a *formal* linguistic universal, if shown to be a general property of natural languages. Recent attempts to specify the abstract conditions that a generative grammar must meet have produced a variety of proposals concerning formal universals, in this sense. For example, consider the proposal that the syntactic component of a grammar must contain transformational rules (these being operations of a highly special kind) mapping semantically interpreted deep structures into phonetically interpreted surface structures, or the proposal that the phonological component of a grammar consists of a sequence of rules, a subset of which may apply cyclically to successively more dominant constituents of the surface structure (a transformational cycle, in the sense of much recent work on phonology). Such proposals make claims of a quite different sort from the claim that certain substantive phonetic elements are available for phonetic representation in all languages, or that certain specific categories must be central to the syntax of all languages, or that certain semantic features or categories provide a universal framework for semantic description. Substantive universals such as these concern the vocabulary for the description of language; formal universals involve rather the character of the rules that appear in grammars and the ways in which they can be interconnected.

On the semantic level, too, it is possible to search for what might be called formal universals, in essentially the sense just described. Consider, for example, the assumption that proper names, in any language, must designate objects meeting a condition of spatiotemporal contiguity,[15] and that the same is true of other terms designating objects; or the condition that the color words of any language must subdivide the color spectrum into continuous segments; or the condition that artifacts are defined in terms of certain human goals, needs, and functions instead of solely in terms of physical qualities.[16] Formal constraints of this sort on a system of concepts may severely limit the choice (by the child, or the linguist) of a descriptive grammar, given primary linguistic data.

The existence of deep-seated formal universals, in the sense suggested by such examples as these, implies that all languages are cut to the same pattern, but does not imply that there is any point by point correspondence between particular languages. It does not, for example, imply that there must be some reasonable procedure for translating between languages.[17]

In general, there is no doubt that a theory of language, regarded as a hypothesis about the innate "language-forming capacity" of humans, should concern itself with both substantive and formal universals. But whereas substantive universals have been the traditional concern of general linguistic theory, investigations of the abstract conditions that must be satisfied by any generative grammar have been undertaken only quite recently. They seem to offer extremely rich and varied possibilities for study in all aspects of grammar.

§ 6. FURTHER REMARKS ON DESCRIPTIVE AND EXPLANATORY THEORIES

Let us consider with somewhat greater care just what is involved in the construction of an "acquisition model" for language. A child who is capable of language learning must have

(12) (i) a technique for representing input signals
  (ii) a way of representing structural information about these signals
  (iii) some initial delimitation of a class of possible hypotheses about language structure
  (iv) a method for determining what each such hypothesis implies with respect to each sentence
  (v) a method for selecting one of the (presumably, infinitely many) hypotheses that are allowed by (iii) and are compatible with the given primary linguistic data

Correspondingly, a theory of linguistic structure that aims for explanatory adequacy must contain

(13) (i) a universal phonetic theory that defines the notion "possible sentence"
  (ii) a definition of "structural description"
  (iii) a definition of "generative grammar"
  (iv) a method for determining the structural description of a sentence, given a grammar
  (v) a way of evaluating alternative proposed grammars

Putting the same requirements in somewhat different terms, we must require of such a linguistic theory that it provide for

(14) (i) an enumeration of the class $s_1, s_2, \cdots$ of possible sentences
  (ii) an enumeration of the class $SD_1, SD_2, \cdots$ of possible structural descriptions
  (iii) an enumeration of the class $G_1, G_2, \cdots$ of possible generative grammars
  (iv) specification of a function f such that $SD_{f(i,j)}$ is the structural description assigned to sentence s_i by grammar G_j, for arbitrary i,j[18]
  (v) specification of a function m such that $m(i)$ is an integer associated with the grammar G_i as its value (with, let us say, lower value indicated by higher number)

Conditions of at least this strength are entailed by the decision to aim for explanatory adequacy.

A theory meeting these conditions would attempt to account for language learning in the following way. Consider first the nature of primary linguistic data. This consists of a finite amount of information about sentences, which, furthermore, must be rather restricted in scope, considering the time limitations that are in effect, and fairly degenerate in quality (cf. note 14). For example, certain signals might be accepted as properly formed sentences, while others are classed as nonsentences, as a result of correction of the learner's attempts on the part of the linguistic community. Furthermore, the conditions of use might be such as to require that structural descriptions be assigned to these objects in certain ways. That the latter is a prerequisite for language acquisition seems to follow from the widely accepted (but, for the moment, quite unsupported) view that there must be a partially semantic basis for the acquisition of syntax or for the justification of hypotheses about the syntactic component of a grammar. Incidentally, it is often not realized how strong a claim this is about the innate concept-forming abilities of the child and the system of linguistic universals that these abilities imply. Thus what is maintained, presumably, is that the child has an innate theory of potential structural descriptions that is sufficiently rich and fully developed so that he is able to determine, from a real situation in which a signal occurs, which structural descriptions may be appropriate to this signal, and also that he is able to do this in part in advance of any assumption as to the linguistic structure of this signal. To say that the assumption about innate capacity is extremely strong is, of course, not to say that it is incorrect. Let us, in any event, assume tentatively that the primary linguistic data consist of signals classified as sentences and nonsentences, and a partial and tentative pairing of signals with structural descriptions.

A language-acquisition device that meets conditions (i)–(iv) is capable of utilizing such primary linguistic data as the empirical basis for language learning. This device must search through the set of possible hypotheses G_1, G_2, $\cdots$, which are available to it by virtue of condition (iii), and must select grammars that are compatible with the primary linguistic data, represented in terms of (i) and (ii). It is possible to test compatibility by virtue of the fact that the device meets condition (iv). The device would then select one of these potential grammars by the evaluation measure guaranteed by (v).[19] The selected grammar now provides the device with a method for interpreting an arbitrary sentence, by virtue of (ii) and (iv). That is to say, the device has now constructed a theory of the language of which the primary linguistic data are a sample. The theory that the device has now selected and internally represented specifies its tacit competence, its knowledge of the language. The child who acquires a language in this way of course knows a great deal more than he has "learned." His knowledge of the language, as this is determined by his internalized grammar, goes far beyond the presented primary linguistic data and is in no sense an "inductive generalization" from these data.

This account of language learning can, obviously, be paraphrased directly as a description of how the linguist whose work is guided by a linguistic theory meeting conditions (i)–(v) would justify a grammar that he constructs for a language on the basis of given primary linguistic data.[20]

Notice, incidentally, that care must be taken to distinguish several different ways in which primary linguistic data may be necessary for language learning. In part, such data determine to which of the possible languages (that is, the languages provided with grammars in accordance with the a priori constraint (iii)) the language learner is being exposed, and it is this function of the primary linguistic data that we are considering here. But such data may play an entirely different role as well; namely, certain kinds of data and experience may be required in order to set the language-acquisition device into operation, although they may not affect the manner of its functioning in the least. Thus it has been found that semantic reference may greatly facilitate performance in a syntax-learning experiment, even though it does not, apparently, affect the *manner* in which acquisition of syntax proceeds; that is, it plays no role in determining which hypotheses are selected by the learner (Miller and Norman, 1964). Similarly, it would not be at all surprising to find that normal language learning requires use of language in real-life situations, in some way. But this, if true, would not be sufficient to show that information regarding situational context (in particular, a pairing of signals with structural descriptions that is at least in part prior to assumptions about syntactic structure) plays any role in determining how language is acquired, once the mechanism is put to work and the task of language learning is undertaken by the child. This distinction is quite familiar outside of the domain of language acquisition. For example, Richard Held has shown in numerous experiments that under certain circumstances reafferent stimulation (that is, stimulation resulting from voluntary activity) is a prerequisite to the development of a concept of visual space, although it may not determine the character of this concept (cf. Held and Hein, 1963; Held and Freedman, 1963, and references cited there). Or, to take one of innumerable examples from studies of animal learning, it has been observed (Lemmon and Patterson, 1964) that depth perception in lambs is considerably facilitated by mother-neonate contact, although again there is no reason to suppose that the nature of the lamb's "theory of visual space" depends on this contact.

In studying the actual character of learning, linguistic or otherwise, it is of course necessary to distinguish carefully between these two functions of external data — the function of initiating or facilitating the operation of innate mechanisms and the function of determining in part the direction that learning will take.[21]

Returning now to the main theme, we shall call a theory of linguistic structure that meets conditions (i)–(v) an *explanatory theory*, and a theory that meets conditions (i)–(iv) a *descriptive theory*. In fact, a linguistic theory that is concerned only with descriptive adequacy will limit its attention to topics (i)–(iv). Such a theory must, in other words, make available a class of generative grammars containing, for each language, a descriptively adequate grammar of this language — a grammar that (by means of (iv)) assigns structural descriptions to sentences in accordance with the linguistic competence of the native speaker. A theory of language is empirically significant only to the extent that it meets conditions (i)–(iv). The further question of explanatory adequacy arises only in connection with a theory that also meets condition (v) (but see p. 36). In other words, it arises only to the extent that the theory provides a principled basis for selecting a descriptively adequate grammar on the basis of primary linguistic data by the use of a well-defined evaluation measure.

This account is misleading in one important respect. It suggests that to raise a descriptively adequate theory to the level of explanatory adequacy one needs only to define an appropriate evaluation measure. This is incorrect, however. A theory may be descriptively adequate, in the sense just defined, and yet provide such a wide range of potential grammars that there is no possibility of discovering a formal property distinguishing the descriptively adequate grammars, in general, from among the mass of grammars compatible with whatever data are available. In fact, the real problem is almost always to restrict the range of possible hypotheses by adding additional structure to the notion "generative grammar." For the construction of a reasonable acquisition model, it is necessary to reduce the class of attainable[22] grammars compatible with given primary linguistic data to the point where selection among them can be made by a formal evaluation measure. This requires a precise and narrow delimitation of the notion "generative grammar" — a restrictive and rich hypothesis concerning the universal properties that determine the form of language, in the traditional sense of this term.

The same point can be put in a somewhat different way. Given a variety of descriptively adequate grammars for natural languages, we are interested in determining to what extent they are unique and to what extent there are deep underlying similarities among them that are attributable to the form of language as such. Real progress in linguistics consists in the discovery that certain features of given languages can be reduced to universal properties of language, and explained in terms of these deeper aspects of linguistic form. Thus the major endeavor of the linguist must be to enrich the theory of linguistic form by formulating more specific constraints and conditions on the notion "generative grammar." Where this can be done, particular grammars can be simplified by eliminating from them descriptive statements that are attributable to the general theory of grammar (cf. § 5). For example, if we conclude that the transformational cycle[23] is a universal feature of the phonological component, it is unnecessary, in the grammar of English, to describe the manner of functioning of those phonological rules that involve syntactic structure. This description will now have been abstracted from the grammar of English and stated as a formal linguistic universal, as part of the theory of generative grammar. Obviously, this conclusion, if justified, would represent an important advance in the theory of language, since it would then have been shown that what appears to be a peculiarity of English is actually explicable in terms of a general and deep empirical assumption about the nature of language, an assumption that can be refuted, if false, by study of descriptively adequate grammars of other languages.

In short, the most serious problem that arises in the attempt to achieve explanatory adequacy is that of characterizing the notion "generative grammar" in a sufficiently rich, detailed, and highly structured way. A theory of grammar may be descriptively adequate and yet leave unexpressed major features that are defining properties of natural language and that distinguish natural languages from arbitrary symbolic systems. It is for just this reason that the attempt to achieve explanatory adequacy — the attempt to discover linguistic universals — is so crucial at every stage of understanding of linguistic structure, despite the fact that even descriptive adequacy on a broad scale may be an unrealized goal. It is not necessary to achieve descriptive adequacy before raising questions of explanatory adequacy. On the contrary, the crucial questions, the questions that have the greatest bearing on our concept of language and on descriptive practice as well, are almost always those involving explanatory adequacy with respect to particular aspects of language structure.

To acquire language, a child must devise a hypothesis compatible with presented data — he must select from the store of potential grammars a specific one that is appropriate to the data available to him. It is logically possible that the data might be sufficiently rich and the class of potential grammars sufficiently limited so that no more than a single permitted grammar will be compatible with the available data at the moment of successful language acquisition, in our idealized "instantaneous" model (cf. notes 19 and 22). In this case, no evaluation procedure will be necessary as a part of linguistic theory — that is, as an innate property of an organism or a device capable of language acquisition. It is rather difficult to imagine how in detail this logical possibility might be realized, and all concrete attempts to formulate an empirically adequate linguistic theory certainly leave ample room for mutually inconsistent grammars, all compatible with primary data of any conceivable sort. All such theories therefore require supplementation by an evaluation measure if language acquisition is to be accounted for and selection of specific grammars is to be justified; and I shall continue to assume tentatively, as heretofore, that this is an empirical fact about the innate human *faculté de langage* and consequently about general linguistic theory as well.

§ 7. *ON EVALUATION PROCEDURES*

The status of an evaluation procedure for grammars (see condition (v) of (12)–(14)) has often been misconstrued. It must first of all be kept clearly in mind that such a measure is not given a priori, in some manner. Rather, any proposal concerning such a measure is an empirical hypothesis about the nature of language. This is evident from the preceding discussion. Suppose that we have a descriptive theory, meeting conditions (i)–(iv) of (12)–(14) in some fixed way. Given primarily linguistic data D, different choices of an evaluation measure will assign quite different ranks to alternative hypotheses (alternative grammars) as to the language of which D is a sample, and will therefore lead to entirely different predictions as to how a person who learns a language on the basis of D will interpret new sentences not in D. Consequently, choice of an evaluation measure is an empirical matter, and particular proposals are correct or incorrect.

Perhaps confusion about this matter can be traced to the use of the term "simplicity measure" for particular proposed evaluation measures, it being assumed that "simplicity" is a general notion somehow understood in advance outside of linguistic theory. This is a misconception, however. In the context of this discussion, "simplicity" (that is, the evaluation measure m of (v)) is a notion to be defined within linguistic theory along with "grammar," "phoneme," etc. Choice of a simplicity measure is rather like determination of the value of a physical constant. We are given, in part, an empirical pairing of certain kinds of primary linguistic data with certain grammars that are in fact constructed by people presented with such data. A proposed simplicity measure constitutes part of the attempt to determine precisely the nature of this association. If a particular formulation of (i)–(iv) is assumed, and if pairs (D_1, G_1), (D_2, G_2), $\cdots$ of primary linguistic data and descriptively adequate grammars are given, the problem of defining "simplicity" is just the problem of discovering how G_i is determined by D_i, for each i. Suppose, in other words, that we regard an acquisition model for language as an input-output device that determines a particular generative grammar as "output," given certain primary linguistic data as input. A proposed simplicity measure, taken together with a specification of (i)–(iv), constitutes a hypothesis concerning the nature of such a device. Choice of a simplicity measure is therefore an empirical matter with empirical consequences.

All of this has been said before. I repeat it at such length because it has been so grossly misunderstood.

It is also apparent that evaluation measures of the kinds that have been discussed in the literature on generative grammar cannot be used to compare different theories of grammar; comparison of a grammar from one class of proposed grammars with a grammar from another class, *by such a measure*, is utterly without sense. Rather, an evaluation measure of this kind is an essential part of a particular theory of grammar that aims at explanatory adequacy. It is true that there is a sense in which alternative theories of language (or alternative theories in other domains) can be compared as to simplicity and elegance. What we have been discussing here, however, is not this general question but rather the problem of comparing two theories of a language — two grammars of this language — in terms of a particular general linguistic theory. This is, then, a matter of formulating an explanatory theory of language; it is not to be confused with the problem of choosing among competing theories of language. Choice among competing theories of language is of course a fundamental question and should also be settled, insofar as possible, on empirical grounds of descriptive and explanatory adequacy. But it is not the question involved in the use of an evaluation measure in the attempt to achieve explanatory adequacy.

As a concrete illustration, consider the question of whether the rules of a grammar should be unordered (let us call this the linguistic theory T_U) or ordered in some specific way (the theory T_0). A priori, there is no way to decide which of the two is correct. There is no known absolute sense of "simplicity" or "elegance," developed within linguistic theory or general epistemology, in accordance with which T_U and T_0 can be compared. It is quite meaningless, therefore, to maintain that in some absolute sense T_U is "simpler" than T_0 or conversely. One can easily invent a general concept of "simplicity" that will prefer T_U to T_0, or T_0 to T_U; in neither case will this concept have any known justification. Certain measures of evaluation have been proposed and in part empirically justified within linguistics — for example, minimization of feature specification (as discussed in Halle, 1959a, 1961, 1962a, 1964) or the measure based on abbreviatory notations (discussed on pp. 42f.). These measures do not apply, because they are internal to a specific linguistic theory and their empirical justification relies essentially on this fact. To choose between T_U and T_0, we must proceed in an entirely different way. We must ask whether T_U or T_0 provides descriptively adequate grammars for natural languages, or leads to explanatory adequacy. This is a perfectly meaningful empirical question if the theories in question are stated with sufficient care. For example, if $T_U{}^s$ is the familiar theory of phrase structure grammar and $T_0{}^s$ is the same theory, with the further condition that the rules are linearly ordered and apply cyclically, with at least one rule $A \rightarrow X$ being obligatory for each category A, so as to guarantee that each cycle is nonvacuous, then it can be shown that $T_U{}^s$ and $T_0{}^s$ are incomparable in descriptive power (in "strong generative capacity" — see § 9; see Chomsky, 1955, Chapters 6 and 7, and Chomsky, 1956, for some discussion of such systems). Consequently, we might ask whether natural languages in fact fall under $T_U{}^s$ or $T_0{}^s$, these being non-equivalent and empirically distinguishable theories. Or, supposing $T_U{}^P$ and $T_0{}^P$ to be theories of the phonological component (where $T_U{}^P$ holds phonological rules to be unordered and $T_0{}^P$ holds them to be partially ordered), it is easy to invent hypothetical "languages" for which significant generalizations are expressible in terms of $T_0{}^P$ but not $T_U{}^P$, or conversely. We can therefore try to determine whether there are significant generalizations that are expressible in terms of one but not the other theory in the case of empirically given languages. In principle, either result is possible; it is an entirely factual question, having to do with the properties of natural languages. We shall see later that $T_0{}^S$ is rather well motivated as a theory of the base, and strong arguments have been offered to show that $T_0{}^P$ is correct and $T_U{}^P$ is wrong, as a theory of phonological processes (cf. Chomsky, 1951, 1964; Halle, 1959a, 1959b, 1962a, 1964). In both cases, the argument turns on the factual question of expressibility of linguistically significant generalizations in terms of one or the other theory, not on any presumed absolute sense of "simplicity" that might rank T_U and T_0 relative to one another. Failure to appreciate this fact has led to a great deal of vacuous and pointless discussion.

Confusion about these questions may also have been engendered by the fact that there are several different senses in which one can talk of "justifying" a grammar, as noted on pp. 26–27. To repeat the major point: on the one hand, the grammar can be justified on external grounds of descriptive adequacy — we may ask whether it states the facts about the language correctly, whether it predicts correctly how the idealized native speaker would understand arbitrary sentences and gives a correct account of the basis for this achievement; on the other hand, a grammar can be justified on internal grounds if, given an explanatory linguistic theory, it can be shown that this grammar is the highest-valued grammar permitted by the theory and compatible with given primary linguistic data. In the latter case, a principled basis is presented for the construction of this grammar, and it is therefore justified on much deeper empirical grounds. Both kinds of justification are of course necessary; it is important, however, not to confuse them. In the case of a linguistic theory that is merely descriptive, only one kind of justification can be given — namely, we can show that it permits grammars that meet the external condition of descriptive adequacy.[24] It is only when all of the conditions (i)–(v) of (12)–(14) are met that the deeper question of internal justification can be raised.

It is also apparent that the discussion as to whether an evaluation measure is a "necessary" part of linguistic theory is quite without substance (see, however, pp. 36–37). If the linguist is content to formulate descriptions one way or another with little concern for justification, and if he does not intend to proceed from the study of facts about particular languages to an investigation of the characteristic properties of natural language as such, then construction of an evaluation procedure and the associated concerns that relate to explanatory adequacy need not concern him. In this case, since interest in justification has been abandoned, neither evidence nor argument (beyond minimal requirements of consistency) has any bearing on what the linguist presents as a linguistic description. On the other hand, if he wishes to achieve descriptive adequacy in his account of language structure, he must concern himself with the problem of developing an explanatory theory of the form of grammar, since this provides one of the main tools for arriving at a descriptively adequate grammar in any particular case. In other words, choice of a grammar for a particular language L will always be much underdetermined by the data drawn from L alone. Moreover, other relevant data (namely, successful grammars for other languages or successful fragments for other subparts of L) will be available to the linguist only if he possesses an explanatory theory. Such a theory limits the choice of grammar by the dual method of imposing formal conditions on grammar and providing an evaluation procedure to be applied for the language L with which he is now concerned. Both the formal conditions and the evaluation procedure can be empirically justified by their success in other cases. Hence, any far-reaching concern for descriptive adequacy must lead to an attempt to develop an explanatory theory that fulfills these dual functions, and concern with explanatory adequacy surely requires an investigation of evaluation procedures.

The major problem in constructing an evaluation measure for grammars is that of determining which generalizations about a language are significant ones; an evaluation measure must be selected in such a way as to favor these. We have a generalization when a set of rules about distinct items can be replaced by a single rule (or, more generally, partially identical rules) about the whole set, or when it can be shown that a "natural class" of items undergoes a certain process or set of similar processes. Thus, choice of an evaluation measure constitutes a decision as to what are "similar processes" and "natural classes" — in short, what are significant generalizations. The problem is to devise a procedure that will assign a numerical measure of valuation to a grammar in terms of the degree of linguistically significant generalization that this grammar achieves. The obvious numerical measure to be applied to a grammar is length, in terms of number of symbols. But if this is to be a meaningful measure, it is necessary to devise notations and to restrict the form of rules in such a way that significant considerations of complexity and generality are converted into considerations of length, so that real generalizations shorten the grammar and spurious ones do not. Thus it is the notational conventions used in presenting a grammar that define "significant generalization," if the evaluation measure is taken as length.

This is, in fact, the rationale behind the conventions for use of parentheses, brackets, etc., that have been adopted in explicit (that is, generative) grammars. For a detailed discussion of these, see Chomsky (1951, 1955), Postal (1962a), and Matthews (1964). To take just one example, consider the analysis of the English Verbal Auxiliary. The facts are that such a phrase must contain Tense (which is, furthermore, *Past* or *Present*), and then may or may not contain a Modal and either the *Perfect* or *Progressive* Aspect (or both), where the elements must appear in the order just given. Using familiar notational conventions, we can state this rule in the following form:

(15)   Aux → Tense (Modal)(*Perfect*)(*Progressive*)

(omitting details that are not relevant here). Rule (15) is an abbreviation for eight rules that analyze the element Aux into its eight possible forms. Stated in full, these eight rules would involve twenty symbols, whereas rule (15) involves four (not counting Aux, in both cases). The parenthesis notation, in this case, has the following meaning. It asserts that the difference between four and twenty symbols is a measure of the degree of linguistically significant generalization achieved in a language that has the forms given in list (16), for the Auxiliary Phrase, as compared with a language that has, for example, the forms given in list (17) as the representatives of this category:

(16)   Tense, Tense⌢Modal, Tense⌢*Perfect*, Tense⌢*Progressive*, Tense⌢Modal⌢*Perfect*, Tense⌢Modal⌢*Progressive*, Tense ⌢*Perfect*⌢*Progressive*, Tense⌢Modal⌢*Perfect*⌢*Progressive*

(17)   Tense⌢Modal⌢*Perfect*⌢*Progressive*, Modal⌢*Perfect*⌢*Progressive*⌢Tense, *Perfect*⌢*Progressive*⌢Tense⌢Modal, *Progressive*⌢Tense⌢Modal⌢*Perfect*, Tense⌢*Perfect*, Modal⌢*Progressive*

In the case of both list (16) and list (17), twenty symbols are involved. List (16) abbreviates to rule (15) by the notational convention; list (17) cannot be abbreviated by this convention. Hence, adoption of the familiar notational conventions involving the use of parentheses amounts to a claim that there is a linguistically significant generalization underlying the set of forms in list (16) but not the set of forms in list (17). It amounts to the empirical hypothesis that regularities of the type exemplified in (16) are those found in natural languages, and are of the type that children learning a language will expect; whereas cyclic regularities of the type exemplified in (17), though perfectly genuine, abstractly, are not characteristic of natural language, are not of the type for which children will intuitively search in language materials, and are much more difficult for the language-learner to construct on the basis of scattered data or to use. What is claimed, then, is that when given scattered examples from (16), the language learner will construct the rule (15) generating the full set with their semantic interpretations, whereas when given scattered examples that could be subsumed under a cyclic rule, he will not incorporate this "generalization" in his grammar — he will not, for example, conclude from the existence of "yesterday John arrived" and "John arrived yesterday" that there is a third form "arrived yesterday John," or from the existence of "is John here" and "here is John" that there is a third form "John here is," etc. One might easily propose a different notational convention that would abbreviate list (17) to a shorter rule than list (16), thus making a different empirical assumption about what constitutes a linguistically significant generalization. There is no a priori reason for preferring the usual convention; it simply embodies a factual claim about the structure of natural language and the predisposition of the child to search for certain types of regularity in natural language.

The illustrative examples of the preceding paragraph must be regarded with some caution. It is the full set of notational conventions that constitute an evaluation procedure, in the manner outlined earlier. The factual content of an explanatory theory lies in its claim that the most highly valued grammar of the permitted form will be selected, on the basis of given data. Hence, descriptions of particular subsystems of the grammar must be evaluated in terms of their effect on the entire system of rules. The extent to which particular parts of the grammar can be selected independently of others is an empirical matter about which very little is known, at present. Although alternatives can be clearly formulated, deeper studies of particular languages than are presently available are needed to settle the questions that immediately arise when these extremely important issues are raised. To my knowledge, the only attempt to evaluate a fairly full and complex subsystem of a grammar is in Chomsky (1951), but even here all that is shown is that the value of the system is a "local maximum" in the sense that interchange of adjacent rules decreases value. The effect of modifications on a larger scale is not investigated. Certain aspects of the general question, relating to lexical and phonological structure, are discussed in Halle and Chomsky (forthcoming).

One special case of this general approach to evaluation that has been worked out in a particularly convincing way is the condition of minimization of distinctive feature specifications in the phonological component of the grammar. A very plausible argument can be given to the effect that this convention defines the notions of "natural class" and "significant generalization" that have been relied on implicitly in descriptive and comparative-historical phonological investigations, and that determine the intuitively given distinction between "phonologically possible" and "phonologically impossible" nonsense forms. For discussion, see Halle (1959a, 1959b, 1961, 1962a, 1964), Halle and Chomsky (forthcoming). It is important to observe that the effectiveness of this particular evaluation measure is completely dependent on a strong assumption about the form of grammar, namely, the assumption that only feature notation is permitted. If phonemic notation is allowed in addition to feature notation, the measure gives absurd consequences, as Halle shows.

It is clear, then, that choice of notations and other conventions is not an arbitrary or "merely technical" matter, if length is to be taken as the measure of valuation for a grammar. It is, rather, a matter that has immediate and perhaps quite drastic empirical consequences. When particular notational devices are incorporated into a linguistic theory of the sort we are discussing, a certain empirical claim is made, implicitly, concerning natural language. It is implied that a person learning a language will attempt to formulate generalizations that can easily be expressed (that is, with few symbols) in terms of the notations available in this theory, and that he will select grammars containing these generalizations over other grammars that are also compatible with the given data but that contain different sorts of generalization, different concepts of "natural class," and so on. These may be very strong claims, and need by no means be true on any a priori grounds.

To avoid any possible lingering confusion on this matter,

let me repeat once more that this discussion of language learning in terms of formulation of rules, hypotheses, etc., does not refer to conscious formulation and expression of these but rather to the process of arriving at an internal representation of a generative system, which can be appropriately described in these terms.

In brief, it is clear that no present-day theory of language can hope to attain explanatory adequacy beyond very restricted domains. In other words, we are very far from being able to present a system of formal and substantive linguistic universals that will be sufficiently rich and detailed to account for the facts of language learning. To advance linguistic theory in the direction of explanatory adequacy, we can attempt to refine the evaluation measure for grammars or to tighten the formal constraints on grammars so that it becomes more difficult to find a highly valued hypothesis compatible with primary linguistic data. There can be no doubt that present theories of grammar require modification in both of these ways, the latter, in general, being the more promising. Thus the most crucial problem for linguistic theory seems to be to abstract statements and generalizations from particular descriptively adequate grammars and, wherever possible, to attribute them to the general theory of linguistic structure, thus enriching this theory and imposing more structure on the schema for grammatical description. Whenever this is done, an assertion about a particular language is replaced by a corresponding assertion, from which the first follows, about language in general. If this formulation of a deeper hypothesis is incorrect, this fact should become evident when its effect on the description of other aspects of the language or the description of other languages is ascertained. In short, I am making the obvious comment that, wherever possible, general assumptions about the nature of language should be formulated from which particular features of the grammars of individual languages can be deduced. In this way, linguistic theory may move toward explanatory adequacy and contribute to the study of human mental processes and intellectual capacity — more specifically, to the determination of the abilities that make language learning possible under the empirically given limitations of time and data.

§ 8. *LINGUISTIC THEORY AND LANGUAGE LEARNING*

In the preceding discussion, certain problems of linguistic theory have been formulated as questions about the construction of a hypothetical language-acquisition device. This seems a useful and suggestive framework within which to pose and consider these problems. We may think of the theorist as given an empirical pairing of collections of primary linguistic data associated with grammars that are constructed by the device on the basis of such data. Much information can be obtained about both the primary data that constitute the input and the grammar that is the "output" of such a device, and the theorist has the problem of determining the intrinsic properties of a device capable of mediating this input-output relation.

It may be of some interest to set this discussion in a somewhat more general and traditional framework. Historically, we can distinguish two general lines of approach to the problem of acquisition of knowledge, of which the problem of acquisition of language is a special and particularly informative case. The empiricist approach has assumed that the structure of the acquisition device is limited to certain elementary "peripheral processing mechanisms" — for example, in recent versions, an innate "quality space" with an innate "distance" defined on it (Quine, 1960, pp. 83f.),[25] a set of primitive unconditioned reflexes (Hull, 1943), or, in the case of language, the set of all "aurally distinguishable components" of the full "auditory impression" (Bloch, 1950). Beyond this, it assumes that the device has certain analytical data-processing mechanisms or inductive principles of a very elementary sort, for example, certain principles of association, weak principles of "generalization" involving gradients along the dimensions of the given quality space, or, in our case, taxonomic principles of segmentation and classification such as those that have been developed with some care in modern linguistics, in accordance with the Saussurian emphasis on the fundamental character of such principles. It is then assumed that a preliminary analysis of experience is provided by the peripheral processing mechanisms, and that one's concepts and knowledge, beyond this, are acquired by application of the available inductive principles to this initially analyzed experience.[26] Such views can be formulated clearly in one way or another as empirical hypotheses about the nature of mind.

A rather different approach to the problem of acquisition of knowledge has been characteristic of rationalist speculation about mental processes. The rationalist approach holds that beyond the peripheral processing mechanisms,[27] there are innate ideas and principles of various kinds that determine the form of the acquired knowledge in what may be a rather restricted and highly organized way. A condition for innate mechanisms to become activated is that appropriate stimulation be presented. Thus for Descartes (1647), the innate ideas are those arising from the faculty of thinking rather than from external objects:

... nothing reaches our mind from external objects through the organs of sense beyond certain corporeal movements ... but even these movements, and the figures which arise from them, are not conceived by us in the shape they assume in the organs of sense. ... Hence it follows that the ideas of the movements and figures are themselves innate in us. So much the more must the ideas of pain, colour, sound and the like be innate, that our mind may, on occasion of certain corporeal movements, envisage these ideas, for they have no likeness to the corporeal movements ... [p. 443].

Similarly, such notions as that things equal to the same thing are equal to each other are innate, since they cannot arise as necessary principles from "particular movements." In general,

sight ... presents nothing beyond pictures, and hearing nothing beyond voices or sounds, so that all these things that we think of, beyond these voices or pictures, as being symbolized by them, are presented to us by means of ideas which come from no other source than our faculty of thinking, and are accordingly together with that faculty innate in us, that is, always existing in us potentially; for existence in any faculty is not actual but merely potential existence, since the very word "faculty" designates nothing more or less than a potentiality. ... [Thus ideas are innate in the sense that] in some families generosity is innate, in others certain diseases like gout or gravel, not that on this account the babes of these families suffer from these diseases in their mother's womb, but because they are born with a certain disposition or propensity for contracting them . . . [p. 442].

Still earlier, Lord Herbert (1624) maintains that innate ideas and principles "remain latent when their corresponding objects are not present, and even disappear and give no sign of their existence"; they "must be deemed not so much the outcome of experience as principles without which we should have no experience at all . . . [p. 132]." Without these principles, "we could have no experience at all nor be capable of observations"; "we should never come to distinguish between things, or to grasp any general nature . . . [p. 105]." These notions are extensively developed throughout seventeenth-century rationalist philosophy. To mention just one example, Cudworth (1731) gives an extensive argument in support of his view that "there are many ideas of the mind, which though the cogitations of them be often occasionally invited from the motion or appulse of sensible objects without made upon our bodies; yet notwithstanding the ideas themselves could not possibly be stamped or impressed upon the soul from them, because sense takes no cognizance at all of any such things in those corporeal objects, and therefore they must needs arise from the innate vigour and activity of the mind itself . . . [Book IV]." Even in Locke one finds essentially the same conception, as was pointed out by Leibniz and many commentators since.

In the Port-Royal *Logic* (Arnauld, 1662), the same point of view is expressed in the following way:

It is false, therefore, that all our ideas come through sense. On the contrary, it may be affirmed that no idea which we have in our minds has taken its rise from sense, except on occasion of those movements which are made in the brain through sense, the impulse from sense giving occasion to the mind to form different ideas which it would not have formed without it, though these ideas have very rarely any resemblance to what takes place in the sense and in the brain; and there are at least a very great number of ideas which, having no connection with any

bodily image, cannot, without manifest absurdity, be referred to sense
. . . [Chapter 1].

In the same vein, Leibniz refuses to accept a sharp distinction
between innate and learned:

I agree that we learn ideas and innate truths either in considering their
source or in verifying them through experience. . . . And I cannot
admit this proposition: *all that one learns is not innate.* The truths of
numbers are in us, yet nonetheless one learns them,[28] either by drawing
them from their source when we learn them through demonstrative
proof (which shows that they are innate), or by testing them in examples, as do ordinary arithmeticians . . . [*New Essays,* p. 75]. [Thus] all
arithmetic and all geometry are in us virtually, so that we can find them
there if we consider attentively and set in order what we already have
in the mind . . . [p. 78]. [In general,] we have an infinite amount of
knowledge of which we are not always conscious, not even when we
need it [p. 77]. The senses, although necessary for all our actual knowledge, are not sufficient to give it all to us, since the senses never give us
anything but examples, i.e., particular or individual truths. Now all the
examples which confirm a general truth, whatever their number, do not
suffice to establish the universal necessity of that same truth . . .
[pp. 42–43]. Necessary truths . . . must have principles whose proof does
not depend on examples, nor consequently upon the testimony of the
senses, although without the senses it would never have occurred to us
to think of them. . . . It is true that we must not imagine that these
eternal laws of the reason can be read in the soul as in an open book
. . . but it is sufficient that they can be discovered in us by dint of attention, for which the senses furnish occasions, and successful experience
serves to confirm reason . . . [p. 44]. [There are innate general principles that] enter into our thoughts, of which they form the soul and the
connection. They are as necessary thereto as the muscles and sinews are
for walking, although we do not at all think of them. The mind leans
upon these principles every moment, but it does not come so easily to
distinguish them and to represent them distinctly and separately, because that demands great attention to its acts. . . . Thus it is that one
possesses many things without knowing it . . . [p. 74].

(as, for example, the Chinese possess articulate sounds, and
therefore the basis for alphabetic writing, although they have
not invented this).

Notice, incidentally, that throughout these classical discussions of the interplay between sense and mind in the formation of ideas, no sharp distinction is made between perception and acquisition, although there would be no inconsistency in the assumption that latent innate mental structures, once "activated," are then available for interpretation of the data of sense in a way in which they were not previously.

Applying this rationalist view to the special case of language learning, Humboldt (1836) concludes that one cannot really teach language but can only present the conditions under which it will develop spontaneously in the mind in its own way. Thus the *form of a language,* the schema for its grammar, is to a large extent given, though it will not be available for use without appropriate experience to set the language-forming processes into operation. Like Leibniz, he reiterates the Platonistic view that, for the individual, learning is largely a matter of *Wiedererzeugung,* that is, of drawing out what is innate in the mind.[29]

This view contrasts sharply with the empiricist notion (the prevailing modern view) that language is essentially an adventitious construct, taught by "conditioning" (as would be maintained, for example, by Skinner or Quine) or by drill and explicit explanation (as was claimed by Wittgenstein), or built up by elementary "data-processing" procedures (as modern linguistics typically maintains), but, in any event, relatively independent in its structure of any innate mental faculties.

In short, empiricist speculation has characteristically assumed that only the procedures and mechanisms for the acquisition of knowledge constitute an innate property of the mind. Thus for Hume, the method of "experimental reasoning" is a basic instinct in animals and humans, on a par with the instinct "which teaches a bird, with such exactness, the art of incubation, and the whole economy and order of its nursery" — it is derived "from the original hand of nature" (Hume, 1748, § IX). The form of knowledge, however, is otherwise quite free. On the other hand, rationalist speculation has assumed that the general form of a system of knowledge is fixed in advance as a disposition of the mind, and the function of experience is to cause this general schematic structure to be realized and more fully differentiated. To follow Leibniz's enlightening analogy, we may make

... the comparison of a block of marble which has veins, rather than a block of marble wholly even, or of blank tablets, i.e., of what is called among philosophers a *tabula rasa*. For if the soul resembled these blank tablets, truths would be in us as the figure of Hercules is in the marble, when the marble is wholly indifferent to the reception of this figure or some other. But if there were veins in the block which should indicate the figure of Hercules rather than other figures, this block would be more determined thereto, and Hercules would be in it as in some sense innate, although it would be needful to labor to discover these veins, to clear them by polishing, and by cutting away what prevents them from appearing. Thus it is that ideas and truths are for us innate, as inclinations, dispositions, habits, or natural potentialities, and not as actions; although these potentialities are always accompanied by some actions, often insensible, which correspond to them [Leibniz, *New Essays*, pp. 45–46].

It is not, of course, necessary to assume that empiricist and rationalist views can always be sharply distinguished and that these currents cannot cross. Nevertheless, it is historically accurate as well as heuristically valuable to distinguish these two very different approaches to the problem of acquisition of knowledge. Particular empiricist and rationalist views can be made quite precise and can then be presented as explicit hypotheses about acquisition of knowledge, in particular, about the innate structure of a language-acquisition device. In fact, it would not be inaccurate to describe the taxonomic, data-processing approach of modern linguistics as an empiricist view that contrasts with the essentially rationalist alternative proposed in recent theories of transformational grammar. Taxonomic linguistics is empiricist in its assumption that general linguistic theory consists only of a body of procedures for determining the grammar of a language from a corpus of data, the form of language being unspecified except insofar as restrictions on possible grammars are determined by this set of procedures. If we interpret taxonomic linguistics as making an empirical claim,[30] this claim must be that the grammars that result from application of the postulated procedures to a sufficiently rich selection of data will be descriptively adequate — in other words, that the set of procedures can be regarded as constituting a hypothesis about the innate language-acquisition system. In contrast, the discussion of language acquisition in preceding sections was rationalistic in its assumption that various formal and substantive universals are intrinsic properties of the language-acquisition system, these providing a schema that is applied to data and that determines in a highly restricted way the general form and, in part, even the substantive features of the grammar that may emerge upon presentation of appropriate data. A general linguistic theory of the sort roughly described earlier, and elaborated in more detail in the following chapters and in other studies of transformational grammar, must therefore be regarded as a specific hypothesis, of an essentially rationalist cast, as to the nature of mental structures and processes. See Chomsky (1959b, 1962b, 1964) and Katz (forthcoming) for some further discussion of this point.

When such constrasting views are clearly formulated, we may ask, as an empirical question, which (if either) is correct. There is no a priori way to settle this issue. Where empiricist and rationalist views have been presented with sufficient care so that the question of correctness can be seriously raised, it cannot, for example, be maintained that in any clear sense one is "simpler" than the other in terms of its potential physical realization,[31] and even if this could be shown, one way or the other, it would have no bearing on what is completely a factual issue. This factual question can be approached in several ways. In particular, restricting ourselves now to the question of language acquisition, we must bear in mind that any concrete empiricist proposal does impose certain conditions on the form of the grammars that can result from application of its inductive principles to primary data. We may therefore ask whether the grammars that these principles can provide, in principle, are at all close to those which we in fact discover when we investigate real languages. The same question can be asked about a concrete rationalist proposal. This has, in the past, proved to be a useful way to subject such hypotheses to one sort of empirical test.

If the answer to this question of adequacy-in-principle is positive, in either case, we can then turn to the question of feasibility: can the inductive procedures (in the empiricist case) or the mechanisms of elaboration and realization of innate schemata (in the rationalist case) succeed in producing grammars within the given constraints of time and access, and within the range of observed uniformity of output? In fact, the second question has rarely been raised in any serious way in connection with empiricist views (but cf. Miller, Galanter, and Pribram, 1960, pp. 145–148, and Miller and Chomsky, 1963, p. 430, for some comments), since study of the first question has been sufficient to rule out whatever explicit proposals of an essentially empiricist character have emerged in modern discussions of language acquisition. The only proposals that are explicit enough to support serious study are those that have been developed within taxonomic linguistics. It seems to have been demonstrated beyond any reasonable doubt that, quite apart from any question of feasibility, methods of the sort that have been studied in taxonomic linguistics are intrinsically incapable of yielding the systems of grammatical knowledge that must be attributed to the speaker of a language (cf. Chomsky, 1956, 1957, 1964; Postal, 1962b, 1964a, 1964c; Katz and Postal, 1964, § 5.5, and many other publications for discussion of these questions that seems unanswerable and is, for the moment, not challenged). In general, then, it seems to me correct to say that empiricist theories about language acquisition are refutable wherever they are clear, and that further empiricist speculations have been quite empty and uninformative. On the other hand, the rationalist approach exemplified by recent work in the theory of transformational grammar seems to have proved fairly productive, to be fully in accord with what is known about language, and to offer at least some hope of providing a hypothesis about the intrinsic structure of a language-acquisition system that will meet the condition of adequacy-in-principle and do so in a sufficiently narrow and interesting way so that the question of feasibility can, for the first time, be seriously raised.

One might seek other ways of testing particular hypotheses about a language-acquisition device. A theory that attributes possession of certain linguistic universals to a language-acquisition system, as a property to be realized under appropriate external conditions, implies that only certain kinds of symbolic systems can be acquired and used as languages by this device. Others should be beyond its language-acquisition capacity. Systems can certainly be invented that fail the conditions, formal and substantive, that have been proposed as tentative linguistic universals in, for example, Jakobsonian distinctive-feature theory or the theory of transformational grammar. In principle, one might try to determine whether invented systems that fail these conditions do pose inordinately difficult problems for language learning, and do fall beyond the domain for which the language-acquisition system is designed. As a concrete example, consider the fact that, according to the theory of transformational grammar, only certain kinds of formal operations on strings can appear in grammars — operations that, furthermore, have no a priori justification. For example, the permitted operations cannot be shown in any sense to be the most "simple" or "elementary" ones that might be invented. In fact, what might in general be considered "elementary operations" on strings do not qualify as grammatical transformations at all, while many of the operations that do qualify are far from elementary, in any general sense. Specifically, grammatical transformations are necessarily "structure-dependent" in that they manipulate substrings only in terms of their assignment to categories. Thus it is possible to formulate a transformation that can insert all or part of the Auxiliary Verb to the left of a Noun Phrase that precedes it, independently of what the length or internal complexity of the strings belonging to these categories may be. It is impossible, however, to formulate as a transformation such a simple operation as reflection of an arbitrary string (that is, replacement of any string $a_1 \cdots a_n$, where each a_i is a single symbol, by $a_n \cdots a_1$), or interchange of the $(2n-1)^{\text{th}}$ word with the $2n^{\text{th}}$ word throughout a string of arbitrary length, or insertion of a symbol in the middle of a string of even length. Similarly, if the structural analyses that define transformations are restricted to Boolean conditions on *Analyzability*, as suggested later, it will be impossible to formulate many "structure-dependent" operations as transformations — for example, an operation that will iterate a symbol that is the leftmost member of a category (impossible, short of listing all categories of the grammar in the structural analysis), or an operation that will iterate a symbol that belongs to as many rightmost as leftmost categories). Hence, one who proposes this theory would have to predict that although a language might form interrogatives, for example, by interchanging the order of certain categories (as in English), it could not form interrogatives by reflection, or interchange of odd and even words, or insertion of a marker in the middle of the sentence. Many other such predictions, none of them at all obvious in any a priori sense, can be deduced from any sufficiently explicit theory of linguistic universals that is attributed to a language-acquisition device as an intrinsic property. For some initial approaches to the very difficult but tantalizing problem of investigating questions of this sort, see Miller and Stein (1963), Miller and Norman (1964).

Notice that when we maintain that a system is not learnable by a language-acquisition device that mirrors human capacities, we do not imply that this system cannot be mastered by a human in some other way, if treated as a puzzle or intellectual exercise of some sort. The language-acquisition device is only one component of the total system of intellectual structures that can be applied to problem solving and concept formation; in other words, the *faculté de langage* is only one of the faculties of the mind. What one would expect, however, is that there should be a qualitative difference in the way in which an organism with a functional language-acquisition system[32] will approach and deal with systems that are languagelike and others that are not.

The problem of mapping the intrinsic cognitive capacities of an organism and identifying the systems of belief and the organization of behavior that it can readily attain should be central to experimental psychology. However, the field has not developed in this way. Learning theory has, for the most part, concentrated on what seems a much more marginal topic, namely the question of species-independent regularities in acquisition of items of a "behavioral repertoire" under experimentally manipulable conditions. Consequently, it has necessarily directed its attention to tasks that are extrinsic to an organism's cognitive capacities — tasks that must be approached in a devious, indirect, and piecemeal fashion. In the course of this work, some incidental information has been obtained about the effect of intrinsic cognitive structure and intrinsic organization of behavior on what is learned, but this has rarely been the focus of serious attention (outside of ethology). The sporadic exceptions to this observation (see, for example, the discussion of "instinctual drift" in Breland and Breland, 1961) are quite suggestive, as are many ethological studies of lower organisms. The general question and its many ramifications, however, remain in a primitive state.

In brief, it seems clear that the present situation with regard to the study of language learning is essentially as follows. We have a certain amount of evidence about the character of the generative grammars that must be the "output" of an acquisition model for language. This evidence shows clearly that taxonomic views of linguistic structure are inadequate and that knowledge of grammatical structure cannot arise by application of step-by-step inductive operations (segmentation, classification, substitution procedures, filling of slots in frames, association, etc.) of any sort that have yet been developed within linguistics, psychology, or philosophy. Further empiricist speculations contribute nothing that even faintly suggests a way of overcoming the intrinsic limitations of the methods that have so far been proposed and elaborated. In particular, such speculations have not provided any way to account for or even to express the fundamental fact about the normal use of language, namely the speaker's ability to produce and understand instantly new sentences that are not similar to those previously heard in any physically defined sense or in terms of any notion of frames or classes of elements, nor associated with those previously heard by conditioning, nor obtainable from them by any sort of "generalization" known to psychology or philosophy. It seems plain that language acquisition is based on the child's discovery of what from a formal point of view is a deep and abstract theory — a generative grammar of his language — many of the concepts and principles of which are only remotely related to experience by long and intricate chains of unconscious quasi-inferential steps. A consideration of the character of the grammar that is acquired, the degenerate quality and narrowly limited extent of the available data, the striking uniformity of the resulting grammars, and their independence of intelligence, motivation, and emotional state, over wide ranges of variation, leave little hope that much of the structure of the language can be learned by an organism initially uninformed as to its general character.

It is, for the present, impossible to formulate an assumption about initial, innate structure rich enough to account for the fact that grammatical knowledge is attained on the basis of the evidence available to the learner. Consequently, the empiricist effort to show how the assumptions about a language-acquisition device can be *reduced to a conceptual minimum*[33] is quite misplaced. The real problem is that of developing a hypothesis about initial structure that is sufficiently rich to account for acquisition of language, yet not so rich as to be inconsistent with the known diversity of language. It is a matter of no concern and of only historical interest that such a hypothesis will evidently not satisfy the preconceptions about learning that derive from centuries of empiricist doctrine. These preconceptions are not only quite implausible, to begin with, but are without factual support and are hardly consistent with what little is known about how animals or humans construct a "theory of the external world."

It is clear why the view that all knowledge derives solely from the senses by elementary operations of association and "generalization" should have had much appeal in the context of eighteenth-century struggles for scientific naturalism. However, there is surely no reason today for taking seriously a position that attributes a complex human achievement entirely to months (or at most years) of experience, rather than to millions of years of evolution or to principles of neural organization that may be even more deeply grounded in physical law — a position that would, furthermore, yield the conclusion that man is, apparently, unique among animals in the way in which he acquires knowledge. Such a position is particularly implausible with regard to language, an aspect of the child's world that is a human creation and would naturally be expected to reflect intrinsic human capacity in its internal organization.

In short, the structure of particular languages may very well be largely determined by factors over which the individual has no conscious control and concerning which society may have little choice or freedom. On the basis of the best information now available, it seems reasonable to suppose that a child cannot help constructing a particular sort of transformational grammar to account for the data presented to him, any more than he can control his perception of solid objects or his attention to line and angle. Thus it may well be that the general features of language structure reflect, not so much the course of one's experience, but rather the general character of one's capacity to acquire knowledge—in the traditional sense, one's innate ideas and innate principles. It seems to me that the problem of clarifying this issue and sharpening our understanding of its many facets provides the most interesting and important reason for the study of descriptively adequate grammars and, beyond this, the formulation and justification of a general linguistic theory that meets the condition of explanatory adequacy. By pursuing this investigation, one may hope to give some real substance to the traditional belief that "the principles of grammar form an important, and very curious, part of the philosophy of the human mind" (Beattie, 1788).

§ 9. GENERATIVE CAPACITY AND ITS LINGUISTIC RELEVANCE

It may be useful to make one additional methodological observation in connection with the topics discussed in the last few sections. Given a descriptive theory of language structure,[34] we can distinguish its *weak generative capacity* from its *strong generative capacity* in the following way. Let us say that a grammar *weakly generates* a set of sentences and that it *strongly generates* a set of structural descriptions (recall that each structural description uniquely specifies a sentence, but not necessarily conversely), where both weak and strong generation are determined by the procedure f of (12iv) = (13iv) = (14iv). Suppose that the linguistic theory T provides the class of grammars $G_1, G_2, \cdots$, where G_i weakly generates the language L_i and strongly generates the system of structural descriptions Σ_i. Then the class $\{L_1, L_2, \cdots\}$ constitutes the *weak generative capacity* of T and the class $\{\Sigma_1, \Sigma_2, \cdots\}$ constitutes the *strong generative capacity* of T.[35]

The study of strong generative capacity is related to the study of descriptive adequacy, in the sense defined. A grammar is descriptively adequate if it strongly generates the correct set of structural descriptions. A theory is descriptively adequate if its strong generative capacity includes the system of structural descriptions for each natural language; otherwise, it is descriptively inadequate. Thus inadequacy of strong generative capacity, on empirical grounds, shows that a theory of language is seriously defective. As we have observed, however, a theory of language that appears to be empirically adequate in terms of strong generative capacity is not necessarily of any particular theoretical interest, since the crucial question of explanatory adequacy goes beyond any consideration of strong generative capacity.

The study of weak generative capacity is of rather marginal linguistic interest. It is important only in those cases where some proposed theory fails even in weak generative capacity — that is, where there is some natural language even the *sentences* of which cannot be enumerated by any grammar permitted by this theory. In fact, it has been shown that certain fairly elementary theories (in particular, the theory of context-free phrase-structure grammar and the even weaker theory of finite-state grammar) do not have the weak generative capacity required for the description of natural language, and thus fail empirical tests of adequacy in a particularly surprising way.[36] From this observation we must conclude that as linguistic theory progresses to a more adequate conception of grammatical structure, it will have to permit devices with a weak generative capacity that differs, in certain respects, from that of these severely defective systems.

It is important to note, however, that the fundamental defect of these systems is not their limitation in weak generative capacity but rather their many inadequacies in strong generative capacity. Postal's demonstration that the theory of context-free grammar (simple phrase-structure grammar) fails in weak generative capacity was preceded by over a half-dozen years of discussion of the strong generative capacity of this theory, which showed conclusively that it cannot achieve descriptive adequacy. Furthermore, these limitations in strong generative capacity carry over to the theory of context-sensitive phrase-structure grammar, which probably does not fail in weak generative capacity. Presumably, discussion of weak generative capacity marks only a very early and primitive stage of the study of generative grammar. Questions of real linguistic interest arise only when strong generative capacity (descriptive adequacy) and, more important, explanatory adequacy become the focus of discussion.

As observed earlier, the critical factor in the development of a fully adequate theory is the limitation of the class of possible grammars. Clearly, this limitation must be such as to meet empirical conditions on strong (and, a fortiori, weak) generative capacity, and, furthermore, such as to permit the condition of explanatory adequacy to be met when an appropriate evaluation measure is developed. But beyond this, the problem is to impose sufficient structure on the schema that defines "generative grammar" so that relatively few hypotheses will have to be tested by the evaluation measure, given primary linguistic data. We want the hypotheses compatible with fixed data to be "scattered" in value, so that choice among them can be made relatively easily.

This requirement of "feasibility" is the major empirical constraint on a theory, once the conditions of descriptive and explanatory adequacy are met. It is important to keep the requirements of explanatory adequacy and feasibility in mind when weak and strong generative capacities of theories are studied as mathematical questions. Thus one can construct hierarchies of grammatical theories in terms of weak and strong generative capacity, but it is important to bear in mind that these hierarchies do *not* necessarily correspond to what is probably the empirically most significant dimension of increasing power of linguistic theory. This dimension is presumably to be defined in terms of the scattering in value of grammars compatible with fixed data. Along this empirically significant dimension, we should like to accept the least "powerful" theory that is empirically adequate. It might conceivably turn out that this theory is extremely powerful (perhaps even universal, that is, equivalent in generative capacity to the theory of Turing machines)[37] along the dimension of weak generative capacity, and even along the dimension of strong generative capacity. It will not necessarily follow that it is very powerful (and hence to be discounted) in the dimension which is ultimately of real empirical significance.

In brief, mathematical study of formal properties of grammars is, very likely, an area of linguistics of great potential. It has already provided some insight into questions of empirical interest and will perhaps some day provide much deeper insights. But it is important to realize that the questions presently being studied are primarily determined by feasibility of mathematical study, and it is important not to confuse this with the question of empirical significance.

2

Categories and Relations in Syntactic Theory

§ *1. THE SCOPE OF THE BASE*

WE now return to the problem of refining and elaborating the sketch (in Chapter 1, § 3) of how a generative grammar is organized. Putting off to the next chapter any question as to the adequacy of earlier accounts of grammatical transformations, we shall consider here only the formal properties of the base of the syntactic component. We are therefore concerned primarily with extremely simple sentences.

The investigation of generative grammar can profitably begin with a careful analysis of the kind of information presented in traditional grammars. Adopting this as a heuristic procedure, let us consider what a traditional grammar has to say about a simple English sentence such as the following:

(1) sincerity may frighten the boy

Concerning this sentence, a traditional grammar might provide information of the following sort:

(2) (i) the string (1) is a Sentence (S); *frighten the boy* is a Verb Phrase (VP) consisting of the Verb (V) *frighten* and the Noun Phrase (NP) *the boy; sincerity* is also an NP; the NP *the boy* consists of the Determiner (Det) *the*, followed by a Noun (N); the NP *sincerity* consists of just an N; *the* is, furthermore, an Article (Art); *may* is a Verbal Auxiliary (Aux) and, furthermore, a Modal (M).

(ii) the NP *sincerity* functions as the Subject of the sentence
(1), whereas the VP *frighten the boy* functions as the Predicate of this sentence; the NP *the boy* functions as the
Object of the VP, and the V *frighten* as its Main Verb;
the grammatical relation Subject-Verb holds of the pair
(*sincerity, frighten*), and the grammatical relation Verb-
Object holds of the pair (*frighten, the boy*).[1]

(iii) the N *boy* is a Count Noun (as distinct from the Mass
Noun *butter* and the Abstract Noun *sincerity*) and a
Common Noun (as distinct from the Proper Noun *John*
and the Pronoun *it*); it is, furthermore, an Animate Noun
(as distinct from *book*) and a Human Noun (as distinct
from *bee*); *frighten* is a Transitive Verb (as distinct from
occur), and one that does not freely permit Object deletion (as distinct from *read, eat*); it takes Progressive Aspect
freely (as distinct from *know, own*); it allows Abstract
Subjects (as distinct from *eat, admire*) and Human Objects (as distinct from *read, wear*).

It seems to me that the information presented in (2) is, without question, substantially correct and is essential to any account
of how the language is used or acquired. The main topic I should
like to consider is how information of this sort can be formally
presented in a structural description, and how such structural
descriptions can be generated by a system of explicit rules. The
next three subsections (§§ 2.1, 2.2, 2.3) discuss these questions in
connection with (2i), (2ii), and (2iii), respectively.

§ 2. *ASPECTS OF DEEP STRUCTURE*

§ 2.1. *Categorization*

The remarks given in (2i) concern the subdivision of the
string (1) into continuous substrings, each of which is assigned to
a certain category. Information of this sort can be represented
by a labeled bracketing of (1), or, equivalently, by a tree-diagram
such as (3). The interpretation of such a diagram is transparent,

(3)

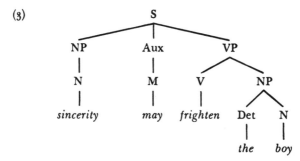

and has been discussed frequently elsewhere. If one assumes now that (1) is a basic string, the structure represented as (3) can be taken as a first approximation to its (base) Phrase-marker.

A grammar that generates simple Phrase-markers such as (3) may be based on a vocabulary of symbols that includes both *formatives* (*the, boy,* etc.) and *category symbols* (S, NP, V, etc.). The formatives, furthermore, can be subdivided into *lexical* items (*sincerity, boy*) and *grammatical* items (*Perfect, Possessive,* etc.; except possibly for *the,* none of these are represented in the simplified example given).

A question arises at once as to the choice of symbols in Phrase-markers. That is, we must ask whether the formatives and category symbols used in Phrase-markers have some language-independent characterization, or whether they are just convenient mnemonic tags, specific to a particular grammar.

In the case of the lexical formatives, the theory of phonetic distinctive features taken together with the full set of conditions on phonological representation does, in fact, give a language-independent significance to the choice of symbols, though it is by no means a trivial problem to establish this fact (or to select the proper universal set of substantive phonetic features). I shall assume, henceforth, that an appropriate phonological theory of this sort is established and that, consequently, the lexical formatives are selected in a well-defined way from a fixed universal set.

The question of substantive representation in the case of the grammatical formatives and the category symbols is, in effect, the traditional question of universal grammar. I shall assume that these elements too are selected from a fixed, universal vocabulary, although this assumption will actually have no significant effect on any of the descriptive material to be presented. There is no reason to doubt the importance or reasonableness of the study of this question. It is generally held to involve extrasyntactic considerations of a sort that are at present only dimly perceived. This may very well be true. However, I shall later suggest several general definitions that appear to be correct for English and for other cases with which I am acquainted.[2]

The natural mechanism for generating Phrase-markers such as (3) is a system of *rewriting rules*. A rewriting rule is a rule of the form

(4) $A \rightarrow Z/X - Y$

where X and Y are (possibly null) strings of symbols, A is a single category symbol, and Z is a nonnull string of symbols. This rule is interpreted as asserting that the category A is realized as the string Z when it is in the environment consisting of X to the left and Y to the right. Application of the rewriting rule (4) to a string $\cdots XAY \cdots$ converts this to the string $\cdots XZY \cdots$. Given a grammar, we say that a sequence of strings is a *W-derivation of V* if W is the first and V the last string in the sequence, and each string of the sequence is derived from the one preceding it by application of one of the rewriting rules (with an ordering condition to be added later). Where V is a string of formatives, we say that a W-derivation of V is *terminated*. We call V a *terminal string* if there is an #S#-derivation of #V#, where S is the designated *initial symbol* of the grammar (representing the category "Sentence"), and # is the *boundary symbol* (regarded as a grammatical formative). Thus we construct a derivation of a *terminal string* by successively applying the rewriting rules of the grammar, beginning with the string #S#, until the final string of the derivation consists only of formatives and therefore no further rewriting is possible. If several other conditions are imposed on the system of rewriting rules,[3] it is easy to provide a simple method for assigning a unique and appropriate Phrase-marker to a terminal string, given its derivation. Thus a system of rewriting rules, appropriately constrained, can serve as a part of a generative grammar.

An *unordered* set of rewriting rules, applied in the manner described loosely here (and precisely elsewhere), is called a *constituent structure grammar* (or *phrase structure grammar*). The grammar is, furthermore, called *context-free* (or *simple*) if in each rule of the form (4), X and Y are null, so that the rules apply independently of context. As noted earlier (pp. 60 f., 208), the formal properties of constituent structure grammars have been studied fairly intensively during the past few years; and it has also been shown that almost all of the nontransformational syntactic theories that have been developed within modern linguistics, pure or applied, fall within this framework. In fact, such a system is apparently what is implicit in modern taxonomic ("structuralist") grammars, if these are reformulated as explicit systems for presenting grammatical information (but see note 30, Chapter 1). The inadequacy of such systems as grammars for natural languages seems to me to have been established beyond any reasonable doubt,[4] and I shall not discuss the issue here.

It seems clear that certain kinds of grammatical information are presented in the most natural way by a system of rewriting rules, and we may therefore conclude that rewriting rules constitute part of the base of the syntactic component. Furthermore, we shall assume that these rules are arranged in a linear sequence, and shall define a *sequential derivation* as a derivation formed by a series of rule applications that preserves this ordering. Thus, suppose that the grammar consists of the sequence of rules $R_1, \cdots, R_n$ and that the sequence $\#S\#, \#X_1\#, \cdots, \#X_m\#$ is a derivation of the terminal string X_m. For this to be a sequential derivation, it must be the case that if rule R_i was used to form line $\#X_j\#$ from the line that precedes it, then no rule R_k (for $k > i$) can have been used to form a line $\#X_l\#$ (for $l < j$) from $\#X_{l-1}\#$. We stipulate now that only sequential derivations are generated by the sequence of rules constituting this part of the base.[5]

To provide a Phrase-marker such as (3), the base component might contain the following sequence of rewriting rules:

(5) (I) S→ NP⌒Aux⌒VP
    VP → V⌒NP
    NP → Det⌒N
    NP → N
    Det → *the*
    Aux → M

  (II) M → *may*
    N → *sincerity*
    N → *boy*
    V → *frighten*

Notice that the rules (5), although they do suffice to generate (3), will also generate such deviant strings as *boy may frighten the sincerity*. This is a problem to which we shall turn in § 2.3.

There is a natural distinction in (5) between rules that introduce lexical formatives (class (II)) and the others. In fact, we shall see in § 2.3 that it is necessary to distinguish these sets and to assign the lexical rules to a distinct subpart of the base of the syntactic component.

In the case of the information in (2i), then, we see quite clearly how it is to be formally represented, and what sorts of rules are required to generate these representations.

§ 2.2. *Functional notions*

Turning now to (2ii), we can immediately see that the notions in question have an entirely different status. The notion "Subject," as distinct from the notion "NP," designates a *grammatical function* rather than a *grammatical category*. It is, in other words, an inherently relational notion. We say, in traditional terms, that in (1) *sincerity* is an NP (not that it is the NP of the sentence), and that it is (functions as) the *Subject-of* the sentence (not that it is a Subject). Functional notions like "Subject," "Predicate" are to be sharply distinguished from categorial notions such as "Noun Phrase," "Verb," a distinction that is not to be obscured by the occasional use of the same term for notions of both kinds. Thus it would merely confuse the issue to attempt to represent the information presented in (2ii) formally by extending the

(6)

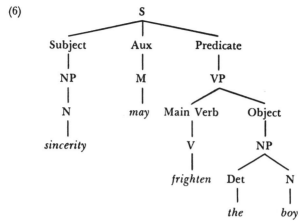

Phrase-marker (3) to (6), adding the necessary rewriting rules to (5I). This approach is mistaken in two ways. For one thing, it confuses categorial and functional notions by assigning categorial status to both, and thus fails to express the relational character of the functional notions. For another, it fails to observe that both (6) and the grammar on which it is based are redundant, since the notions Subject, Predicate, Main-Verb, and Object, being relational, are already represented in the Phrase-marker (3), and no new rewriting rules are required to introduce them. It is necessary only to make explicit the relational character of these notions by defining "Subject-of," for English, as the relation holding between the NP of a sentence of the form NP⌒Aux⌒VP and the whole sentence,[6] "Object-of" as the relation between the NP of a VP of the form V⌒NP and the whole VP, etc. More generally, we can regard any rewriting rule as defining a set of grammatical functions, in this way, only some of which (namely, those that involve the "higher-level," more abstract grammatical categories) have been provided, traditionally, with explicit names.

The fundamental error of regarding functional notions as categorial is somewhat masked in such examples as (6), in which there is only a single Subject, a single Object, and a single Main-Verb. In this case, the relational information can be supplied, intuitively, by the reader. But consider such sentences as (7), in which many grammatical functions are realized, several by the same phrase:

(7) (a) John was persuaded by Bill to leave
    (b) John was persuaded by Bill to be examined
    (c) what disturbed John was being regarded as incompetent

In (7a), *John* is simultaneously Object-of *persuade* (*to leave*) and Subject-of *leave*; in (7b), *John* is simultaneously Object-of *persuade* (*to be examined*) and Object-of *examine*; in (7c), *John* is simultaneously Object-of *disturb*, Object-of *regard* (*as incompetent*), and Subject-of the predication *as incompetent*. In both (7a) and (7b), *Bill* is the ("logical") Subject-of the Sentence, rather than *John*, which is the so-called "grammatical" Subject-of the Sentence, that is, the Subject with respect to the surface structure (cf. note 32). In such cases as these, the impossibility of a categorial interpretation of functional notions becomes at once apparent; correspondingly, the deep structure in which the significant grammatical functions are represented will be very different from the surface structure. Examples of this sort, of course, provide the primary motivation and empirical justification for the theory of transformational grammar. That is, each sentence of (7) will have a basis consisting of a sequence of base Phrase-markers, each of which represents some of the semantically relevant information concerning grammatical function.

Returning now to the main question, let us consider the problem of presenting information about grammatical function in an explicit and adequate way, restricting ourselves now to base Phrase-markers. To develop a uniform approach to this question, we may proceed as follows. Suppose that we have a sequence of rewriting rules, such as (5), including in particular the rule

(8) $A \rightarrow X$

Associated with this rule is each grammatical function

(9) $[B, A]$

where B is a category and $X = YBZ$, for some Y, Z (possibly null).[7] Given a Phrase-marker of the terminal string W, we say that the substring U of W bears the grammatical relation $[B, A]$ to the substring V of W if V is dominated by a node labeled A which directly dominates YBZ, and U is dominated by this occurrence of B.[8] Thus the Phrase-marker in question contains the subconfiguration (10). In particular, given the Phrase-marker

(10)

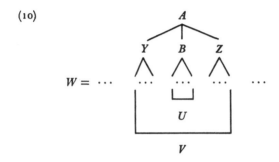

(3) generated by the rules (5), we should have the result that *sincerity* bears the relation [NP, S] to *sincerity may frighten the boy*, *frighten the boy* bears the relation [VP, S] to *sincerity may frighten the boy*, *the boy* bears the relation [NP, VP] to *frighten the boy*, and *frighten* bears the relation [V, VP] to *frighten the boy*.

Suppose further that we propose the following general definitions:

(11) (i) Subject-of: [NP, S]
   (ii) Predicate-of: [VP, S]
   (iii) Direct-Object-of: [NP, VP]
   (iv) Main-Verb-of: [V, VP]

In this case, we can now say that with respect to the Phrase-marker (3) generated by the rules (5), *sincerity* is the Subject-of the sentence *sincerity may frighten the boy* and *frighten the boy* is its Predicate; and *the boy* is the Direct-Object-of the Verb Phrase *frighten the boy* and *frighten* is its Main-Verb. With these definitions, the information presented in the redundant representation (6) is derivable directly from (3), that is, from the grammar (5) itself. These definitions must be thought of as belonging to general linguistic theory; in other words, they form part of the general procedure for assigning a full structural description to a sentence, given a grammar (the procedure f of (12iv), (13iv), (14iv) in § 6, Chapter 1).

In such examples as (7), the grammatical functions will also be given directly by the system of rewriting rules that generate the base Phrase-markers that underlie these sentences, though these grammatical functions are not represented in the configurations of the surface structures in these cases. For example (details aside), the basis for (7a) will contain base Phrase-markers for the strings *Bill persuaded John Sentence, John left*, and these base Phrase-markers present the semantically relevant functional information exactly as in the case of (3).

Notice that the same grammatical function may be defined by several different rewriting rules of the base. Thus suppose that a grammar were to contain the rewriting rules

(12) (i) S → Adverbial⌢NP⌢   (*Naturally, John will leave*)
        Aux⌢VP
  (ii) S → NP⌢Aux⌢VP   (*John will leave*)
 (iii) VP → V⌢NP   (*examine Bill*)
 (iv) VP → V   (*leave*)
  (v) VP → V⌢NP⌢Sentence   (*persuade Bill that John left*)
 (vi) VP → Copula⌢Predicate   (*be President*)
(vii) Predicate → N   (*President*)

Then Subject-of is defined by both (i) and (ii), so that *John* is Subject-of the sentences accompanying both (i) and (ii); Object-of is defined by both (iii) and (v), so that *Bill* is the Object-of the Verb Phrases given as examples to both (iii) and (v); Main-Verb-of is defined by (iii), (iv), and (v), so that *examine, leave, persuade* are the Main-Verbs of the accompanying examples. But notice that "President" is not the Object-of *John is President*, if the rules are as in (12). It is definitions of this sort that were presupposed in the discussion of *persuade* and *expect* in Chapter 1, § 4.

Notice that the general significance of the definitions (11)

depends on the assumption that the symbols S, NP, VP, N, and V have been characterized as grammatical universals. We shall return to this question later. Quite apart from this, it is likely that these definitions are too restricted to serve as general explications for the traditionally designated grammatical functions in that they assume too narrow a substantive specification of the form of grammar. They can be generalized in various ways, but I do not, at the moment, see any strong empirical motivation for one or another specific extension or refinement (but see § 2.3.4). In any event, these questions aside, it is clear that information concerning grammatical functions of the sort exemplified in (2ii) can be extracted directly from the rewriting rules of the base, without any necessity for *ad hoc* extensions and elaborations of these rules to provide specific mention of grammatical function. Such extensions, aside from their redundancy, have the defect of failing to express properly the relational character of the functional notions and are thus useless in all but the simplest cases.

However, we have not yet exhausted the information presented in (2ii). Thus it is still necessary to define grammatical relations of the sort that hold between *sincerity* and *frighten* (Subject-Verb) and between *frighten* and *the boy* (Verb-Object) in (1). Such relations can be defined derivatively in terms of the functional notions suggested earlier. Thus Subject-Verb can be defined as the relation between the Subject-of a Sentence and Main-Verb-of the Predicate-of the Sentence, where Subject-of, Main-Verb-of, and Predicate-of are the notions of (11); and Verb-Object can be defined as the relation between the Main-Verb-of and the Direct-Object-of a VP. However, there is still something missing in this account. Thus we have no basis, as yet, for distinguishing the legitimate and traditionally recognized grammatical relation Subject-Verb, as just defined, from the irrelevant pseudorelation Subject-Object, which is definable just as easily in the same terms. Traditional grammar seems to define such relations where there are selectional restrictions governing the paired categories. Thus the choice of Main-Verb is determined by the choice of Subject and Object, though Subject and Object are in general chosen independently of one another and, correspondingly, have no grammatical relation of the sort in question holding between them. I shall defer the discussion of selectional relations until § 4.2, and at that point we can return to the question of grammatical relations. But in any event, it is fairly clear that nothing essentially new is involved here beyond the rules that generate strings and Phrase-markers.

In summary, then, it seems unnecessary to extend the system of rewriting rules in order to accommodate information of the sort presented in (2ii). With appropriate general definitions of the relational notions involved, this information can be extracted directly from Phrase-markers that are generated by simple rewriting rules such as (5) and (12). This information is already contained, implicitly, in the system of elementary rewriting rules. Representations such as (6) and new or elaborated rewriting rules to generate them are unnecessary, as well as misleading and inappropriate.

Finally, I should like to call attention, once again, to the fact that various modifications and extensions of these functional notions are possible, and that it is important to find empirical motivation for such improvements. For example, the characterization might be sharpened somewhat in terms of several notions that will be useful later on. Suppose again that we have a base grammar consisting of a sequence of rewriting rules, and that (as in (5)) we have distinguished lexical rules (such as (5II)), which introduce lexical formatives, from the others. We shall see later that this distinction is formally quite clearly marked. A category that appears on the left in a lexical rule we shall call a *lexical category*; a lexical category or a category that dominates a string $\cdots X \cdots$, where X is a lexical category, we shall call a *major category*. Thus in the grammar (5), the categories N, V, and M are lexical categories,[9] and all categories except Det (and possibly M and Aux — see note 9) are major categories. It would, then, be in accord with traditional usage to limit the functional notions to major categories. We shall consider a further refinement in the final paragraph of § 2.3.4.

§ 2.3. Syntactic features

§ 2.3.1. The problem.

Information of the sort presented in (2iii) raises several difficult and rather vexing questions. First, it is not obvious to what extent this information should be provided by the syntactic component at all. Second, it is an interesting question whether or to what extent semantic considerations are relevant in determining such subcategorizations as those involved in (2iii). These are distinct questions, though they are often confused. They are connected only in that if the basis for making the distinctions is purely syntactic, then surely the information must be presented in the syntactic component of the grammar. We might call these the questions of *presentation* and *justification*, respectively.

As far as the question of justification is concerned, a linguist with a serious interest in semantics will presumably attempt to deepen and extend syntactic analysis to the point where it can provide the information concerning subcategorization, instead of relegating this to unanalyzed semantic intuition, there being, for the moment, no other available proposal as to a semantic basis for making the necessary distinctions. Of course, it is an open question whether this attempt can succeed, even in part.

I shall be concerned here only with the question of *presentation* of information of the sort given in (2iii). I am assuming throughout that the semantic component of a generative grammar, like the phonological component, is purely interpretive. It follows that all information utilized in semantic interpretation must be presented in the syntactic component of the grammar (but cf. Chapter 4, § 1.2). Some of the problems involved in presenting this information will be explored later.

Although the question of justification of subcategorizations such as those of (2iii) is beyond the scope of the present discussion, it may nevertheless be useful to touch on it briefly. What is at stake, essentially, is the status of such expressions as

(13) (i) the boy may frighten sincerity
   (ii) sincerity may admire the boy
   (iii) John amazed the injustice of that decision

   (iv) the boy elapsed
   (v) the boy was abundant
  (vi) the harvest was clever to agree
 (vii) John is owning a house
(viii) the dog looks barking
  (ix) John solved the pipe
   (x) the book dispersed

It is obvious to anyone who knows English that these expressions have an entirely different status from such sentences as

(14) (i) sincerity may frighten the boy (=(1))
   (ii) the boy may admire sincerity
  (iii) the injustice of that decision amazed John
  (iv) a week elapsed
   (v) the harvest was abundant
  (vi) the boy was clever to agree
 (vii) John owns a house
(viii) the dog looks terrifying
  (ix) John solved the problem
   (x) the boys dispersed

The distinction between (13) and (14) is not at issue, and clearly must be accounted for somehow by an adequate theory of sentence interpretation (a descriptively adequate grammar). The expressions of (13) deviate in some manner (not necessarily all in the same manner) from the rules of English.[10] If interpretable at all, they are surely not interpretable in the manner of the corresponding sentences of (14). Rather, it seems that interpretations are imposed on them by virtue of analogies that they bear to nondeviant sentences.

There are fairly clear-cut cases of violation of purely syntactic rules, for example,

(15) (i) sincerity frighten may boy the
   (ii) boy the frighten may sincerity

and standard examples of purely semantic (or "pragmatic") incongruity, for example,

(16) (i) oculists are generally better trained than eye-doctors
    (ii) both of John's parents are married to aunts of mine
    (iii) I'm memorizing the score of the sonata I hope to compose some day
    (iv) that ice cube that you finally managed to melt just shattered
    (v) I knew you would come, but I was wrong

The examples of (13), however, have a borderline character, and it is much less clear how their aberrant status is to be explained. In other words, we must face the problem of determining to what extent the results and methods of syntactic or of semantic analysis can be extended to account for the deviance and interpretation of these expressions. It goes without saying that the same answer may not be appropriate in all of these cases, and that purely semantic or purely syntactic considerations may not provide the answer in some particular case. In fact, it should not be taken for granted, necessarily, that syntactic and semantic considerations can be sharply distinguished.

Several suggestions have been made as to how syntactic considerations can provide a subclassification of the appropriate sort. These involve the notion of "degree of grammaticalness," along various dimensions, and concrete proposals involve techniques of subclassifying based on distributional similarities. Although these notions have been advanced only very tentatively, it seems to me that they have some plausibility.[11] The only suggestion as to possible semantic grounds for these distinctions has been that they are based on language-independent semantic absolutes — that in each case, the deviance is attributable to violation of some linguistic universal that constrains the form of the semantic component of any generative grammar. It is possible that this is the right answer; furthermore, there is no reason why some combination of these two extreme approaches should not be attempted.

In any case, what is needed is a systematic account of how application of the devices and methods appropriate to unequivocal cases can be extended and deepened to provide a basis for explaining the status of such expressions as those of (13), and an account of how an ideal listener might assign an interpretation to such sentences, where possible, presumably on the basis of analogy to nondeviant cases. These are real and important questions. A descriptively adequate grammar must account for such phenomena in terms of the structural descriptions provided by its syntactic and semantic components, and a general linguistic theory that aims for explanatory adequacy must show how such a grammar can develop on the basis of data available to the language learner. Vague and unsupported assertions about the "semantic basis for syntax" make no contribution to the understanding of these questions.

Proceeding now from the question of justification to the question of presentation, we must determine how a grammar can provide structural descriptions that will account for such phenomena as those exemplified. A priori there is no way to decide whether the burden of presentation should fall on the syntactic or semantic component of the generative grammar. If the former, we must design the syntactic component so that it does not provide for the sentences of (13) directly, but assigns them Phrase-markers only by virtue of their structural similarities to such perfectly well-formed sentences as those of (14), perhaps in the manner described in the references in note 11. Thus the syntactic component will operate in terms of selectional restrictions involving such categories as animateness and abstractness, and will characterize (13i), for example, as a string generated only by relaxing certain of these restrictions. Alternatively, if we conclude that the semantic component should carry the burden of accounting for these facts, we can allow the syntactic component to generate the sentences of (14) as well as those of (13), with no distinction of grammaticalness, but with lexical items specified in such a way that rules of the semantic component will determine the incongruity of the sentences of (13) and the manner in which they can be interpreted (if at all). Either way, we face a well-defined problem, and it is reasonably clear how to proceed to examine it. I shall, for the present, accept the position of the references of note 11, assuming that the notion "scale of grammaticalness" will be relevant to semantic interpretation, that a distinction should be made between (13) and (14) by rules of the syntactic component, and that the sentences of (13) are assigned Phrase-markers only by relaxation of certain syntactic conditions. Later on, I shall try to indicate the precise point at which this decision affects the form of the syntactic component, and shall discuss briefly some possible alternatives.

§ 2.3.2. *Some formal similarities between syntax and phonology.* Consider now how information of the sort given in (2iii) can be presented in explicit rules. Note that this information concerns *subcategorization* rather than "branching" (that is, analysis of a category into a sequence of categories, as when S is analyzed into NP⌢Aux⌢VP, or NP into Det⌢N). Furthermore, it seems that the only categories involved are those containing lexical formatives as members. Hence, we are dealing with a rather restricted part of grammatical structure, and it is important to bear this in mind in exploring appropriate means for presenting these facts.

The obvious suggestion is to deal with subcategorization by rewriting rules of the type described in § 2.2, and this was the assumption made in the first attempts to formalize generative grammars (cf. Chomsky, 1951,[12] 1955, 1957). However, G. H. Matthews, in the course of his work on a generative grammar of German in 1957–1958, pointed out that this assumption was incorrect and that rewriting rules are not the appropriate device to effect subcategorization of lexical categories.[13] The difficulty is that this subcategorization is typically not strictly hierarchic, but involves rather cross classification. Thus, for example, Nouns in English are either Proper (*John, Egypt*) or Common (*boy, book*) and either Human (*John, boy*) or non-Human (*Egypt, book*). Certain rules (for example, some involving Determiners) apply to the Proper/Common distinction; others (for example, rules involving choice of Relative Pronoun) to the Human/non-Human distinction. But if the subcategorization is given by rewriting rules, then one or the other of these distinctions will have to dominate, and the other will be unstatable in the natural way. Thus if we decide to take Proper/Common as the major distinction, we have such rules as

(17) N → Proper
   N → Common
   Proper → Pr-Human
   Proper → Pr-nHuman
   Common → C-Human
   Common → C-nHuman

where the symbols "Pr-Human," "Pr-nHuman," "C-Human," and "C-nHuman" are entirely unrelated, as distinct from one another as the symbols "Noun," "Verb," "Adjective," and "Modal." In this system, although we can easily state a rule that applies only to Proper Nouns or only to Common Nouns, a rule that applies to Human Nouns must be stated in terms of the unrelated categories Pr-Human and C-Human. This obviously indicates that a generalization is being missed, since this rule would now be no simpler or better motivated than, for example, a rule applying to the unrelated categories Pr-Human and Abstract Nouns. As the depth of the analysis increases, problems of this sort mount to the point where they indicate a serious inadequacy in a grammar that consists only of rewriting rules. Nor is this particular difficulty overcome, as many others are, when we add transformational rules to the grammar.

 Formally, this problem is identical to one that is familiar on the level of phonology. Thus phonological units are also cross-classified, with respect to phonological rules. There are, for example, rules that apply to voiced consonants [b], [z], but not to unvoiced consonants [p], [s], and there are other rules that apply to continuants [s], [z], but not to stops [p], [b], and so on. For this reason it is necessary to regard each phonological unit as a set of features, and to design the phonological component in such a way that each rule applies to all segments containing a certain feature or constellation of features. The same solution suggests itself in the case of the syntactic problem that we are now facing, and it is this method of dealing with the problem that I shall elaborate here.

Before we turn to the use of features on the syntactic level, let us review briefly the operation of the phonological component (cf. Halle, 1959a, 1959b, 1962a, 1964, for discussion of this question). Each lexical formative is represented as a sequence of segments, each segment being a set of features. In other words, each lexical formative is represented by a *distinctive-feature matrix* in which the columns stand for successive segments, and the rows for particular features. An entry in the ith column and jth row of such a matrix indicates how the ith segment is specified with respect to the jth feature. A particular entry may indicate that the segment in question is *unspecified* with respect to the feature in question, or that it is *positively specified* with respect to this feature, or that it is *negatively specified* with respect to this feature. We say that two segments are *distinct* just in case one is positively specified with respect to a feature with respect to which the other is negatively specified, and, more generally, that two matrices with the same number of columns are distinct if the ith segment of one is distinct in this sense from the ith segment of the other, for some i.

Suppose that

(18) $A \rightarrow Z/X - Y$

is a phonological rule, where A, Z, X, and Y are matrices, and A and Z are, furthermore, segments (matrices with just a single column). This is the typical form of a phonological rule. We shall say that the rule (18) is applicable to any string $WX'A'Y'V$, where X', A', Y' are matrices with the same number of columns as X, A, Y, respectively, and $X'A'Y'$ is not distinct from XAY (actually, qualifications are necessary that do not concern us here — cf. Halle and Chomsky, forthcoming, for discussion). The rule (18) converts the string $WX'A'Y'V$ to the string $WX'Z'Y'V$, where Z' is the segment consisting of the feature specifications of Z together with all feature specifications of A' for features with respect to which Z is unspecified.

As an illustration of some of these notions, consider this phonological rule:

(19)   [+continuant] → [+voiced]/ — [+voiced]

This will convert [sm] into [zm], [fd] into [vd], [šg] into [žg], etc.,
but it will not affect [st] or [pd], for example.[14] These conventions
(which can be simplified and generalized in ways that do not
concern us here) allow us to apply rules to any class of segments
specified by a given combination of features, and thus to make
use of the cross classification of segments provided by the feature
representation.

These notions can be adapted without essential change to the
representation of lexical categories and their members, providing
a very natural solution to the cross-classification problem and,
at the same time, contributing to the general unity of grammatical theory. Each lexical formative will have associated with
it a set of *syntactic features* (thus *boy* will have the syntactic
features [+Common], [+Human], etc.). Furthermore, the symbols
representing lexical categories (N, V, etc.) will be analyzed by
the rules into *complex symbols*, each complex symbol being a
set of specified syntactic features, just as each phonological segment is a set of specified phonological features. For example, we
might have the following grammatical rules:

(20) (i) N → [+N, ±Common]
    (ii) [+Common] → [±Count]
    (iii) [+Count] → [±Animate]
    (iv) [−Common] → [±Animate]
    (v) [+Animate] → [±Human]
    (vi) [−Count] → [±Abstract]

We interpret rule (20i) as asserting that the symbol N in a line of
a derivation is to be replaced by one of the two *complex symbols*
[+N, +Common] or [+N, −Common]. The rules (20ii–20vi)
operate under the conventions for phonological rules. Thus rule
(20ii) asserts that any complex symbol Q that is already specified
as [+Common] is to be replaced by the complex symbol containing all of the features of Q along with either the feature
specification [+Count] or [−Count]. The same is true of the other
rules that operate on complex symbols.

The total effect of the rules (20) can be represented by the branching diagram (21). In this representation, each node is

(21)

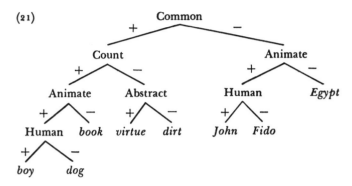

labeled by a feature, and the lines are labeled + or −. Each maximal path corresponds to a category of lexical items; an element of this category has the feature $[\alpha F]$ ($\alpha = +$ or −) if and only if one of the lines constituting this path is labeled α and descends from a node labeled F. Typical members of the categories defined by (20) are given at the terminal points of (21).

A system of complex symbol rules need not be representable by a branching diagram of this sort; e.g., the empirically realized categories defined by the rules (20) are also defined by the rules (22), but in this case there is no representing branching diagram.

(22) (i) N → [+N, ±Animate, ±Common]

   (ii) [+Common] → [±Count]

   (iii) [−Count] → $\begin{bmatrix} \pm\text{Abstract} \\ -\text{Animate} \end{bmatrix}$

   (iv) [+Animate] → [±Human]

If we were to require representability in a branching diagram as a formal condition on these rules, then (22) would be excluded. In this case, the rules could just as well be presented in the form (21) as the form (20). In any event, with rules of this sort that introduce and elaborate complex symbols, we can develop the **full set of lexical categories.**

§ *2.3.3. General structure of the base component.* We now modify the description of the base subcomponent that was presented earlier, and exemplified by (5), in the following way. In addition to rewriting rules that apply to category symbols and that generally involve branching, there are rewriting rules such as (20) that apply to symbols for lexical categories and that introduce or operate on complex symbols (sets of specified syntactic features). The grammar will now contain no rules such as those of (5II) that introduce the formatives belonging to lexical categories. Instead, the base of the grammar will contain a *lexicon*, which is simply an unordered list of all lexical formatives. More precisely, the lexicon is a set of *lexical entries*, each lexical entry being a pair (D, C), where D is a phonological distinctive feature matrix "spelling" a certain lexical formative and C is a collection of specified syntactic features (a complex symbol).[15]

The system of rewriting rules will now generate derivations terminating with strings that consist of grammatical formatives and complex symbols. Such a string we call a *preterminal string*. A terminal string is formed from a preterminal string by insertion of a lexical formative in accordance with the following *lexical rule*:

If Q is a complex symbol of a preterminal string and (D, C) is a lexical entry, where C is not distinct from Q, then Q can be replaced by D.

We now extend the fundamental notion *is a* that relates strings to categories (for example, *the boy* is an NP in (3)) in the following way. We say that in the terminal string formed by replacing the complex symbol Q by the formative D of the lexical entry (D, C), the formative D *is an* $[\alpha F]$ (equivalently, is *dominated by* $[\alpha F]$) if $[\alpha F]$ is part of the complex symbol Q or the complex symbol C, where α is either $+$ or $-$ and F is a feature (but cf. note 15). We also extend the general notion "Phrase-marker" in such a way that the Phrase-marker of a terminal string also contains the new information. With this extension, a Phrase-maker can naturally no longer be represented by a tree-diagram, as before, since it has an additional "dimension" at the level of subcategorization.

As a concrete example, consider again the sentence *sincerity may frighten the boy* (=(1)). Instead of the grammar (5) we now have a grammar containing the branching rules (5I), which I repeat here as (23), along with the subcategorization rules (20), repeated as (24), and containing a lexicon with the entries (25). It is to be understood, here and later on, that the italicized items stand for phonological distinctive feature matrices, that is, "spellings" of formatives.

(23)   S → NP⌢Aux⌢VP
       VP → V⌢NP
       NP → Det⌢N
       NP → N
       Det → *the*
       Aux → M

(24) (i) N → [+N, ±Common]
     (ii) [+Common] → [±Count]
     (iii) [+Count] → [±Animate]
     (iv) [−Common] → [±Animate]
     (v) [+Animate] → [±Human]
     (vi) [−Count] → [±Abstract]

(25) (*sincerity*, [+N, −Count, +Abstract])
     (*boy*, [+N, +Count, +Common, +Animate, +Human])
     (*may*, [+M])

We shall have more to say about these rules and lexical entries later, and they will still undergo significant revision.

These rules allow us to generate the preterminal string

(26)   [+N, −Count, +Abstract]⌢M⌢Q⌢*the*⌢[+N, +Count, +Animate, +Human],

where Q is the complex symbol into which V is analyzed by rules that we shall discuss directly. The lexical rule (which, since it is perfectly general, need not be stated in any grammar — in other words, it constitutes part of the definition of "derivation") now allows us to insert *sincerity* for the first complex symbol and *boy* for the last complex symbol of (26) and, as we shall see, to insert *frighten* for Q (and *may* for M — cf. note 9). Except for the case of *frighten*, the information about the sentence (1) that is given in (2) is now explicitly provided in full by the Phrase-marker generated by the grammar consisting of the rules (23), (24), and the lexicon (25). We might represent this Phrase-marker in the form shown in (27). If the lexicon includes ad-

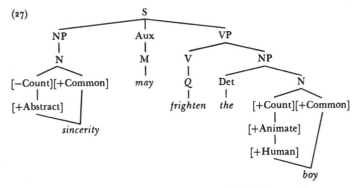

ditional specific information about the lexical items that appear in (26), this information will also appear in the Phrase-marker, represented in terms of features that appear in the Phrase-marker in a position dominated by the lexical categories N and V and dominating the formative in question.

Given this Phrase-maker, we can derive all of the information (2i) and (2iii), which concerns assignment of substrings to categories, in terms of the relation *is a*; and the functional information (2ii) is derivable from the Phrase-marker in the manner described in § 2.2.

We shall return in Chapter 4, § 2 to questions concerning the proper formulation of lexical entries. However, we can see immediately that separating the lexicon from the system of rewriting rules has quite a number of advantages. For one thing, many of the grammatical properties of formatives can now be specified directly in the lexicon, by association of syntactic features with lexical formatives, and thus need not be represented

in the rewriting rules at all. In particular, morphological properties of various kinds can be treated in this way — for example,
membership of lexical items in derivational classes (declensional
classes, strong or weak verbs, nominalizable adjectives, etc.).
Since many such properties are entirely irrelevant to the
functioning of the rules of the base and are, furthermore, highly
idiosyncratic, the grammar can be significantly simplified if
they are excluded from the rewriting rules and listed in lexical
entries, where they most naturally belong. Or, returning to
(2iii), notice that it is now unnecessary to use rewriting rules
to classify Transitive Verbs into those that do and those that do
not normally permit Object deletion. Instead, the lexical entries
for *read, eat,* on the one hand, and *frighten, keep,* on the other,
will differ in specification for the particular syntactic feature of
Object deletion, which is not mentioned in the rewriting rules
at all. The transformational rule that deletes Objects will now
be applicable only to those words positively specified with respect
to this feature, this information now being contained in the
Phrase-marker of the strings in which these words appear. Any
attempt to construct a careful grammar will quickly reveal that
many formatives have unique or almost unique grammatical
characteristics, so that the simplification of the grammar that
can be effected in these ways will certainly be substantial.

In general, all properties of a formative that are essentially
idiosyncratic will be specified in the lexicon.[16] In particular, the
lexical entry must specify: (*a*) aspects of phonetic structure that
are not predictable by general rule (for example, in the case
of *bee,* the phonological matrix of the lexical entry will specify
that the first segment is a voiced labial stop and the second an
acute vowel, but it will not specify the degree of aspiration of the
stop or the fact that the vowel is voiced, tense, and unrounded);[17]
(*b*) properties relevant to the functioning of transformational
rules (as the example of the preceding paragraph, and many
others); (*c*) properties of the formative that are relevant for
semantic interpretation (that is, components of the dictionary
definition); (*d*) lexical features indicating the positions in which
a lexical formative can be inserted (by the lexical rule) in a

preterminal string. In short, it contains information that is required by the phonological and semantic components of the grammar and by the transformational part of the syntactic component of the grammar, as well as information that determines the proper placement of lexical entries in sentences, and hence, by implication, the degree and manner of deviation of strings that are not directly generated (see § 2.3.1 and Chapter 4, § 1.1). Notice, incidentally, that the purely semantic lexical features constitute a well-defined set, in a given grammar. A feature belongs to this set just in case it is not referred to by any rule of the phonological or syntactic component. This may be important for the theory of semantic interpretation. See Katz (1964*b*).

It is important to observe that the base system no longer is, strictly speaking, a phrase structure (constituent structure) grammar. As described informally in § 2.3.1 and more carefully in the references cited there, a phrase structure grammar consists of an unordered set of rewriting rules, and assigns a structural description that can be represented as a tree-diagram with nodes labeled by symbols of the vocabulary. This theory formalizes a conception of linguistic structure that is substantive and interesting, and that has been quite influential for at least half a century, namely the "taxonomic" view that syntactic structure is determined exclusively by operations of segmentations and classification (see § 2.3.1; Postal, 1964*a*; and Chomsky, 1964). Of course, we have already departed from this theory by assuming that the rewriting rules apply in a prescribed sequence to generate a restricted set of (base) strings, rather than freely to generate the full set of actual sentences. This modification restricted the role of the phrase structure grammar. But introduction of complex symbols constitutes another radical departure from this theory, and the separate treatment of the lexicon just suggested is again an essential revision. These modifications affect the strong generative capacity of the theory. It is no longer true that a Phrase-marker can be represented as a labeled tree-diagram, where each label stands for a category of strings. Furthermore, the conventions for the use of complex symbols in effect allow the use of quasi-transformational rules in the base component.

To see why this is so, notice that a derivation involving only phrase structure rules (rewriting rules) has a strict "Markovian" character. That is, in a derivation consisting of the successive lines $\sigma_1, \cdots, \sigma_n$ ($\sigma_1 = \#S\#$; $\sigma_n = \#a_1 \cdots a_k\#$, where each a_i is a terminal or nonterminal symbol of the vocabulary on which the grammar is based), the rules that can be applied to form the next line σ_{n+1} are independent of $\sigma_1, \cdots, \sigma_{n-1}$ and depend completely on the string σ_n. A grammatical transformation, on the other hand, typically applies to a string *with a particular structural description*. Thus application of such a rule to the last line of a derivation depends in part on earlier lines. A grammatical transformation is, in other words, a rule that applies to Phrasemarkers rather than to strings in the terminal and nonterminal vocabulary of the grammar.

Suppose, however, that we were to include labeled brackets in the strings that constitute a derivation and were to allow the "rewriting rules" to refer to these symbols. We should now have a kind of transformational grammar, and we should have entirely lost the intuition about language structure that motivated the development of phrase structure grammar. In fact, incorporation of brackets into strings provides the most appropriate notation for the transformational rules of the phonological component (see Halle and Chomsky, 1960, forthcoming; Chomsky and Miller, 1963, § 6), though not for the transformational rules of the syntactic component, which are not "local transformations" of the sort that appear, exclusively, in the transformational cycle in phonology.[18] But with the availability of complex symbols, aspects of the earlier steps of a derivation can also be carried along to later steps, just as in the case of the notation for transformational rules that involves carrying along labeled brackets in lines of a derivation; and, to some extent, global operations on strings can be coded into complex category symbols and carried along in derivations until the point of "application" of these operations. Consequently, rules applying to complex symbols are, in effect, transformational rules, and a grammar using complex symbols is a kind of transformational grammar rather than a phrase structure grammar. Notice, incidentally, that the conventions established for the use of complex symbols do not provide systems with greater *weak* generative capacity than phrase structure grammars (even if appropriate conventions are established to permit complex symbols to appear at any point in a derivation, rather than only in lexical categories — see note 4). This fact, of course, has no bearing on the observation that such a theory is no longer a version of the theory of phrase structure grammar.

§ *2.3.4. Context-sensitive subcategorization rules.* We have not yet considered how the category V is analyzed into a complex symbol. Thus suppose that we have the grammar (23)–(25). We must still give rules to determine whether a V may or may not be transitive, and so on, and must add to the lexicon appropriate entries for individual verbal formatives. It would not do simply to add to the grammar the rule (28), analogous to (24):

(28)   V → [+V, ±Progressive, ±Transitive, ±Abstract-Subject, ±Animate-Object]

The problem is that an occurrence of the category symbol V can be replaced by a complex symbol containing the feature [+Transitive] just in case it is in the environment — NP. Similarly, the Verb can be positively specified for the feature [Abstract-Subject] just in case it is the environment [+Abstract] ··· — ; and it can be positively specified for the feature [Animate-Object] just in case it is in the environment — ··· [+Animate]; and so on, in the case of all of those lexical features that are involved in the statement of contextual restrictions. Hence, the features [Transitive], [Abstract-Subject], [Animate-Object] must be introduced by rewriting rules that are restricted with respect to context, as distinct from the context-free rules (22) that subcategorize Nouns.[19]

As a first approximation, we might consider rules of the following sort, for the analysis of V:

(29) (i) V → [+V, +Transitive]/ — NP
 (ii) V → [+V, −Transitive]/ — #

(30) (i) [+V] → [+[+Abstract]-Subject]/[+N, +Abstract] Aux —
 (ii) [+V] → [+[−Abstract]-Subject]/[+N, −Abstract] Aux —
 (iii) [+V] → [+[+Animate]-Object]/ — Det [+N, +Animate]
 (iv) [+V] → [+[−Animate]-Object]/ — Det [+N, −Animate]

We can now introduce the standard conventions for expressing generalizations in the case of context-sensitive rewriting rules such as (4), (29), (30) (cf., for example, Chomsky, 1957, Appendix; cf. § 7, Chapter 1, for discussion of the role of these conventions in linguistic theory), in particular, the convention that

$$(31) \qquad A \to Z/ \left\{ \begin{array}{c} X_1 - Y_1 \\ \cdot \\ \cdot \\ \cdot \\ X_n - Y_n \end{array} \right\}$$

is an abbreviation for the sequence of rules

(32) (i) $A \to Z/X_1 - Y_1$
  ·
  ·
  ·
 (n) $A \to Z/X_n - Y_n$

and other familiar related conventions. These allow us to restate (29) and (30) as (33) and (34), respectively.

$$(33) \begin{array}{c} \text{(i)} \\ \text{(ii)} \end{array} \Bigg\} \quad V \to [+V, \left\{ \begin{array}{l} +\text{Transitive}]/ - \text{NP} \\ -\text{Transitive}]/ - \# \end{array} \right\}$$

$$(34) \begin{array}{c} \text{(i)} \\ \\ \text{(ii)} \\ \\ \text{(iii)} \\ \\ \text{(iv)} \end{array} \Bigg\} \ [+V] \to \left\{ \begin{array}{l} [+[+\text{Abstract}]\text{-Subject}]/ \\ \qquad\qquad [+N, +\text{Abstract}]\ \text{Aux} - \\ [+[-\text{Abstract}]\text{-Subject}]/ \\ \qquad\qquad [+N, -\text{Abstract}]\ \text{Aux} - \\ [+[+\text{Animate}]\text{-Object}]/ \\ \qquad\qquad - \text{Det}\ [+N, +\text{Animate}] \\ [+[-\text{Animate}]\text{-Object}]/ \\ \qquad\qquad - \text{Det}\ [+N, -\text{Animate}] \end{array} \right\}$$

It is immediately apparent that the rules (33) and (34), though formally adequate, are extremely clumsy and leave important generalizations unexpressed. This becomes still more obvious when we observe that alongside of (34) there are many other rules of the same kind; and that alongside of (33) there are rules specifying various other choices of subcategories of Verbs, for example, in such environments as: — Adjective [e.g., *grow (old)*, *feel (sad)*], — Predicate-Nominal [*become (president)*], — *like⌢* Predicate-Nominal [*look (like a nice person)*, *act (like a fool)*], — S' [*think (that he will come)*, *believe (it to be unlikely)*], where S' is a variant of a sentence, — NP⌢S' [*persuade (John that it is unlikely)*] (omitting certain refinements).

In other words, the schema for grammatical description that we have so far developed still does not permit us to state the actual processes at work in determining the form of sentences. In the present case, there is a large set of rules (of which (34) mentions just four) that, in effect, assign features of the Subject and Object to the Verb, somewhat in the manner of ordinary rules of agreement in many languages; and there are also many rules (of which (33) presents just two) that impose a subclassification on the category Verb in terms of the set of frames in which this category appears at the stage of a derivation where it is to be subcategorized. These generalizations are not expressible in terms of the schema for grammatical description so far developed, an inadequacy that reveals itself in the redundancy and clumsiness of the systems of rules of which (33) and (34) are samples.

Our present difficulty can be seen clearly by comparing the rules (34) with the hypothetical set (35):

$$(35) \left.\begin{array}{r} \text{(i)} \\ \text{(ii)} \\ \text{(iii)} \\ \text{(iv)} \end{array}\right\} [+V] \rightarrow \left\{\begin{array}{l} [+F_1]/[+N, +\text{Abstract}]\ \text{Aux} \text{—} \\ [+F_2]/[+N, -\text{Abstract}]\ \text{Aux} \text{—} \\ [+F_1]/ \text{—}\ \text{Det}\ [+N, +\text{Animate}] \\ [-F_2]/ \text{—}\ \text{Det}\ [+N, -\text{Animate}] \end{array}\right\}$$

where F_1 and F_2 are certain syntactic features. Rules such as (34) systematically select the Verb in terms of the choice of Subject and Object, whereas the rules (35) determine the subcategorization of Verbs in some essentially haphazard way in terms of choice of Subject and Object. However, the system (34) is not, in our present terms, more highly valued than (35); in fact, the opposite would be true in this case if the familiar notational conventions are applied to evaluate these systems. In other words, the linguistically significant generalization underlying (34) is not expressible within our present framework, which is therefore shown to be inadequate (in this case, at the level of explanatory adequacy).

Let us consider how a more natural and revealing expression of these processes can be developed. Observe that the feature specification [+Transitive] can be regarded as merely a notation indicating occurrence in the environment — NP. A more expressive notation would be simply the symbol " — NP" itself.[20] Generalizing, let us allow certain features to be designated in the form $[X - Y]$, where X and Y are strings (perhaps null) of symbols. We shall henceforth call these *contextual features*. Let us regard Transitive Verbs as positively specified for the contextual feature [— NP], pre-Adjectival Verbs such as *grow*, *feel*, as positively specified for the contextual feature [— Adjective], and so on. We then have a general rule of subcategorization to the effect that *a Verb is positively specified with respect to the contextual feature associated with the context in which it occurs.* We thus introduce the notation

(36) $A \rightarrow X^\frown CS^\frown Y/Z - W$

as an abbreviation for the rewriting rule

(37) $A \rightarrow X^\frown [+A, +Z - W]^\frown Y/Z - W,$

where "CS" stands for "complex symbol." Utilizing the bracket conventions, we can now have

$$(38) \quad A \rightarrow X^\frown CS^\frown Y/ \left\{ \begin{array}{c} Z_1 - W_1 \\ \cdot \\ \cdot \\ \cdot \\ Z_n - W_n \end{array} \right.$$

as an abbreviation for the sequence of rules

(39) $A \to X^\frown [+A, +Z_1 - W_1]^\frown Y/Z_1 - W_1$

.

.

.

$A \to X^\frown [+A, +Z_n - W_n]^\frown Y/Z_n - W_n$

The notation introduced in (35) allows us to express the fact that a set of frames in which the symbol A occurs imposes a corresponding subclassification on A, with one subdivision corresponding to each listed context. Thus in the case of Verb subclassification, we shall have, instead of (33), the rule (40), as a better approximation:

(40) $V \to CS/ -$ $\begin{cases} \text{NP} \\ \# \\ \text{Adjective} \\ \text{Predicate-Nominal} \\ like^\frown\text{Predicate-Nominal}] \\ \text{Prepositional-Phrase} \\ that^\frown S' \\ \text{NP } (of^\frown Det^\frown N) \ S' \\ \text{etc.} \end{cases}$ [21]

The lexicon might now contain the items

(41)   *eat*, $[+V, + - \text{NP}]$
       elapse, $[+V, + - \#]$
       grow, $[+V, + - \text{NP}, + - \#, + - \text{Adjective}]$
       become, $[+V, + - \text{Adjective}, + - \text{Predicate-Nominal}]$
       seem, $[+V, + - \text{Adjective}, + - like^\frown\text{Predicate-Nominal}]$
       look, $[+V, + - (\text{Prepositional-Phrase}) \#, + - \text{Adjective},$
       $+ - like^\frown\text{Predicate-Nominal}]$
       believe, $[+V, + - \text{NP}, + - that^\frown S']$
       persuade, $[+V, + - \text{NP } (of^\frown Det^\frown N) \ S']$

and so on.[22] The rules (40) supplemented by the lexicon (41) will permit such expressions as *John eats food, a week elapsed, John grew a beard, John grew, John grew sad, John became sad, John became president, John seems sad, John seems like a nice fellow,*

John looked, John looked at Bill, John looks sad, John looks like a nice fellow, John believes me, John believes that it is unlikely, John persuaded Bill that we should leave, John persuaded Bill of the necessity for us to leave.

We see that with a slight extension of conventional notations the systematic use of complex symbols permits a fairly simple and informative statement of one of the basic processes of subclassification.

We can use the same notational device to express the kinds of selectional restriction expressed in such rules as (34), which assign features of the Subject and Object to the Verb. Thus we can replace (34) by the rules

$$
(42) \begin{matrix} \text{(i)} \\ \text{(ii)} \\ \text{(iii)} \\ \text{(iv)} \end{matrix} \Bigg\} [+V] \rightarrow CS/ \begin{cases} [+\text{Abstract}]\ \text{Aux} \, — \\ [-\text{Abstract}]\ \text{Aux} \, — \\ — \ \text{Det}\ [+\text{Animate}] \\ — \ \text{Det}\ [-\text{Animate}] \end{cases}
$$

where now [[+Abstract] Aux —] is the feature denoted in (34) as [[+Abstract]-Subject], etc. The notational convention (36)–(37) shows in what respect a system of rules such as (34), but not (35), expresses a linguistically significant generalization.

The rules of (40) and (42) analyze a category into a complex symbol in terms of the frame in which this category appears. The rules differ in that in the case of (40) the frame is stated in terms of category symbols, whereas in the case of (42) the frame is stated in terms of syntactic features. Rules such as (40), which analyze a symbol in terms of its categorial context, I shall henceforth call *strict subcategorization rules*. Rules such as (42), which analyze a symbol (generally, a complex symbol) in terms of syntactic features of the frames in which it appears, I shall call *selectional rules*. The latter express what are usually called "selectional restrictions" or "restrictions of cooccurrence." We shall see later that there are important syntactic and semantic differences between strict subcategorization rules and selectional rules with respect to both their form and function, and that consequently this distinction may be an important one.

In the case of both the strict subcategorization rules (40) and the selectional rules (42), there are still deeper generalizations that are not yet expressed. Consider first the case of (40). This set of rules imposes a categorization on the symbol V in terms of a certain set of frames in which V occurs. It fails to express the fact that *every frame in which V appears, in the VP,* is relevant to the strict subcategorization of V, and the further fact that *no frame which is not part of the VP* is relevant to the strict subcategorization of V. Thus the symbol VP will dominate such strings as the following, in derivations generated by rewriting rules of the base:

(43) (i) V   (*elapse*)
   (ii) V NP   (*bring the book*)
  (iii) V NP *that*-S   (*persuade John that there was no hope*)
  (iv) V Prep-Phrase   (*decide on a new course of action*)
   (v) V Prep-Phrase Prep-Phrase   (*argue with John about the plan*)
  (vi) V Adj   (*grow sad*)
 (vii) V like Predicate-Nominal (*feel like a new man*)
(viii) V NP Prep-Phrase   (*save the book for John*)
  (ix) V NP Prep-Phrase Prep-Phrase (*trade the bicycle to John for a tennis racket*)

and so on. Corresponding to each such string dominated by VP, there is a strict subcategorization of Verbs. On the other hand, Verbs are not strictly subcategorized in terms of types of Subject NP's or type of Auxiliary, apparently.[23] This observation suggests that at a certain point in the sequence of base rewriting rules, we introduce the rule that strictly subcategorizes Verbs in the following form:

(44) V → CS/ — α, where α is a string such that Vα is a VP

The rule schema (44) expresses the actual generalization that determines strict categorization of Verbs in terms of the set of syntactic frames in which V appears.

We have now discussed the problem of formulating the generalizations that actually underlie the strict subcategorization rules (40), and have presented informally a device that would accomplish this result. It remains to consider the selectional rules, of which (42) presents a sample. Here too it is evident that there are linguistically significant generalizations that are not expressed in the rules as given in this form. Thus the rules (42) do not make use of the fact that *every* syntactic feature of the Subject and Object imposes a corresponding classification on the Verb,[24] not just certain arbitrarily chosen features. Once again, a certain extension of the notational devices for formulating rules is called for so that the evaluation measure will operate correctly. In this case, the most natural way to formulate the underlying generalization would be by such rule schemata as

(45) $[+V] \rightarrow CS/ \left\{ \begin{array}{l} \alpha^\frown Aux\, - \\ -\, Det^\frown \alpha \end{array} \right\}$, where α is an N,

α being a variable ranging over specified features. We interpret these schemata as abbreviating the sequence of all rules derived from (45) by replacing α by a symbol meeting the stated condition, namely dominance by N (with some ordering that is apparently inconsequential). The rules abbreviated by the schemata (45) assert, simply, that each feature of the preceding and following Noun is assigned to the Verb and determines an appropriate selectional subclassification of it. Thus if the rule (45) appears in the sequence of base rules after the rules (20), then each of the lexical features that was introduced by the rules of (20) would determine a corresponding subclassification of the complex symbol $[+V]$.

The rule schemata (44) and (45) deal with a situation in which an element (in this case, the Verb) is subcategorized in terms of the contexts in which this element appears, where these contexts all meet some syntactic condition. In all cases, an important generalization would be missed if the relevant contexts were merely listed. The theory of grammar would fail to express the fact that a grammar is obviously more highly valued if subcategorization is determined by a set of contexts that is syntactically definable. The appropriate sense of "syntactically definable" is suggested by the examples just given. A precise account of "syntactically definable" can be given quite readily within the framework of transformational grammar.

At the conclusion of § 2.3.3 we pointed out that a system of rewriting rules that makes use of complex symbols is no longer a phrase structure grammar (though it does not differ from such a grammar in weak generative capacity), but rather is more properly regarded as a kind of transformational grammar. The rule schemata (44) and (45) take on the character of transformational rules even more clearly. Rules of this type are essentially of the form

(46) $A \rightarrow CS/X - Y$, where XAY is analyzable as $Z_1, \cdots, Z_n$,

where the expression "X is analyzable as $Y_1, \cdots, Y_n$," means that X can be segmented into $X = X_1 \cdots X_n$ in such a way that X_i is dominated by Y_i, in the Phrase-marker of the derivation under construction. Analyzability, in this sense, is the basic predicate in terms of which the theory of transformational grammar is developed (see Chomsky, 1955, 1956, and many other references). Thus, for example, we can often restate the rules in question with the use of labeled brackets (regarding these as carried along in the course of a derivation), or by allowing complex symbols to appear at arbitrary points of a derivation, with certain features being carried over to certain of the "descendants" of a particular category symbol in the manner of Matthews's system referred to in note 13, or in various other similar ways.[25]

Along with a lexicon, then, the base component of the grammar contains: (i) rewriting rules that typically involve branching and that utilize only categorial (noncomplex) symbols and (ii) rule schemata that involve only lexical categories, except in the statement of context, and that utilize complex symbols. The rules (i) are ordinary phrase structure rules, but the rules (ii) are transformational rules of an elementary sort. One might, in fact, suggest that even the rules (i) must be replaced, in part, by

rule schemata that go beyond the range of phrase structure rules
in strong generative capacity (cf., for example, Chomsky and
Miller, 1963, p. 298, Chomsky and Schützenberger, 1963, p. 133,
where such operations as conjunction are discussed in terms of
a framework of this sort), or by local transformations (cf. note 18).
In short, it has become clear that it was a mistake, in the first
place, to suppose that the base component of a transformational
grammar should be strictly limited to a system of phrase structure rules, although such a system does play a fundamental role
as a subpart of the base component. In fact, its role is that of
defining the grammatical relations that are expressed in the
deep structure and that therefore determine the semantic interpretation of a sentence.

The descriptive power of the base component is greatly en-
riched by permitting transformational rules; consequently, it is
important to see what limitations can be imposed on their
use — that is, to see to what extent freedom to use such devices
is actually empirically motivated. From the examples just given,
it seems that there are indeed heavy restrictions. Thus the strict
subcategorization of V involves only frames that are dominated
by the symbol VP, and there are also obvious restrictions (to
which we return in § 4.2) involved in the use of selectional rules.
Putting these aside for the moment, let us continue with the
investigation of strict subcategorization rules.

The symbol V is introduced by rules of the form: $VP \rightarrow V \cdots$,
and it is frames dominated by VP that determine strict subcategorization of Verbs. This suggests that we impose the following general condition on strict subcategorization rules: each such
rule must be of the form

(47) $A \rightarrow CS/\alpha - \beta$, where $\alpha A \beta$ is a σ,

where, furthermore, σ is the category symbol that appears on
the left in the rule $\sigma \rightarrow \cdots A \cdots$ that introduces A. Thus (47),
reformulated within the framework of the theory of grammatical
transformations, would be what we have called a "local transformation." Cf. note 18. The italicized condition guarantees that

the transformation is, furthermore, "strictly local" in the sense of note 18. If this condition of strict local subcategorization is adopted as a general condition on the form of grammar, then the strict subcategorization rules can simply be given in the form

(48) $A \rightarrow CS$

the rest being supplied automatically by a convention. In other words, the only characteristic of these rules that must be explicitly indicated in the grammar is their position in the sequence of rules. This position fixes the set of frames that determine subcategorization.

Suppose that the rule that introduces Nouns into the grammar is, essentially, the following:

(49)   NP $\rightarrow$ (Det) N(S′)

In this case, we should expect strict subcategorization of Nouns into the categories [Det — S′], [Det —], [— S′], and [—] (continuing with the notational conventions for features introduced earlier). The category [Det — S′] is the category of Nouns with sentential Complements (such as "the *idea* that he might succeed," "the *fact* that he was guilty," "the *opportunity* for him to leave," "the *habit* of working hard" — the latter involving a sentential Complement with an obligatorily deleted Subject). The category [Det —] is simply the category of Common Nouns. The category [—] is the category of Proper Nouns, that is, Nouns with no Determiner (or, as in the case of "The Hague," "The Nile," with a fixed Determiner that may just as well be taken as part of the Noun itself, rather than as part of a freely and independently selected Determiner system).[26] If this is correct, then the Proper/Common distinction is strict subcategorial, and does not fall together with the other features introduced in (20). The category [— S′] is not realized in so obvious a way as the others. Perhaps one should utilize this category to account for "quotes contexts" and, more importantly, for the impersonal *it* of such sentences as "it strikes me that he had no choice," "it surprised me that he left," "it is obvious that the attempt must fail," which derive from underlying strings with NP's of the form: it⌢Sentence (the Sentence Complement either being separated from it by a transformation, as in the examples cited, or substituting for it by a strictly local transformation in the manner described in note 18).

Returning, once again, to Verb subcategorization, we note one further consequence of accepting the general condition suggested in connection with (47). It is well known that in Verb–Prepositional-Phrase constructions one can distinguish various degrees of "cohesion" between the Verb and the accompanying Prepositional-Phrase. The point can be illustrated clearly by such ambiguous constructions as

(50) he decided on the boat

which may mean "he chose the boat" or "he made his decision while on the boat." Both kinds of phrase appear in

(51) he decided on the boat on the train

that is, "he chose the boat while on the train." Clearly, the second Prepositional-Phrase in (51) is simply a Place Adverbial, which, like a Time Adverbial, has no particular connection with the Verb, but in fact modifies the entire Verb Phrase or perhaps the entire sentence. It can, in fact, be optionally preposed to the sentence, although the first Prepositional-Phrase of (51), which is in close construction to the Verb, cannot — that is, the sentence "on the train, he decided" is unambiguous. There are many other examples of the same kind (for example, "he worked at the office" versus "he worked at the job"; "he laughed at ten o'clock" versus "he laughed at the clown"; "he ran after dinner" versus "he ran after John"). Clearly, Time and Place Adverbials can occur quite freely with various types of Verb Phrase, on the one hand, whereas many types of Prepositional-Phrase appear in much closer construction to Verbs. This observation suggests that we modify slightly the first several rules of the base, replacing them by

(52) (i) S → NP⌒Predicate-Phrase

   (ii) Predicate-Phrase → Aux⌒VP (Place) (Time)

   (iii) VP →
$\left\{ \begin{array}{l} be \text{ Predicate} \\ V \left\{ \begin{array}{l} \text{(NP) (Prep-Phrase) (Prep-Phrase) (Manner)} \\ \text{Adj} \\ \text{S}' \\ (like) \text{ Predicate-Nominal} \end{array} \right\} \end{array} \right\}$

   (iv) Prep-Phrase →
$\left\{ \begin{array}{l} \text{Direction} \\ \text{Duration} \\ \text{Place} \\ \text{Frequency} \\ \text{etc.} \end{array} \right\}$

   (v) V → CS

The conventions governing complex symbols will interpret (v) as strictly subcategorizing Verbs with respect to all contexts introduced in the second part of rule (iii) and in rule (iv).

It will follow, then, that Verbs are subcategorized with respect to the Prepositional-Phrases introduced by (52iii) but not with respect to those introduced by (52ii) — namely, the Place and Time Adverbials that are associated with the full Predicate-Phrase, and that might, in fact, be in part more closely associated with the Auxiliary (cf. note 23) or with Sentence Adverbials which form a "pre-Sentence" unit in the underlying structure. Thus Verbs will be subcategorized with respect to Verbal Complements, but not with respect to Verb Phrase Complements. That this is essentially the case is clear from the examples given. To illustrate, once again, in connection with the four types of Adverbials listed in (52iv), we have such phrases as (53), but not (54):[27]

(53) dash — into the room (V — Direction)
     last — for three hours (V — Duration)
     remain — in England (V — Place)
     win — three times a week (V — Frequency)

(54) dash — in England
     last — three times a week
     remain — into the room
     win — for three hours

Similarly, the italicized phrases in "he argued *with John (about politics)*," "he aimed (the gun) *at John*," "he talked *about Greece*," "he ran *after John*," "he decided *on a new course of action*," and so on, are of types that induce a subcategorization of Verbs, whereas the italicized phrases in "John died *in England*," "John played Othello *in England*," "John always runs *after dinner*," and so on, do not play a role in Verb subcategorization, since they are introduced by a rule (namely (52ii)) the left-hand symbol of which does not directly dominate V.

Similarly, the other contexts introduced in (52iii) will play a role in strict subcategorization of Verbs. In particular, the Manner Adverbial participates in Verb subcategorization. Thus Verbs generally take Manner Adverbials freely, but there are some that do not — for example: *resemble, have, marry* (in the sense of "John married Mary," not "the preacher married John and Mary," which does take Manner Adverbials freely); *fit* (in the sense of "the suit fits me," not "the tailor fitted me," which does take Manner Adverbials freely); *cost, weigh* (in the sense of "the car weighed two tons," not "John weighed the letter," which does take Manner Adverbials freely); and so on. The Verbs that do not take Manner Adverbials freely Lees has called "middle Verbs" (Lees, 1960a, p. 8), and he has also observed that these are, characteristically, the Verbs with following NP's that do not undergo the passive transformation. Thus we do not have "John is resembled by Bill," "a good book is had by John," "John was married by Mary," "I am fitted by the suit," "ten dollars is cost by this book," "two tons is weighed by this car," and so on (although of course "John was married by Mary" is acceptable in the sense of "John was married by the preacher," and we can have "I was fitted by the tailor," "the letter was weighed by John," etc.).[28]

These observations suggest that the Manner Adverbial should have as one of its realizations a "dummy element" signifying that the passive transformation must obligatorily apply. That is, we may have the rule (55) as a rewriting rule of the base and may formulate the passive transformation so as to apply to strings of the form (56), with an elementary transformation that sub-

stitutes the first NP for the dummy element *passive* and places
the second NP in the position of the first NP:

(55)   Manner → by⌢*passive*

(56)   NP — Aux — V — ⋯ — NP — ⋯ — by⌢*passive* — ⋯

(where the leftmost ⋯ in (56) requires further specification —
e.g., it cannot contain an NP).

This formulation has several advantages over that presented
in earlier work on transformational grammar (such as Chomsky,
1957). First of all, it accounts automatically for the restriction of
passivization to Verbs that take Manner Adverbials freely. That
is, a Verb will appear in the frame (56) and thus undergo the
passive transformation only if it is positively specified, in the
lexicon, for the strict subcategorization feature [— NP⌢Manner],
in which case it will also take Manner Adverbials freely. Second,
with this formulation it is possible to account for the derived
Phrase-marker of the passive by the rules for substitution transformations. This makes it possible to dispense entirely with an
ad hoc rule of derived constituent structure that, in fact, was
motivated solely by the passive construction (cf. Chomsky, 1957,
pp. 73–74). Third, it is now possible to account for "pseudopassives," such as "the proposal was vehemently argued against,"
"the new course of action was agreed on," "John is looked up to
by everyone," by a slight generalization of the ordinary passive
transformation. In fact, the schema (56) already permits these
passives. Thus "everyone looks up to John by *passive*" meets
the condition (56), with *John* as the second NP, and it will be
converted into "John is looked up to by everyone" by the same
elementary transformation that forms "John was seen by everyone" from "everyone saw John." In the earlier formulation (cf.
Chomsky, 1955, Chapter IX), it was necessary to treat pseudopassives by a new transformation. The reason was that V of (56)
had to be limited to transitive Verbs, for the ordinary passive
transformation, so as to exclude the "middle" Verbs *have*,
resemble, etc. But if passivization is determined by a Manner
Adverbial, as just suggested, then V in (56) can be quite free, and

can be an intransitive as well as a transitive Verb. Thus "John is looked up to" and "John was seen" are formed by the same rule despite the fact that only in the latter case is *John* the Direct-Object of the deep structure.

Notice, however, that the Adverbial introduced by (52ii) is not subject to the passive transformation as defined by (56), since it will *follow* the Adverbial *by⌢passive*. This accounts for the fact that we can have "this job is being worked at quite seriously" from "Unspecified-Subject is working at this job quite seriously," where "at this job" is a Verb-Complement introduced by (52iii), but not "the office is being worked at" from "Unspecified-Subject is working at the office," where the phrase "at the office" is a VP-Complement introduced by (52ii) and therefore follows the Manner Adverbial. Similarly, we can have "the boat was decided on" in the sense of "he chose the boat," but not in the sense of "he decided while on the boat." Thus the passive sentence corresponding to (50) is unambiguous, though (50) itself is ambiguous. Many other facts can be explained in the same way.

The fact that we are able, in this way, to account for the nonambiguity of "the boat was decided on by John" as contrasted with the ambiguity of "John decided on the boat," along with many similar examples, provides an indirect justification for the proposal (cf. p. 99) that strict subcategorization rules be limited to strictly local transformations. It is perhaps worth while to trace through the argument again to see why this is so. By the "strictly local subcategorization" principle we know that certain categories must be internal to the VP and others must be external to it. One of the elements that must be internal to the VP, in accordance with this principle, is the marker for passivization, since it plays a role in strict subcategorization of the Verb. Furthermore, the marker for passivization is associated with the presence of the Manner Adverbial, which is internal to the VP by the strictly local subcategorization principle. Since the passive transformation must be formulated with the structure index (56), it follows that NP's in VP-Complements are not subject to "pseudopassivization" while NP's in V-Complements may be subject to this operation. In particular, where "on the boat" is a

V-Complement in "John decided on the boat" (meaning "John chose the boat"), it is subject to pseudopassivization by the passive transformation; but where "on the boat" is a VP-Complement in "John decided on the boat" (meaning "John decided while he was on the boat," equivalently, "on the boat, John decided"), it is not subject to pseudopassivization since it does not meet the condition (56). Therefore, observing that "the boat was decided on by John" is unambiguous and means only that John chose the boat, we conclude that the premise of this argument — namely the assumption that strict subcategorization is limited to strictly local transformations — has empirical support.

The reanalysis (52) requires that the definitions of functional notions proposed in § 2.2 (cf. (11)) be slightly altered. Thus we might perhaps define the notion "Predicate-of" as [Predicate-Phrase, S] rather than as [VP, S]. This revised formulation of the rules, incidentally, illustrates another property of the traditional functional notions. We observed in § 2.2 that these notions are defined only for what we called "major categories." Furthermore, it seems that they are defined only for those major categories A that appear in rules of the form $X \to \cdots A \cdots B \cdots$ or $X \to \cdots B \cdots A \cdots$, where B is also a major category. This seems quite natural, considering the relational character of these notions.

§ 3. AN ILLUSTRATIVE FRAGMENT OF THE BASE COMPONENT

Let us now summarize this discussion by returning to the original problem, posed in § 1, of presenting structural information of the sort illustrated in (2) of § 1 in a set of rules that are designed to express precisely the basic linguistic processes involved.

We may now consider a generative grammar with a base component containing, among many others, the rules and rule schemata (57) and the lexicon (58):

(57) (i) S → NP⌒Predicate-Phrase
(ii) Predicate-Phrase → Aux⌒VP (Place) (Time)

(iii) VP → $\left\{ \begin{array}{l} \text{Copula}^\frown\text{Predicate} \\ \text{V} \left\{ \begin{array}{l} \text{(NP) (Prep-Phrase) (Prep-Phrase) (Manner)} \\ \text{S}' \\ \text{Predicate} \end{array} \right. \end{array} \right\}$

(iv) Predicate → $\left\{ \begin{array}{l} \text{Adjective} \\ (like) \text{ Predicate-Nominal} \end{array} \right\}$

(v) Prep-Phrase → Direction, Duration, Place, Frequency, etc.

(vi) V → CS

(vii) NP → (Det) N (S')

(viii) N → CS

(ix) [+Det —] → [±Count]

(x) [+Count] → [±Animate]

(xi) [+N, + —] → [±Animate]

(xii) [+Animate] → [±Human]

(xiii) [−Count] → [± Abstract]

(xiv) [+V] → CS/$\alpha^\frown$Aux — (Det$^\frown\beta$) $\Big\}$, where α is an N and

(xv) Adjective → CS/α $\cdots$ — $\Big\}$ β is an N

(xvi) Aux → Tense (M) (Aspect)

(xvii) Det → (pre-Article$^\frown$of) Article (post-Article)

(xviii) Article → [±Definite]

(58) (*sincerity*, [+N, +Det —, − Count, +Abstract, $\cdots$])
  (*boy*, [+N, +Det —, +Count, +Animate, +Human, $\cdots$])
  (*frighten*, [+V, + — NP, +[+Abstract] Aux — Det
    [+Animate], +Object-deletion, $\cdots$])
  (*may*, [+M, $\cdots$])

This system of rules will generate the Phrase-marker (59).

Adding the rules that realize Definite as *the* and non-Definite as null before a following non-Count Noun, we derive the sentence "sincerity may frighten the boy" of § 1, with the Phrase-marker (59). Notice that this fragment of the base is "sequential" in the sense of § 2.1.

We have only sketched the procedure for constructing a Phrase-marker of the required sort from a derivation. However, this is a relatively minor matter of appropriate formalization and involves nothing of principle. In particular, (59) represents not only all information involving the relation "is a," holding

(59)

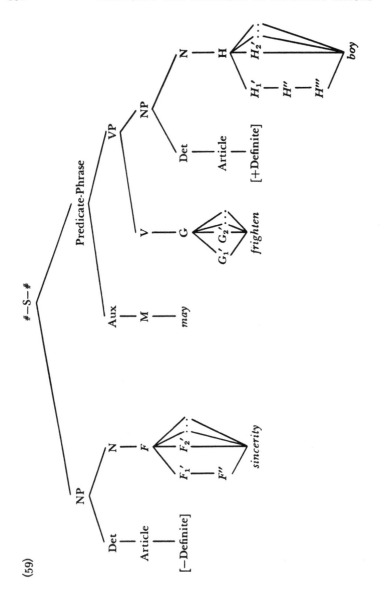

$$F = [+\text{Det}\text{—}] = \text{Common}$$
$$F_1' = [-\text{Count}]$$

$\cdot \quad \cdot \quad \cdot$

$$F'' = [+\text{Abstract}]$$

$$G = [+\text{—}\text{NP}] = \text{Transitive}$$
$$G_1' = [+[+\text{Abstract}]\text{Aux}\text{—}\text{Det}[+\text{Animate}]]$$

$$G_2' = [+\text{Object-deletion}]$$

$\cdot \quad \cdot \quad \cdot$

$$H = [+\text{Det}\text{—}] = F$$
$$H_1' = [+\text{Count}] = -F_1'$$

$\cdot \quad \cdot \quad \cdot$

$$H'' = [+\text{Animate}]$$
$$H''' = [+\text{Human}]$$

between strings and the categories (many of them now represented by features) to which they belong but also the hierarchic relation among these categories that is provided by the rules and mirrored precisely in the derivation.

The Phrase-marker (59) provides directly all information of the sort specified in (2i) and (2iii); and, as we have observed, functional information of the sort specified in (2ii) is derivable from this Phrase-marker as well. If the analysis that we have given is correct, then it is devices of the sort just exhibited that are implicit in the informal statements of traditional grammar summarized in (2), with one exception, to which we shall turn in the next section.

Notice that neither the lexicon (58) nor the Phrase-marker (59) is fully specified. There are clearly other syntactic features that must be indicated, and we have given no semantic features in either (58) or (59). In part, it is clear how these gaps can be filled, but it would be a serious mistake, in this case, to suppose that this is in general merely a question of added detail.

One final comment is necessary in connection with the lexicon (58). Given a lexical entry (D,C), where D is a phonological feature matrix and C a complex symbol, the lexical rule (cf. p. 84) permits substitution of D for any complex symbol K that is not distinct from C. Consequently, lexical entries must be specified negatively for features corresponding to contexts in which they may not occur. Thus in (58), for example, *boy* must be specified as $[-V]$, so as to exclude it from the position of *frighten* in "sincerity may frighten the boy," and not only must *frighten* be specified as $[-N]$, to exclude it from the position of *boy* in this sentence, but it must also be specified negatively for the feature $[-\text{Adjective}]$, so as to exclude it from the position of *turn* in "his hair turned gray," and so on. These negative specifications were not actually given in (58).

We can deal with this matter by adopting several additional conventions governing the base component. First of all, we may assume that a base rule that analyzes the lexical category A into a complex symbol automatically includes the feature $[+A]$ as one of the elements of this complex symbol (see (20), § 2.3.2).

Second, we may assume that each lexical entry automatically, by convention, contains the feature [−A] for every lexical category *A*, unless it is explicitly provided with the feature [+*A*]. Thus in (58), the entry for *boy* contains [−V], [−Adjective], [−M] (cf. note 9).[29] Third, in the case of features introduced by strict subcategorization or selectional rules (what we have called the "contextual features"), we may adopt one of the following conventions:

(i) list in the lexicon only the features corresponding to frames in which the item in question *cannot* appear (rather than, as in (58), those corresponding to features in which it *can* appear)

(ii) list only the features corresponding to frames in which the item *can* appear, as in (58) (in case (i) or case (ii) we add the further convention that an item is specified in the opposite way for every contextual feature not mentioned in its lexical entry)

(iii) adopt (i) for the strict subcategorization features and (ii) for the selectional features

(iv) adopt (ii) for the strict subcategorization features and (i) for the selectional features. In any case, the distinctness requirement of the lexical rule will now exclude items from certain contexts, and permit them in others.

These conventions embody alternative empirical hypotheses concerning valuation of grammar. Thus (i) is correct if the most highly valued grammar is that in which the distribution of items is least constrained, and (ii) is correct if the most highly valued grammar is that in which the distribution of items is most constrained (similarly, (iii) and (iv)). For the time being, I have no strong examples to support one or another of these assumptions, and thus prefer to leave the question open. We shall return briefly to the problem in Chapter 4.

§ 4. TYPES OF BASE RULES

§ 4.1. Summary

The fragment presented in § 3 illustrates the kinds of rules that apparently are to be found in the base component. There is a fundamental distinction between the rewriting rules (57) and the lexicon (58). The lexical rule need not be stated in the grammar since it is universal and hence part of the theory of grammar. Its status is just like that of the principles that define "derivation" in terms of a system of rewriting rules, for example. It thus has the status of a convention determining the interpretation of the grammar, rather than the status of a rule of the grammar. In terms of the framework of § 6, Chapter 1, we may say that the lexical rule in fact constitutes part of the general, language-independent definition of the function f of (14iv), § 6, Chapter 1.

Among the rewriting rules of the base component we can distinguish *branching rules*, such as (i), (ii), (iii), (iv), (v), (vii), (xvi), (xvii), from *subcategorization rules*, such as all others of (57). All rewriting rules are of the form

(60) $A \rightarrow Z/X - W$

The branching rules are those rules of the form (60) in which neither A nor Z involves any complex symbols. Thus a branching rule analyzes a category symbol A into a string of (one or more) symbols each of which is either a terminal symbol or a nonterminal category symbol. A subcategorization rule, on the other hand, introduces syntactic features, and thus forms or extends a complex symbol. We have, so far, restricted the subcategorization rules to lexical categories. In particular, we have not permitted rules of the form (60) in which A is a complex symbol and Z a terminal or category symbol or a string of more than one symbol. This restriction may be a bit too severe, and we must apparently weaken it slightly. See Chapter 4, § 2. Notice that these two sets of rules (branching and subcategorization) are not ordered with respect to one another, although once a subcategorization rule has been applied to a certain category symbol σ no branching rule can be applied to any of the symbols that are derived from σ.

Branching rules and subcategorization rules may be *context-free* (such as all of the branching rules of (57) and (x), (xi), (xii), (xiii), (xviii)) or *context-sensitive* (such as (vi), (viii), (xiv), (xv)). Notice that (57) contains no context-sensitive branching rules. Moreover, the subcategorization rules that are context-sensitive are, in effect, strictly local transformational rules (cf. p. 99). These are important facts, to which we return in Chapter 3.

Among the context-sensitive subcategorization rules we have, furthermore, distinguished two important subtypes, namely *strict subcategorization rules* (such as (57vi) and (57viii)), which subcategorize a lexical category in terms of the frame of category symbols in which it appears, and *selectional rules* (such as (57xiv), (57xv)), which subcategorize a lexical category in terms of syntactic features that appear in specified positions in the sentence.

We noted that subcategorization rules may follow branching rules in the sequence of rules constituting the base, but that once a subcategorization rule has applied to form a complex symbol Σ, no branching rule can later apply to Σ (but cf. Chapter 4, § 2). The same relation apparently holds between strict subcategorization rules and selectional rules. That is, these may be interspersed in the base, but once a selectional rule has applied to form the complex symbol Σ, no strict subcategorization rule applies later to develop Σ further. So, at least, it appears from the examples that I have considered. Perhaps this should be imposed as a general, additional condition on the base.

§ 4.2. Selectional rules and grammatical relations

We shall say that a selectional rule, such as (57xiv), (57xv), defines a *selectional relation* between two positions in a sentence — for example, in the case of (57xiv), the position of the Verb and that of the immediately preceding or immediately following Noun. Such selectional relations determine grammatical relations, in one of the senses of this traditional term. We observed earlier that the notion of grammatical function defined in § 2.2 did not yet account for the assignment of the Subject-Verb relation to the pair *sincerity, frighten* and the Verb-Object relation to *frighten, boy* in *sincerity may frighten the boy* (=(1)). The suggested definition of grammatical relation would account for these assertions, given the grammar (57), (58). The same notion of grammatical relation could, in fact, have been defined in terms of the heads of major categories (cf. § 2.2), but the definition in terms of selectional relations seems somewhat more natural and avoids the problem noted on pp. 73–74. With this notion now defined, we have completed the analysis of the informal grammatical statement (2) of § 1.[30]

Consider now the selectional rules (57xiv), (57xv), which constrain the choice of Verb and Adjective in terms of a free choice of certain features of the Noun (in this case, the Subject and Object). Suppose, instead, that we were to subcategorize the Verb by a context-free rule, and then to use a selectional rule to determine the subcategorization of the Subject and Object. We might have, for the Verb, such a rule as

(61) V → [+V, +[+Abstract]-Subject, +[+Animate]-Object][31]

Thus we might in particular form the complex symbol

(62) [+V, +[+Abstract]-Subject, +[+Animate]-Object]

which can be replaced by a lexical item such as *frighten*, lexically marked as allowing an Abstract Subject and an Animate Object. We must now give a context-sensitive selectional rule to determine the choice of Subject and Object, just as in (57) we gave such a rule to determine the choice of Verb in terms of Subject and Object. Thus we would have such rules as

$$(63) \quad N \rightarrow CS/ \left\{ \begin{matrix} - \text{Aux} + \alpha \\ \alpha + \text{Det} - \end{matrix} \right\}, \text{ where } \alpha \text{ is a V}$$

These rules would assign features of the Verb to the Subject and Object, just as (57xiv) assigned features of the Subject and Object to the Verb. For example, if the Verb is (62), the Subject would be specified as having the features

(64) [pre-+[+Abstract]-Subject, pre-+[+Animate]-Object]

Similarly, the Object would have the features

(65) [post-+[+Abstract]-Subject, post-+[+Animate]-Object]

But, clearly, the feature [pre-+[+Animate]-Object] is irrelevant to choice of Subject Noun, and the feature [post-+[+Abstract]-

Subject] is irrelevant to choice of Object Noun. Much more serious than this, however, is the fact that a Noun must be marked in the lexicon for the feature [pre-X-Subject] if and only if it is marked for the feature [post-X-Object], where X is any feature. That is, the choice of elements for the position "Subject of a Verb with Animate Subject" is the same as the choice of elements for the position "Object of a Verb with Animate Object." Animate Nouns appear in both positions. But the feature [Animate] is no longer available for Nouns, only the features [pre-+[+Animate]-Subject] and [post-+[+Animate]-Object]. Consequently, a mass of perfectly *ad hoc* rules must be added to the grammar to assign to Nouns with the feature [pre-X-Subject] also the feature [post-X-Object], for each feature X, and conversely. Moreover, the features [pre-X-Subject], [post-X-Object], for each X, are single symbols, and the fact that X occurs in both of them cannot be referred to by a rule of the grammar (unless we complicate the mechanism further by allowing features to have a feature composition themselves).

In short, the decision to choose the complex symbol analysis of Verbs independently and to select Nouns by a selectional rule in terms of Verbs leads to a quite considerable complication of the grammar. The problems are magnified when we bring into account the independent Noun-Adjective selectional rules. In much the same way we can rule out the possibility of allowing Subject to select Verb but Verb to select Object.

We see, then, that within the framework so far developed, there is no alternative to selecting Verbs in terms of Nouns (and, by a similar argument, Adjectives in terms of Nouns), rather than conversely. Furthermore, this framework seems to be optimal, in that it involves no more mechanism than is actually forced by the linguistic facts. One would imagine that a similar argument can be given for any language. If this is true, it is possible to take another significant step toward a general characterization of the categories Noun, Verb, Adjective, etc. (see §§ 2.1, 2.2).

In § 2.2, I defined "lexical category" and "major category," the latter being a lexical category or a category dominating a string containing a lexical category. Suppose that among the lexical categories, we label as *Noun* the one that is *selectionally dominant* in the sense that its feature composition is determined by a context-free subcategorization rule, its features being carried over by selectional rules to other lexical categories. Among the major categories introduced in the analysis of *Sentence*, we now designate as NP the one that is analyzed as $\cdots$ N $\cdots$. A major category that directly dominates $\cdots$ NP $\cdots$ we can designate VP, and one that directly dominates VP, we can designate Predicate-Phrase. We can define V in various ways — for example, as the lexical category X that appears in a string $\cdots X \cdots$ NP $\cdots$ or $\cdots$ NP $\cdots X \cdots$ directly dominated by VP (assuming that there can be only one such X) or as the lexical category that may obtain its features from selectional rules involving two or more N's (if transitivity is a category that is universally realized). One might now go on to attempt to characterize other lexical, major, and nonmajor categories in general terms. To the extent that we can do this, we shall have succeeded also in giving a substantive specification to the functional notions discussed in § 2.2.

It will be obvious to the reader that this characterization is not intended as definitive in any sense. The reason has already been indicated in note 2. There is no problem in principle of sharpening or generalizing these definitions in one way or another, and there are many formal features of the grammar that can be brought into consideration in doing so. The problem is merely that for the moment there is no strong empirical motivation for one or another suggestion that might be made in these directions. This is a consequence of the fact that there are so few grammars that attempt to give an explicit characterization of the range of sentences and structural descriptions (that is, so few generative grammars), even in a partial sketch. As explicit grammatical descriptions with this goal accumulate, it will no doubt be possible to give empirical justification for various refinements and revisions of such loosely sketched proposals as these, and perhaps to give a substantive characterization to the universal vocabulary from which grammatical descriptions are constructed. However, there is no reason to rule out, a priori, the traditional view that such substantive characterizations must ultimately refer to semantic concepts of one sort or another.

Once again, as in §§ 2.1–2.2, it is clear that this attempt to characterize universal categories depends essentially on the fact that the base of the syntactic component does not, in itself, explicitly characterize the full range of sentences, but only a highly restricted set of elementary structures from which actual sentences are constructed by transformational rules.[32] The base Phrase-markers may be regarded as the elementary content elements from which the semantic interpretations of actual sentences are constructed.[33] Therefore the observation that the semantically significant functional notions (grammatical relations) are directly represented in base structures, and only in these, should come as no surprise; and it is, furthermore, quite natural to suppose that formal properties of the base will provide the framework for the characterization of universal categories.

To say that formal properties of the base will provide the framework for the characterization of universal categories is to assume that much of the structure of the base is common to all languages. This is a way of stating a traditional view, whose origins can again be traced back at least to the *Grammaire générale et raisonnée* (Lancelot *et al.*, 1660). To the extent that relevant evidence is available today, it seems not unlikely that it is true. Insofar as aspects of the base structure are not specific to a particular language, they need not be stated in the grammar of this language. Instead, they are to be stated only in general linguistic theory, as part of the definition of the notion "human language" itself. In traditional terms, they pertain to the form of language in general rather than to the form of particular languages, and thus presumably reflect what the mind brings to the task of language acquisition rather than what it discovers (or invents) in the course of carrying out this task. Thus to some extent the account of the base rules suggested here may not belong to the grammar of English any more than the definition of "derivation" or of "transformation" belongs to the grammar of English. Cf., §§ 6 and 8, Chapter 1.

It is commonly held that modern linguistic and anthropological investigations have conclusively refuted the doctrines of classical universal grammar, but this claim seems to me very much exaggerated. Modern work has, indeed, shown a great diversity in the surface structures of languages. However, since the study of deep structure has not been its concern, it has not attempted to show a corresponding diversity of underlying structures, and, in fact, the evidence that has been accumulated in modern study of language does not appear to suggest anything of this sort. The fact that languages may differ from one another quite significantly in surface structure would hardly have come as a surprise to the scholars who developed traditional universal grammar. Since the origins of this work in the *Grammaire générale et raisonnée*, it has been emphasized that the deep structures for which universality is claimed may be quite distinct from the surface structures of sentences as they actually appear. Consequently, there is no reason to expect uniformity of surface structures, and the findings of modern linguistics are thus not inconsistent with the hypotheses of universal grammarians. Insofar as attention is restricted to surface structures, the most that can be expected is the discovery of statistical tendencies, such as those presented by Greenberg (1963).

In connection with the selectional rule (57xiv), we have now conclusively ruled out one possibility, namely that the Subject or Object may be selected in terms of an independent, or partially independent, choice of Verb. Not quite so simple is the question of whether this rule, which I now repeat in less abbreviated form as (66), should be preferred to the alternative (67).

$$(66) \begin{matrix} \text{(i)} \\ \text{(ii)} \end{matrix} \Bigg\} \quad [+\text{V}] \rightarrow \text{CS}/ \begin{Bmatrix} \alpha^\frown \text{Aux} - {}^\frown\beta \\ \alpha^\frown \text{Aux} - \end{Bmatrix}$$

$$(67) \begin{matrix} \text{(i)} \\ \text{(ii)} \end{matrix} \Bigg\} \quad [+\text{V}] \rightarrow \text{CS}/ \begin{Bmatrix} \alpha^\frown \text{Aux} - \\ - \text{Det}^\frown\beta \end{Bmatrix}$$

In terms of evaluation measures that have so far been proposed (see, for example, Chomsky, 1955, Chapter 3), there is no way of choosing between these. In accordance with the usual conventions for obligatory application of rewriting rules (cf. *ibid.*), (66i) assigns certain features to Transitive Verbs and (66ii) to Intransitive Verbs. On the other hand, (67i) assigns a feature of Subject selection to all Verbs, and (67ii) assigns a feature of Object selection to Transitive Verbs. If we choose (66), the lexical entry for *frighten* will be positively specified for the feature [[+Abstract] Aux — Det [+Animate]]; if we select (67), it will be positively specified for the two features [[+Abstract] Aux —] and [— Det [+Animate]]. It may appear at first that this is little more than a terminological question, but, as in many such cases, this is not at all obvious. Thus consider the following contexts:

(68) (i) he ——— the platoon
   (ii) his decision to resign his commission ——— the platoon
  (iii) his decision to resign his commission ——— our respect

In (68i) we can have the Verb *command* (I neglect, for simplicity of exposition, questions of choice of Auxiliary). In (68iii) we can also have *command*, but in a different though not totally unrelated sense. In (68ii) we cannot have *command*, but we can have, for example, *baffle*, which can also appear in (68i) but not (68iii). If we select the alternative (67), the Verb *command* will be positively marked for the features [[+Animate] Aux —], [— Det [+Animate]], [[+Abstract] Aux —], and [— Det [+Abstract]]. That is, it will be marked in such a way as to permit it to have either an Animate or an Abstract Noun as Subject or Object. But this specification fails to indicate the dependency between Subject and Object illustrated by the deviance of (68ii), when *command* appears in this context. If we select the alternative (66), *command* will be positively marked for the features [[+Animate] Aux — Det [+Animate]] and [[+Abstract] Aux — Det [+Abstract]], but not [[+Abstract] Aux — Det [+Animate]]. Thus *command* would be excluded from the context (66ii), as required. It is for such reasons that I selected the alternative (66) in the grammatical sketch. It should be noted, however, that the grounds for this decision are very weak, since a crucial question

— namely, how to enter lexical items with a range of distinct but related syntactic and semantic features — is far from settled. I have so far not been able to find stronger examples.

It seems at first as though a certain redundancy results from the decision to select (66) over (67), in the case of Verbs for which choice of Subject and Object is independent. However, the same number of features must be indicated in the lexicon, even in this case. With the choice of (66), the features seem more "complicated," in some sense, but this is a misinterpretation of the notational system. Recall that the notation [+Animate] Aux — Det [+Abstract], for example, is a single symbol designating a particular lexical feature, in our framework.

Clearly, this comment does not exhaust the question, by any means. For some further related discussion, see Chapters 3 and 4.

§ 4.3. Further remarks on subcategorization rules

We have distinguished, in the base, between branching rules and subcategorization rules and between context-free and context-sensitive rules. The context-sensitive subcategorization rules are further subdivided into strict subcategorization rules and selectional rules. These rules introduce contextual features, whereas the context-free subcategorization rules introduce inherent features. One might propose, alternatively, that the subcategorization rules be eliminated from the system of rewriting rules entirely and be assigned, in effect, to the lexicon. In fact, this is a perfectly feasible suggestion.

Suppose, then, that the base is divided into two parts, a *categorial* component and a *lexicon*. The categorial component consists solely of branching rules, which are possibly all context-free (see Chapter 3). In particular, the branching rules of (57) would constitute the categorial component of the base of this fragment of English grammar. The primary role of the categorial component is to define implicitly the basic grammatical relations that function in the deep structures of the language. It may well be that to a large extent the form of the categorial component is determined by the universal conditions that define "human language."

The subcategorization rules can be assigned to the lexical component of the base in the following way. First of all, the context-free subcategorization rules, such as (57ix-xiii), can be regarded as syntactic redundancy rules, and hence assigned to the lexicon. Consider, then, the rules that introduce contextual features. These rules select certain frames in which a symbol appears, and they assign corresponding contextual features. A lexical entry may be substituted in these positions if its contextual features match those of the symbol for which it is substituted. Obviously, the contextual features must appear in lexical items. But the rules that introduce contexual features into complex symbols can be eliminated by an appropriate reformulation of the lexical rule, that is, the rule that introduces lexical items into derivations (cf. p. 84). Instead of formulating this as a context-free rule that operates by matching of complex symbols, we can convert it to a context-sensitive rule by conventions of the following sort. Suppose that we have a lexical entry (D, C) where D is a phonological feature matrix and C is a complex symbol containing the feature $[+X - Y]$. We stipulated previously that the lexical rule permits D to replace the symbol Q of the preterminal string $\varphi Q \psi$ provided that Q is not distinct from C. Suppose that we now require, in addition, that this occurrence of Q actually appear in the frame $X - Y$. That is, we require that $\varphi Q \psi$ equal $\varphi_1 \varphi_2 Q \psi_1 \psi_2$, where φ_2 is dominated by X and ψ_1 by Y in the Phrase-marker of $\varphi Q \psi$. This convention can be formulated precisely in terms of the notion "Analyzability" on which the theory of transformations is based. We now eliminate all context-sensitive subcategorization rules from the grammar and rely on the formulation of lexical features, together with the principle just stated, to achieve their effect. Our earlier conditions on subcategorization rules (cf. § 2.3.4) become conditions on the kinds of contextual features that may appear in lexical entries. Thus strict subcategorization features for an item of the category A must involve frames that, together with A, form the single constituent B that immediately dominates A; and the selectional features must involve the lexical categories that are the heads of grammatically related phrases, in the sense outlined earlier.

We now have no subcategorization rules in the categorial component of the base. A preterminal string is generated by the branching rules of the categorial component. Lexical entries substitute for the lexical categories of a preterminal string by the principle just stated. This formulation brings out very clearly the sense in which our utilization of complex symbols was a device for introducing transformational rules into the base component. In fact, suppose that (for uniformity of specification of transformational rules) we add the convention that in the categorial component, there is a rule $A \rightarrow \Delta$ for each lexical category A, where Δ is a fixed "dummy symbol." The rules of the categorial component will now generate Phrase-markers of strings consisting of various occurrences of Δ (marking the positions of lexical categories) and grammatical formatives. A lexical entry is of the form (D, C), where D is a phonological matrix and C a complex symbol. The complex symbol C contains inherent features and contextual features. We can restate this system of features C directly as the structure index I for a certain substitution transformation. This transformation substitutes (D, C) (now regarded as a complex terminal symbol — see note 15) for a certain occurrence of Δ in the Phrase-marker K if K meets the condition I, which is a Boolean condition in terms of Analyzability in the usual sense of transformational grammar. Where strict subcategorization is involved, the substitution transformation is, furthermore, strictly local in the sense of note 18.

Thus the categorial component may very well be a context-free constituent structure grammar (simple phrase structure grammar) with a reduced terminal vocabulary (that is, with all lexical items mapped into the single symbol Δ). The lexicon consists of entries associated with certain substitution transformations that introduce lexical items into strings generated by the categorial component. All contextual restrictions in the base are provided by these transformational rules of the lexicon. The function of the categorial component is to define the system of grammatical relations and to determine the ordering of elements in deep structures.

This way of developing the base component is not quite equivalent to that presented earlier. The earlier proposal was somewhat more restrictive in certain respects. In both formulations, the contextual features (structure indices of substitution transformations) that may appear in the lexicon are limited by the conditions on strict subcategorization and selectional rules previously discussed. But in the earlier formulation, with subcategorization rules given as rewriting rules, there is a further restriction. The ordering of the rewriting rule $A \rightarrow$ CS places an additional limitation on the class of contextual features that may be used. Similarly, the issue discussed in § 4.2 regarding examples (66)–(68) does not arise in the new formulation. Because of the greater flexibility that it allows, certain Verbs can be restricted in terms of Subject and Object selection, some in terms of Subject selection, and some in terms of Object selection. It is an interesting question whether the greater flexibility permitted by the approach of this subsection is ever needed. If so, this must be the preferable formulation of the theory of the base. If not, then the other formulation, in terms of a lexical rule based on the distinctness condition, is to be preferred. We shall return to this question in Chapter 4.

§ 4.4. *The role of categorial rules*

We have defined the *categorial component* as the system of rewriting rules of the base — that is, the system of base rules exclusive of the lexicon and the subcategorization rules that we, for the present, regard as belonging to the lexicon. The rules of the categorial component carry out two quite separate functions: they define the system of grammatical relations, and they determine the ordering of elements in deep structures. At least the first of these functions appears to be carried out in a very general and perhaps universal way by these rules. The transformational rules map deep structures into surface structures, perhaps reordering elements in various ways in the course of this operation.

It has been suggested several times that these two functions of the categorial component be more sharply separated, and that the second, perhaps, be eliminated completely. Such is the import of the proposals regarding the nature of syntactic structure to be found in Curry (1961) and Šaumjan and Soboleva (1963).[34] They propose, in essence, that in place of such rules as (69), the categorial component should contain the corresponding rules (70), where the element on the right is a set rather than a string:

(69) $S \rightarrow NP^\frown VP$
      $VP \rightarrow V^\frown NP$

(70) $S \rightarrow \{NP, VP\}$
      $VP \rightarrow \{V, NP\}$

In (70), no order is assigned to the elements on the right-hand side of the rule; thus $\{NP, VP\} = \{VP, NP\}$, although $NP^\frown VP \neq VP^\frown NP$. The rules (70) can be used to define grammatical relations in exactly the way indicated for the rules (69). The rules (69) convey more information than the corresponding rules (70), since they not only define an abstract system of grammatical relations but also assign an abstract underlying order to the elements. The Phrase-marker generated by such rules as (69) will be representable as a tree-diagram with labeled nodes and labeled lines; the Phrase-marker generated by such rules as (70) will be representable as a tree-diagram with labeled nodes and unlabeled lines.

Proponents of *set-systems* such as (70) have argued that such systems are more "abstract" than *concatenation-systems* such as (69), and can lead to a study of grammatical relations that is independent of order, this being a phenomenon that belongs only to surface structure. The greater abstractness of set-systems, so far as grammatical relations are concerned, is a myth. Thus the grammatical relations defined by (70) are neither more nor less "abstract" or "order-independent" than those defined by (69);

in fact, the systems of grammatical relations defined in the two cases are identical. A priori, there is no way of determining which theory is correct; it is an entirely empirical question, and the evidence presently available is overwhelmingly in favor of concatenation-systems over set-systems, for the theory of the categorial component. In fact, no proponent of a set-system has given any indication of how the abstract underlying unordered structures are converted into actual strings with surface structures. Hence, the problem of giving empirical support to this theory has not yet been faced.

Presumably, the proposal that the categorial component should be a set-system entails that in a set of syntactically related structures with a single network of grammatical relations (for example, "for us to please John is difficult," "it is difficult for us to please John," "to please John is difficult for us," or "John is difficult for us to please"), each member is directly related to the underlying abstract representation, and there is no internal organization — that is, no order of derivation — within the set of structures. But, in fact, whenever an attempt to account for such structures has actually been undertaken, it has invariably been found that there are strong reasons to assign an internal organization and an inherent order of derivation among the items constituting such a set. Furthermore, it has invariably been found that different sets in a single language lead to the *same decision* as to the abstract underlying order of elements. Hence, it seems that a set-system such as (70) must be supplemented by two sets of rules. The first set will assign an intrinsic order to the elements of the underlying unordered Phrase-markers (that is, it will label the lines of the tree-diagrams representing these structures). The second set of rules will be grammatical transformations applying in sequence to generate surface structures in the familiar way. The first set of rules simply converts a set-system into a concatenation-system. It provides the base Phrase-markers required for the application of the sequences of transformations that ultimately form surface structures. There is no evidence at all to suggest that either of these steps can be omitted in the case of natural languages. Consequently, there is no reason to consider the set-system, for the time being, as a possible theory of grammatical structure.

The phenomenon of so-called "free word order" is sometimes mentioned as relevant to this issue, but, so far as I can see, it has no bearing on it at all. Suppose that for some language each permutation of the words of each sentence were to give a grammatical sentence that, in fact, is a paraphrase of the original. In this case, the set-system would be much superior for the categorial component of the grammar of this language. No grammatical transformations would be needed, and the rule for realizing underlying abstract representations would be extremely simple. But there is no known language that remotely resembles this description. In every known language the restrictions on order are quite severe, and therefore rules of realization of abstract structures are necessary. Until some account of such rules is suggested, the set-system simply cannot be considered seriously as a theory of grammar.

Nevertheless, the free word order phenomenon is an interesting and important one, and much too little attention has been given to it. First of all, it should be emphasized that grammatical transformations do not seem to be an appropriate device for expressing the full range of possibilities for stylistic inversion. It seems, rather, that there are several underlying generalizations that determine when such reordering is permissible, and what its semantic functions are. For one thing, richly inflected languages tolerate stylistic reordering much more extensively than languages that are poor in inflection, for obvious reasons. Second, even richly inflected languages do not seem to tolerate reordering when it leads to ambiguity. Thus in a German sentence such as *"Die Mutter sieht die Tochter,"* in which the inflections do not suffice to indicate grammatical function, it seems that the interpretation will invariably be that *"Die Mutter"* is the Subject (unless it has contrastive Stress, in which case it may be taken to be the Subject or the Object). The same seems to be true in other languages as diverse as Russian (cf. Peshkovskii, 1956, p. 42) and Mohawk. In the latter, the Verb contains affixes designating the Subject and Object, but where the reference is ambiguous, the initial NP is taken to be the Subject, under normal intonation (I am indebted to Paul Postal for this information). If this is universal, it suggests the generalization that in any language, stylistic inversion of "major constituents" (in some sense to be defined) is tolerated up to ambiguity — that is, up to the point where a structure is produced that might have been generated independently by the grammatical rules. (As a special case of this, then, it will follow that inflected languages will tolerate reordering much more freely than uninflected ones.) Something of this sort seems to be true, and it is not statable in terms of the theory of transformations.

In general, the rules of stylistic reordering are very different from the grammatical transformations, which are much more deeply embedded in the grammatical system.[35] It might, in fact, be argued that the former are not so much rules of grammar as rules of performance (cf. §§ 1, 2, of Chapter 1). In any event, though this is surely an interesting phenomenon, it is one that has no apparent bearing, for the moment, on the theory of grammatical structure.

3

Deep Structures and Grammatical Transformations

LET us adopt, tentatively, the theory of the base component sketched in § 4.3 of Chapter 2, and continue to use the fragment of § 3, Chapter 2, appropriately modified to exclude sub-categorization rules from the categorial component of the base, as an illustrative example of a grammar.

The base will now generate base Phrase-markers. In § 1, Chapter 1, we defined the basis of a sentence as the sequence of base Phrase-markers that underlies it. The basis of a sentence is mapped into the sentence by the transformational rules, which, furthermore, automatically assign to the sentence a derived Phrase-marker (ultimately, a surface structure) in the process.

For concreteness, consider a base component which generates the Phrase-markers (1)–(3).[1] The base Phrase-marker (3), with a different choice of Auxiliary, would be the basis for the sentence "John was examined by a specialist." The Phrase-marker (1) would be the basis for the sentence "the man was fired," were we to modify it by deleting S′ from the Determiner associated with *man*. (In this case, the passive transformation is followed by the deletion of unspecified agent.) As it stands, however, to form the basis for some sentence, the base Phrase-marker (1) must be supplemented by another Phrase-marker, a transform of which will fill the position of S′ in (1) and thus serve as a relative clause qualifying *man*. Similarly, (2) alone cannot serve as a basis for a sentence because the S′ appearing in the Verbal Complement

(1)

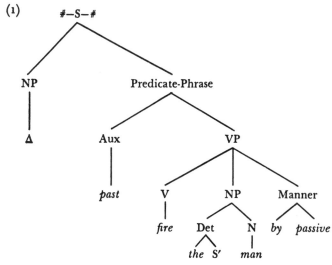

(2)

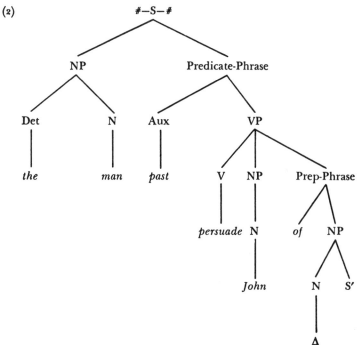

(3)

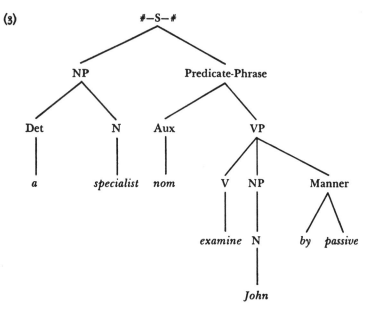

must be replaced by the transform of some other Phrase-marker. In fact, however, the sequence of base Phrase-markers (1), (2), (3) is the basis for the well-formed sentence

(4)   the man who persuaded John to be examined by a specialist was fired

The "transformational history" of (4) by which it is derived from its basis might be represented, informally, by the diagram (5).

(5)

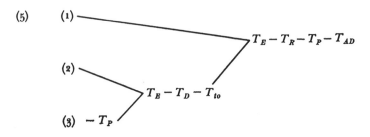

We interpret this as follows: First, apply the Passive transformation T_P to the base Phrase-marker (3); embed the result in the base Phrase-marker (2), in place of S', by a generalized (double-base) substitution transformation T_E, giving a Phrase-marker for "the man persuaded John of Δ John *nom* be examined by a specialist"; to this apply first T_D, which deletes the repeated NP "John," and then T_{to}, which replaces "of Δ *nom*" by "to," giving a Phrase-marker for "the man persuaded John to be examined by a specialist"; next embed this in the position of S' in (1), by T_E; to this apply the relative transformation T_R, which permutes the embedded sentence with the following N and replaces the repeated phrase "the man" by "who," giving a Phrase-marker for "Δ fired the man who persuaded John to be examined by a specialist by *passive*"; to this Phrase-marker apply the passive transformation and agent deletion (T_{AD}), giving (4).

I have left out of this description quite a few transformations that are necessary to give the correct form of (4), as well as other details, but these are, by and large, well known, and introduction of them changes nothing relevant to this discussion.

The diagram (5) is an informal representation of what we may call a *Transformation-marker*. It represents the transformational structure of the utterance (5) very much in the way a Phrase-marker represents the phrase structure of a terminal string. In fact, a Transformation-marker may be formally represented as a set of strings in an alphabet consisting of base Phrase-markers and transformations as its elements, just as a Phrase-marker may be formally represented as a set of strings in an alphabet consisting of terminal symbols, category symbols, and with the developments of the preceding sections, specified features.[2]

The deep structure of an utterance is given completely by its Transformation-marker, which contains its basis. The surface structure of the sentence is the derived Phrase-marker given as the output of the operations represented in the Transformation-marker. The basis of the sentence is the sequence of base Phrase-markers that constitute the terminal points of the tree-diagram (the left-hand nodes, in (5)). When Transformation-markers are represented as in (5), the branching points correspond to generalized transformations that embed a constituent sentence (the lower branch) in a designated position in a matrix sentence (the upper branch).

A theoretical apparatus of this sort, in its essentials, is what underlies the work in transformational generative grammar that has appeared in the last ten years. However, in the course of this work, several important points have gradually emerged which suggest that a somewhat more restricted and conceptually simpler theory of transformations may be adequate.

First, it has been shown that many of the optional singulary transformations of Chomsky (1955, 1957, 1962) must be reformulated as obligatory transformations, whose applicability to a string is determined by presence or absence of a certain marker in the string. This was pointed out by Lees (1960a) for the negation transformation, and by Klima (personal communication) for the question transformation, at about the same time. In fact, it is also true for the passive transformation, as noted in § 2.3.4 of Chapter 2. Katz and Postal (1964) have extended these observations and formulated them in terms of a general principle, namely that *the only contribution of transformations to semantic interpretation is that they interrelate Phrase-markers* (i.e., combine semantic interpretations of already interpreted Phrase-markers in a fixed way).[3] It follows, then, that transformations cannot introduce meaning-bearing elements (nor can they delete lexical items unrecoverably, by the condition mentioned in note 1). Generalizing these remarks to embedding transformations, they conclude also that a sentence transform embedded in a matrix sentence Σ must replace a dummy symbol of Σ. (In the foregoing discussion, adopting this suggestion, we have used S′ as the dummy symbol — this assumption is also implicit in Fillmore, 1963.)

Katz and Postal point out that the principle just stated greatly simplifies the theory of the semantic component, since semantic interpretation will now be independent of all aspects of the Transformation-marker except insofar as this indicates how base structures are interrelated. They have also succeeded in showing that in a large variety of cases, where this general principle has not been met in syntactic description, the description was in fact incorrect on internal syntactic grounds. The principle, then, seems very plausible.

Second, notice that the theory of Transformation-markers permits a great deal of latitude so far as ordering of transformations is concerned. Thus the grammar, in this view, must contain rules generating the possible Transformation-markers by stating conditions that these objects must meet for well-formedness (what Lees, 1960a, calls "traffic rules").[4] These rules may state the ordering of transformations relative to one another, and may designate certain transformations as obligatory, or obligatory relative to certain contexts, by requiring that they appear in specified positions in Transformation-markers. However, only some of the possibilities permitted by this general theory have been realized convincingly with actual linguistic material. In particular, there are no known cases of ordering among generalized embedding transformations although such ordering is permitted by the theory of Transformation-markers. Furthermore, there are no really convincing cases of singulary transformations that must apply to a matrix sentence before a sentence transform is embedded in it, though this too is a possibility, according to the theory.[5] On the other hand, there are many examples of ordering of singulary transformations, and many examples of singulary transformations that must apply to a constituent sentence before it is embedded or that must apply to a matrix sentence after embedding of a constituent structure in it. Thus the diagram (5) is typical of the kind of structure that has actually been discovered in Transformation-markers.

In brief, presently available descriptive studies suggest the following restrictions on ordering of transformations. The singulary transformations are linearly ordered (perhaps only partially ordered). They may apply to a constituent structure before it is embedded, or to a matrix structure, and the constituent structure embedded in it, after this constituent structure is embedded. There is no reason for imposing an extrinsic order on the generalized transformations.[6]

These observations suggest a possible simplification of the theory of transformational grammar. Suppose that we eliminate the notions "generalized transformation" and "Transformation-marker" altogether.[7] In the rewriting rules of the base (in fact, in its categorial component) the string #S# is introduced in the positions where in the illustrative example we introduced the symbol S'. That is, wherever a base Phrase-marker contains a position in which a sentence transform is to be introduced, we fill this position with the string #S#, which initiates derivations. We now allow the rules of the base to apply cyclically, preserving their linear order. Thus, for example, after having generated (1), with #S# in place of S', they reapply to the new occurrence of #S# in the terminal line of the derivation represented by (1). From this occurrence of #S# the rules of the base can generate the derivation represented by (2), with #S# in place of the occurrence of S' in (2). From the latter occurrence of #S#, the same base rules can reapply to form the derivation represented by (3). In this way, the base rules will generate the *generalized Phrase-marker* formed from (1), (2), (3) by replacing S' in (1) by (2) and replacing S' in (2) by (3).

We have thus revised the theory of the base by allowing #S# to appear on the right in certain branching rules, where previously the dummy symbol S' had appeared, and by allowing the rules to reapply (preserving their order) to these newly introduced occurrences of #S#. A generalized Phrase-marker formed in this way contains all of the base Phrase-markers that constitute the basis of a sentence, but it contains more information than a basis in the old sense since it also indicates explicitly how these base Phrase-markers are embedded in one another. That is, the generalized Phrase-marker contains all of the information contained in the basis, as well as the information provided by the generalized embedding transformations.[8]

In addition to the rules of the base, so modified, the grammar contains a linear sequence of singular transformations. These apply to generalized Phrase-markers cyclically, in the following manner. First, the sequence of transformational rules applies to the most deeply embedded base Phrase-marker. (For example, it applies to (3), in the generalized Phrase-marker formed by embedding (3) in (2) and the result in (1), as described earlier.) Having applied to all such base Phrase-markers, the sequence of rules reapplies to a configuration dominated by S in which these base Phrase-markers are embedded (to (2), in the same example), and so on, until finally the sequence of rules applies to the configuration dominated by the initial symbol S of the entire generalized Phrase-marker (to (1), in our example). Notice that in the case of (1)–(3), the effect of this convention is precisely what is described in the Transformation-marker (5). That is, singular transformations are applied to constituent sentences before they are embedded, and to matrix sentences after embedding has taken place. The embedding itself is now provided by the branching rules of the base rather than by generalized transformations. We have, in effect, converted the specific properties of the Transformation-marker (5) into general properties of any possible transformational derivation.

The grammar now consists of a base and a linear sequence of singular transformations. These apply in the manner just described. The ordering possibilities that are permitted by the theory of Transformation-markers but apparently never put to use are now excluded in principle. The notion of Transformation-marker disappears, as does the notion of generalized transformation. The base rules form generalized Phrase-markers that contain just the information contained in the basis and the generalized transformations of the earlier version. But observe that in accordance with the Katz-Postal principle discussed earlier (p. 132), it is precisely this information that should be relevant to semantic interpretation. Consequently, we may take a generalized Phrase-marker, in the sense just defined, to be the deep structure generated by the syntactic component.

Thus the syntactic component consists of a base that generates deep structures and a transformational part that maps them into surface structures. The deep structure of a sentence is submitted to the semantic component for semantic interpretation, and its surface structure enters the phonological component and undergoes phonetic interpretation. The final effect of a grammar, then, is to relate a semantic interpretation to a phonetic representation — that is, to state how a sentence is interpreted. This relation is mediated by the syntactic component of the grammar, which constitutes its sole "creative" part.

The branching rules of the base (that is, its categorial component) define grammatical functions and grammatical relations and determine an abstract underlying order (cf. § 4.4, Chapter 2); the lexicon characterizes the individual properties of particular lexical items that are inserted in specified positions in base Phrase-markers. Thus when we define "deep structures" as "structures generated by the base component," we are, in effect, assuming that the semantic interpretation of a sentence depends only on its lexical items and the grammatical functions and relations represented in the underlying structures in which they appear.[9] This is the basic idea that has motivated the theory of transformational grammar since its inception (cf. note 33, Chapter 2). Its first relatively clear formulation is in Katz and Fodor (1963), and an improved version is given in Katz and Postal (1964), in terms of the modification of syntactic theory proposed there and briefly discussed earlier. The formulation just suggested sharpens this idea still further. In fact, it permits a further simplification of the theory of semantic interpretation presented in Katz and Postal (1964), since Transformation-markers and generalized transformations, as well as "projection rules" to deal with them, need no longer be considered at all. This formulation seems to be a natural extension and summary of the developments of the past few years that have just been summarized.

Notice that in this view one major function of the transformational rules is to convert an abstract deep structure that expresses the content of a sentence into a fairly concrete surface structure that indicates its form.[10] Some possible reasons for such an organization of grammar, in terms of perceptual mechanisms, are suggested in Miller and Chomsky (1963, § 2.2). It is interesting to note, in this connection, that the grammars of the "artificial languages" of logic or theory of programming are, apparently without exception, simple phrase structure grammars in most significant respects.

Looking more closely at the recursive property of the grammar, we have now suggested the following modification of transformational theory. In the earlier version of the theory, the recursive property was assigned to the transformational component, in particular, to the generalized transformations and the rules for forming Transformation-markers. Now the recursive property is a feature of the base component, in particular, of the rules that introduce the initial symbol S in designated positions in strings of category symbols. There are, apparently, no other recursive rules in the base.[11] The transformational component is solely interpretive.

It is worth mentioning that with this formulation of the theory of transformational grammar, we have returned to a conception of linguistic structure that marked the origins of modern syntactic theory, namely that presented in the *Grammaire générale et raisonnée*.[12]

One additional point must be emphasized in connection with the notion "deep structure." When the base rules generate a Phrase-marker from an occurrence of S that is embedded in an already generated Phrase-marker, they cannot take account of the context in which this occurrence of S appears. For example, instead of the generalized Phrase-marker M consisting of (1)–(3) (with (3) embedded in (2) and the result embedded in (1)), we might just as well have constructed the generalized Phrase-marker M' formed from (1), K, and (3), where K is a Phrase-marker differing from (2) only in that *man* in (2) is replaced by *boy* in K. But now, at the stage of derivation at which the relative clause transformation (T_R of (5)) is applied to K with (3) embedded within it, we shall have not the string (6) but rather (7):

(6) Δ fired the man (# the man persuaded John to be examined by a specialist #) by *passive*

(7) Δ fired the man (# the boy persuaded John to be examined by a specialist #) by *passive*

The string (6) (with its Phrase-marker) is of the form that permits the relative clause transformation to apply, replacing "the man" by "who," since the condition of identity of the two Nouns is met and we thus have a recoverable deletion (cf. note 1). But in the case of (7), the transformation will block. Thus the phrase "the boy" cannot be deleted from (7) because of the general condition that only recoverable deletions are permitted — that is, the identity condition of the transformation is not satisfied.[18] This is precisely what we want, for obviously the generalized Phrase-marker formed from (1), K, (3) does not provide the semantic interpretation of (4), as it would if application of the relative clause transformation were permitted in this case. In fact, the generalized Phrase-marker formed from (1), K, and (3), although generated by the base rules, is not the deep structure underlying any surface structure.

We can make this observation precise, in this case, by defining the relative clause transformation in such a way that it deletes the boundary symbol # when it applies. Thus if its application is blocked, this symbol will remain in the string. We can then establish the convention that a well-formed surface structure cannot contain internal occurrences of #. Such occurrences will indicate that certain transformations that should have applied were blocked. The same (or similar) formal devices can be used in a variety of other cases.

Putting aside questions of formalization, we can see that not all generalized Phrase-markers generated by the base will underlie actual sentences and thus qualify as deep structures. What, then, is the test that determines whether a generalized Phrase-marker is the deep structure of some sentence? The answer is very simple. The transformational rules provide exactly such a test, and there is, in general, no simpler test. A generalized Phrase-marker M_D is the deep structure underlying the sentence S, with the surface structure M_S, just in case the transformational rules generate M_S from M_D. The surface structure M_S of S is well formed just in case S contains no symbols indicating the blocking of obligatory transformations. A deep structure is a generalized Phrase-marker underlying some well-formed surface structure. Thus the basic notion defined by a transformational grammar is: *deep structure M_D underlies well-formed surface structure M_S.* The notion "deep structure" itself is derivative from this. The transformational rules act as a "filter" that permits only certain generalized Phrase-markers to qualify as deep structures.

Notice that this filtering function of the transformational component is not an entirely new feature specific to the version of transformational grammar that we are developing now. In fact, it was also true of the earlier version, though this fact was never discussed in exposition. Thus a sequence of base Phrase-markers might have been selected that could not serve as the basis of any sentence; furthermore, any system of rules for generating Transformation-markers would certainly permit certain structures that do not qualify as Transformation-markers because of inconsistencies and blocks arising in the course of carrying out the instructions that they represent. In the present version this filtering function is simply brought out more clearly.

In § 4.3 of Chapter 2 we suggested: (a) that the distributional restrictions of lexical items be determined by contextual features listed in lexical entries, and (b) that these contextual features be regarded as defining certain substitution transformations. Thus strict subcategorial and selectional restrictions of lexical items are defined by transformational rules associated with these items. We have now observed that the transformational rules must also carry the burden of determining the distributional restrictions on base Phrase-markers. Thus the categorial rules that generate the infinite set of generalized Phrase-markers can apparently be context-free, with all distributional restrictions, whether of base Phrase-markers or lexical entries, being determined by the (singulary) transformations.

Such a description of the form of the syntactic component may seem strange if one considers the generative rules as a model for the actual construction of a sentence by a speaker. Thus it seems absurd to suppose that the speaker first forms a generalized Phrase-marker by base rules and then tests it for well-formedness by applying transformational rules to see if it gives, finally, a well-formed sentence. But this absurdity is simply a corollary to the deeper absurdity of regarding the system of generative rules as a point-by-point model for the actual construction of a sentence by a speaker. Consider the simpler case of a phrase structure grammar with no transformations (for example, the grammar of a programming language, or elementary arithmetic, or some small part of English that might be described in these terms). It would clearly be absurd to suppose that the "speaker" of such a language, in formulating an "utterance," first selects the major categories, then the categories into which these are analyzed, and so forth, finally, at the end of the process, selecting the words or symbols that he is going to use (deciding what he is going to talk about). To think of a generative grammar in these terms is to take it to be a model of performance rather than a model of competence, thus totally misconceiving its nature. One can study models of performance that incorporate generative grammars, and some results have been achieved in such studies.[14] But a generative grammar as it stands is no more a model of the speaker than it is a model of the hearer. Rather, as has been repeatedly emphasized, it can be regarded only as a characterization of the intrinsic tacit knowledge or competence that underlies actual performance.

The base rules and the transformational rules set certain conditions that must be met for a structure to qualify as the deep structure expressing the semantic content of some well-formed sentence. Given a grammar containing a base component and a transformational component, one can develop innumerable procedures for actually constructing deep structures. These will vary in exhaustiveness and efficiency, and in the extent to which they can be adapted to the problems of producing or understanding speech. One such constructive procedure is to run through the base rules (observing order) so as to form a generalized Phrase-marker M, and then through the transformational rules (observing order) so as to form a surface structure M' from M. If M' is well formed, then M was a deep structure; otherwise, it was not. All deep structures can be enumerated in this way, just as they can all be enumerated in many other ways, given the grammar. As noted earlier, the grammar defines the relation "the deep structure M underlies the well-formed surface structure M' of the sentence S" and, derivatively, it defines the notions "M is a deep structure," "M' is a well-formed surface structure," "*S* is a well-formed sentence," and many others (such as "*S* is structurally ambiguous," "*S* and *S'* are paraphrases," "*S* is a deviant sentence formed by violating rule *R* or condition *C*"). The grammar does not, in itself, provide any sensible procedure for finding the deep structure of a given sentence, or for producing a given sentence, just as it provides no sensible procedure for finding a paraphrase to a given sentence. It merely defines these tasks in a precise way. A performance model must certainly incorporate a grammar; it is not to be confused with a grammar. Once this point is clear, the fact that transformations act as a kind of filter will occasion no surprise or uneasiness.

To summarize, we have now suggested that the form of grammar may be as follows. A grammar contains a syntactic component, a semantic component, and a phonological component. The latter two are purely interpretive; they play no part in the recursive generation of sentence structures. The syntactic component consists of a base and a transformational component. The base, in turn, consists of a categorial subcomponent and a lexicon. The base generates deep structures. A deep structure enters the semantic component and receives a semantic interpretation; it is mapped by the transformational rules into a surface structure, which is then given a phonetic interpretation by the rules of the phonological component. Thus the grammar assigns semantic interpretations to signals, this association being mediated by the recursive rules of the syntactic component.

The categorial subcomponent of the base consists of a sequence of context-free rewriting rules. The function of these rules is, in essence, to define a certain system of grammatical relations that determine semantic interpretation, and to specify an abstract underlying order of elements that makes possible the functioning of the transformational rules. To a large extent, the rules of the base may be universal, and thus not, strictly speaking, part of particular grammars; or it may be that, although free in part, the choice of base rules is constrained by a universal condition on the grammatical functions that are defined. Similarly, the category symbols appearing in base rules are selected from a fixed universal alphabet; in fact, the choice of symbol may be largely or perhaps completely determined by the formal role the symbol plays in the system of base rules. The infinite generative capacity of the grammar arises from a particular formal property of these categorial rules, namely that they may introduce the initial symbol S into a line of a derivation. In this way, the rewriting rules can, in effect, insert base Phrase-markers into other base Phrase-markers, this process being iterable without limit.

The lexicon consists of an unordered set of lexical entries and certain redundancy rules. Each lexical entry is a set of features (but see note 15 of Chapter 2). Some of these are phonological features, drawn from a particular universal set of phonological features (the distinctive-feature system). The set of phonological features in a lexical entry can be extracted and represented as a phonological matrix that bears the relation "is a" to each of the specified syntactic features belonging to the lexical entry. Some of the features are semantic features. These, too, are presumably drawn from a universal "alphabet," but little is known about this today, and nothing has been said about it here. We call a feature "semantic" if it is not mentioned in any syntactic rule, thus begging the question of whether semantics is involved in syntax.[15] The redundancy rules of the lexicon add and specify features wherever this can be predicted by general rule. Thus the lexical entries constitute the full set of irregularities of the language.

We may construct a derivation of a generalized Phrase-marker by applying the categorial rules in the specified order, beginning with S, reapplying them to each new occurrence of S introduced in the course of the derivation. In this way, we derive a preterminal string, which becomes a generalized Phrase-marker when lexical entries are inserted in accordance with the transformational rules specified by the contextual features that belong to these lexical entries. The base of the syntactic component thus generates an infinite set of generalized Phrase-markers.

The transformational subcomponent consists of a sequence of singular transformations. Each transformation is fully defined by a structure index, which is a Boolean condition on Analyzability, and a sequence of elementary transformations. The notion "Analyzable" is determined in terms of the "is a" relation, which, in turn, is defined by the rewriting rules of the base and by the lexicon. Thus transformations may refer to specified syntactic features as if they were categories. In fact, transformations must also be designed so that they can specify and add syntactic features, but we shall not go into this modification of the theory of transformational grammar here (see Chapter 4, § 2). Given a generalized Phrase-marker, we construct a transformational derivation by applying the sequence of transformational rules sequentially, "from the bottom up" — that is, applying the sequence of rules to a given configuration only if we have already applied it to all base Phrase-markers embedded in this configuration. If none of the transformations blocks, we derive in this way a well-formed surface structure. In this and only this case, the generalized Phrase-marker to which the transformations were originally applied constitutes a deep structure, namely the deep structure of the sentence S, which is the terminal string of the derived surface structure. This deep structure expresses the semantic content of S, whereas the surface structure of S determines its phonetic form.

The interpretive components of a grammar have not been our concern here. Insofar as details of their structure have been worked out, they seem to function in parallel ways. The phonological component consists of a sequence of rules that apply to a surface structure "from the bottom up" in the tree-diagram representing it. That is, these rules apply in a cycle, first to the minimal elements (formatives), then to the constituents of which they are parts (a constituent of a Phrase-marker being a substring of its terminal string dominated by a single category symbol), then to the constituents of which these are parts, and so on, until the maximal domain of phonological processes is reached. (See Chomsky, Halle, and Lukoff, 1956; Halle and Chomsky, 1960, forthcoming; Chomsky, 1962b; Chomsky and Miller, 1963.) In this way a phonetic representation of the entire sentence is formed on the basis of the intrinsic abstract phonological properties of its formatives and the categories represented in the surface structure.

In a somewhat similar way, the projection rules of the semantic component operate on the deep structure generated by the base, assigning a semantic interpretation (a "reading") to each constituent, on the basis of the readings assigned to its parts (ultimately, the intrinsic semantic properties of the formatives) and the categories and grammatical relations represented in the deep structure. (See Katz and Fodor, 1963; Katz and Postal, 1964; and other papers by Katz listed in the bibliography.) To the extent that grammatical categories and relations can be described in language-independent terms, one may hope to find universal projection rules, which need not, therefore, be stated as part of a specific grammar.

Throughout this discussion, we have simply been presupposing the theory of grammatical transformations as presented in the references cited, but it is perhaps worth mentioning that this theory, too, can apparently be simplified in various ways. First, it appears that permutations can be eliminated from the set of elementary transformations in favor of substitutions, deletions, and adjunctions. That is, the derived Phrase-markers that would be provided by permutations may not be necessary in addition to those provided by the other elementary transformations. Elimination of permutations from the base set would greatly simplify the theory of derived constituent structure.[16] Second, it seems that the structural analyses that determine the domain of transformations can be limited to Boolean conditions on Analyzability. That is, quantifiers can be eliminated from the formulation of transformations in favor of a general convention on deletion, as mentioned in note 13. If so, this places a severe additional restriction on the theory of transformations.

The latter point deserves some further clarification. We shall discuss it briefly here and then return to the question in Chapter 4, § 2.2. We are proposing the following convention to guarantee recoverability of deletion: a deletion operation can eliminate only a dummy element, or a formative explicitly mentioned in the structure index (for example, *you* in imperatives), or the designated representative of a category (for example, the *wh*-question transformations that delete Noun Phrases are in fact limited to indefinite Pronouns — cf. Chomsky, 1964, § 2.2), or an element that is otherwise represented in the sentence in a fixed position. To clarify the latter point further, let us define an *erasure transformation* as one that substitutes a term X of its proper analysis for a term Y of its proper analysis (leaving X intact), and then deletes this new occurrence of X which replaced Y. In the example of relativization discussed earlier (pp. 128 f.), if we have the string

$$\overset{1}{\overbrace{\text{the man}}} - \overset{2}{\overbrace{[\#wh\text{-}}} - \overset{3}{\overbrace{\text{the man}}} - \overset{4}{\overbrace{\text{had been fired}\#]\ \text{returned to work}}}$$

(8)

the relative transformation can be formulated as an erasure operation that substitutes the first term X of the proper analysis for the third term Y, erasing the latter[17] in the process. Avoiding details of formalization, which are straightforward within the general theory of transformations, we may say briefly that the erasure operation *uses the term X to delete Y* in such a case. We say, then, that an erasure operation can use the term X to delete Y just in case X and Y are identical. We shall investigate the exact nature of the required relation between X and Y somewhat more fully in Chapter 4, pp. 177f.

As an additional illustration, consider the reflexivization operation (see Lees and Klima, 1963, for a detailed discussion). It has frequently been observed that in a sentence such as "John hurt John" or "the boy hurt the boy," the two phonetically identical Noun Phrases are necessarily interpreted as differing in reference; sameness of reference requires reflexivization of the second Noun Phrase (this is also true of pronominalization). Various attempts have been made to build an account of this into the syntactic component, but none has been very convincing. The availability of lexical features suggests a new approach that might be explored. Suppose that certain lexical items are designated as "referential" and that by a general convention, each occurrence of a referential item is assigned a marker, say, an integer, as a feature.[18] The reflexivization rule can be formulated as an erasure operation that uses one Noun Phrase to delete another. As in the case of relativization (cf. note 17), the erasure leaves a residue, in particular, the feature [±Human], and it introduces the new phonetic element *self*. Thus when applied to "I hurt I," the first Noun Phrase is used to delete the second, finally giving, "I hurt myself." But by the recoverability condition on deletion, the reflexivization rule (similarly, the pronominalization rule) will apply only when the integers assigned to the two items are the same. The semantic component will then interpret two referential items as having the same reference just in case they are strictly identical — in particular, in case they have been assigned the same integer in the deep structure. This gives the right answer in many cases, but there are interesting problems that arise when the referential items are plural, and of course there are problems in specifying the notion "referential" properly.

Notice, incidentally, that the reflexivization rule does not always apply (though pronominalization does) even when the two Nouns are strictly identical and hence coreferential. Thus we have "I kept it near me" alongside of "I aimed it at myself," and so on. The difference is that in the first, but not the second, the repeated Noun is in a Sentence-Complement to the Verb. Thus "I kept it near me" has a deep structure of the form "I — kept — it — # S #," where S dominates "it is near me." But "I aimed it at myself" has a deep structure of the form "I — aimed — it — at me" (there is no underlying sentence "it is at me"). The reflexivization rule does not apply to a repeated N dominated by an occurrence of S that does not dominate the "antecedent" occurrence of N. This particular remark about English is, apparently, a consequence of a more general condition on transformations, namely that no morphological material (in this case, *self*) can be introduced into a configuration dominated by S once the cycle of transformational rules has already completed its application to this configuration (though items can still be extracted from this constituent of a larger "matrix structure," in the next cycle of transformational rules). There are a few examples that seem to conflict with this analysis (such as "I pushed it away from me," "I drew it toward me"), for reasons that I do not understand, but it covers a large number of convincing cases, and, in the distinction it makes between superficially analogous cases that differ only in that one but not the other is based on an independently existing embedded sentence, it provides an interesting confirmation of the theory of transformational grammar.

Returning to the main theme, we can apparently define a grammatical transformation in terms of a "structure index" that is a Boolean condition on Analyzability and a sequence of elementary transformations drawn from a base set including substitutions, deletions, and adjunctions. It seems also that these form larger repeated units (for example, substitution-deletions, erasures) and that the limitations on their application can be given by general conventions of the sort just mentioned. If this is correct, then the formal properties of the theory of transformations become fairly clear and reasonably simple, and it may be possible to undertake abstract study of them of a sort that has not been feasible in the past.

4

Some Residual Problems

§ *1. THE BOUNDARIES OF SYNTAX AND SEMANTICS*

§ *1.1. Degrees of grammaticalness*

IT is quite apparent that current theories of syntax and semantics are highly fragmentary and tentative, and that they involve open questions of a fundamental nature. Furthermore, only very rudimentary grammatical descriptions are available, for any language, so that no satisfactory answers can be given for many factual questions. Consequently, the problem suggested by the title of this section can, for the present, be at best a source for speculation. Nevertheless, some of the topics of the preceding chapters relate to the question of the proper balance between syntax and semantics in a way that deserves at least some further comment.

The distinction between strict subcategorization features and selectional features, which is formally well defined, appears to correlate rather closely with an important distinction in language use. Each such contextual feature is associated with a certain rule that limits lexical entries containing this feature to certain contexts.[1] We can, in each case, construct a deviant sentence by breaking the rule. Thus in § 3 of Chapter 2, Verbs are strictly subcategorized into Intransitives, Transitives, pre-Adjectival, pre-Sentence, etc. In these cases, violation of the rules will give such strings as:

(1) (i) John found sad
    (ii) John elapsed that Bill will come

    (iii) John compelled
    (iv) John became Bill to leave
    (v) John persuaded great authority to Bill

On the other hand, failure to observe a selectional rule will give such typical examples as

(2) (i) colorless green ideas sleep furiously
    (ii) golf plays John
    (iii) the boy may frighten sincerity
    (iv) misery loves company
    (v) they perform their leisure with diligence

(cf. § 2.3.1 of Chapter 2). Clearly, strings such as (1) that break strict subcategorization rules and strings such as (2) that break selectional rules are deviant. It is necessary to impose an interpretation on them somehow — this being a task that varies in difficulty or challenge from case to case — whereas there is no question of imposing an interpretation in the case of such strictly well-formed sentences as

(3) (i) revolutionary new ideas appear infrequently
    (ii) John plays golf
    (iii) sincerity may frighten the boy
    (iv) John loves company
    (v) they perform their duty with diligence

Nevertheless, the manner of deviation illustrated in (2) is rather different from that in (1). Sentences that break selectional rules can often be interpreted metaphorically (particularly, as personification — cf. Bloomfield, 1963) or allusively in one way or another, if an appropriate context of greater or less complexity is supplied. That is, these sentences are apparently interpreted by a direct analogy to well-formed sentences that observe the selectional rules in question. Clearly, one would proceed in quite a different way if forced to assign an interpretation to sentences that break strict subcategorization rules, for example, the sentences of (1).

These examples are, I think, typical of a fairly wide class of cases. A descriptively adequate grammar should make all of these distinctions on some formal grounds, and a grammar of the type just described seems to make them in some measure, at least. It distinguishes perfectly well-formed sentences such as (3) from the sentences of (1) and (2), which are not directly generated by the system of grammatical rules. It further separates the sentences of (1), generated by relaxing strict subcategorization rules, from sentences such as (2), which are generated when selectional rules are relaxed. Thus it takes several steps toward the development of a significant theory of "degree of grammaticalness."[2]

It seems that sentences deviating from selectional rules that involve "higher-level" lexical features such as [Count] are much less acceptable and are more difficult to interpret than those that involve such "lower-level" features as [Human]. At the same time, it is important to bear in mind that not all rules involving low-level syntactic features tolerate deviation as readily as do selectional rules involving these features.[3] Thus both of the sentences

(4) (i) the book who you read was a best seller
    (ii) who you met is John

result from failure to observe rules involving the feature [Human], but are totally unacceptable — although of course an interpretation can easily, and no doubt uniformly, be imposed on them. Both in degree of acceptability and manner of interpretation, they differ completely from sentences that result from a failure to observe selectional rules involving the feature [Human]. Thus no matter how selectional rules are treated, there is no doubt that such features as [Human] play a role in purely syntactic rules (since surely the examples of (4) are ruled out on purely syntactic grounds).

Similarly, consider the selectional feature [[+Abstract] $\cdots$ — $\cdots$ [+Animate]] assigned to such Verbs as *frighten, amuse, charm,* $\cdots$. This feature is involved in rules that are as inviolable as those that give *the book which you read was a best seller* and *what you found was my book,* while excluding (4). Thus items that are positively specified with respect to this feature can appear in the position of pure Adjectives, so that we have such sentences as *a very frightening (amusing, charming, ···) person suddenly appeared*, but not, for example,

(5) (i) a very walking person appeared
    (ii) a very hitting person appeared

These sentences, like those of (4), are immediately and perhaps uniquely interpretable, but are obviously much more seriously ungrammatical, in the intuitive sense that we are now attempting to explicate, than the examples of violation of selectional rules given earlier. Thus it seems that this selectionally introduced contextual feature is also involved in rules that cannot be violated without serious departure from grammaticalness.[4]

Examples such as (4) and (5) therefore support two important observations. First, it is clear that features such as [Human] and [[+Abstract] ··· — ··· [+Animate]] play a role in the functioning of the syntactic component, no matter how narrowly syntax is conceived, as long as it is agreed that (4) and (5) are syntactically deviant. The special character of the examples of (2) is not attributable to the fact that these sentences violate rules involving "low-level features," but rather to the fact that the rules that they violate are selectional rules. Second, it is clear from such examples as (4) and (5) that the notion "grammaticalness" cannot be related to "interpretability" (ease, uniqueness, or uniformity of interpretation), in any simple way, at least. There are sentences such as (4) and (5) that are uniquely, uniformly, and immediately interpretable, no doubt, although they are paradigm examples of departure from well-formedness. On the other hand, there are also perfectly well-formed sentences that may pose great difficulties for interpretation, and may be subject to a variety of perhaps conflicting interpretations. More generally, it is clear that the intuitive notion of grammatical well-formedness is by no means a simple one and that an adequate explication of it will involve theoretical constructs of a highly abstract nature, just as it is clear that various diverse factors determine how and whether a sentence can be interpreted.

The attempts described in the references of note 2 to give a precise definition to at least one dimension of degree of grammaticalness are much more plausible if limited to the question of deviation from selectional rules than if extended to the full range of examples of deviation from well-formedness. In fact, following this suggestion, we might conclude that the *only* function of the selectional rules is to impose a hierarchy of deviation from grammaticalness on a certain set of sentences, namely those sentences that can be generated by relaxing selectional constraints while otherwise keeping the grammer unchanged.

Observe that the rules of the grammar impose a partial ordering in terms of dominance among the features that constitute a complex symbol in a Phrase-marker. For example, referring again to the sample Phrase-marker (59) of Chapter 2 and the formative *frighten*, we have a complex symbol consisting of the features $[+V, + — NP, +[+Abstract] \cdots — \cdots [+Animate]]$, and others, The rules of the grammar impose the dominance order $[+V]$, $[+ — NP]$, $[+[+Abstract] \cdots — \cdots [+Animate]]$, as indicated in (59). In terms of this order, we can define the *degree of deviation* of a string that results from substituting a lexical item in the position of *frighten* in this Phrase-marker. The deviation is greater the higher in the dominance hierarchy is the feature corresponding to the rule that is relaxed. In the example given, then, deviance would be greatest if the item substituted for *frighten* is a non-Verb, less great if it is a Verb but a non-Transitive Verb, and still less great if it is a Transitive Verb that does not take an Abstract Subject. Thus we should have the following order of deviance:

(6) (i) sincerity may virtue the boy
    (ii) sincerity may elapse the boy
    (iii) sincerity may admire the boy

This seems to give a natural explication for at least one sense of the term "deviance." In this connection, compare the suggestions of the references of note 2, which consider size of category within which substitution takes place in determining the degree of grammaticalness (the extent of syntactic deviance) of a string.

At the end of § 4.1 of Chapter 2, it was pointed out that features introduced by strict subcategorization rules dominate features introduced by selectional rules; and in the same section it was further noted that all lexical features are dominated by the symbols for lexical categories. Furthermore, deviation from selectional rules involving high-level features is apparently more serious than deviation from selectional rules involving lower-level features. These various observations combine to make the definition of "degree of deviance" just proposed a rather natural one. If the distinction between strict subcategorization rules and selectional rules noted earlier is generally valid, we might go on to superimpose on the scale of deviance a split into perhaps three general types, namely the types that result from: (i) violation of lexical category (such as (6i)); (ii) conflict with a strict subcategorization feature (such as (6ii) and (1)); and (iii) conflict with a selectional feature (such as (6iii) and (2)). There are, furthermore, subdivisions within at least the third type. Of course, there are also many other types (such as (4), (5)).[5] This is not surprising, since there are rules of many kinds that can be violated.

§ 1.2. Further remarks on selectional rules

Selectional rules play a rather marginal role in the grammar, although the features that they deal with may be involved in many purely syntactic processes (cf. (4), (5)). One might propose, therefore, that selectional rules be dropped from the syntax and that their function be taken over by the semantic component. Such a change would do little violence to the structure of grammar as described earlier. Of course, the features that are utilized and introduced by selectional rules would still appear in lexical entries for strings. That is, *boy* would be specified as [+Human] and *frighten* as permitting an Abstract Subject and Animate Object, etc., in the lexical entries for these items. Furthermore, if we continue to call a feature of the lexical entry a "syntactic feature" when it is involved in a strictly syntactic rule, then these features of the lexical entry will be syntactic rather than semantic features (cf. the discussion of (4), (5)). Nevertheless, in accordance with this proposal, the grammar will directly generate even such sentences as (2), though not, of course, (1), as syntactically well formed. The syntactic component of the grammar would not, in other words, impose a hierarchy of degree of grammaticalness at these lower levels of deviation. This task would now have to be taken over by the semantic component.

Let us continue to suppose that the semantic component is an interpretive device based on projection rules of the type discussed earlier, following Katz, Fodor, and Postal. The projection rules must now be adapted to detect and interpret conflicts in feature composition between grammatically related lexical items and, more generally, grammatically related constituents of base strings. The earlier discussion of deviance, in particular the definition of "degree of deviance," can be carried over with little change. The same is true of the comments regarding Noun-Verb and Noun-Adjective selectional dominance. With slight reformulation, the same arguments will hold under this revision of the structure of grammar.

In § 4.3 of Chapter 2, we discussed two alternative proposals for dealing with contextual features. The first was to introduce them by rewriting rules and to have lexical items introduced into derivations by matching of nondistinct complex symbols (as in Chapter 2, § 3). The second was to regard the contextual features of the lexicon as defining certain substitution transformations that insert lexical items. As noted there, this is not merely a notational question.

We have, then, two open questions in connection with selectional rules, in particular: (i) Do they belong in the syntactic or the semantic component? (ii) Should they be rewriting rules introducing complex symbols or substitution transformations? Without attempting any exhaustive investigation of these questions, I shall now mention briefly some considerations that seem relevant to them.

Suppose that we were to introduce selectional features by

rewriting rules, in accordance with § 3 of Chapter 2. Notice that the selectional rules differ from the strict subcategorization rules in that they typically involve irrelevant symbols standing between the items that they relate. The rule (57xiv) of Chapter 2 is characteristic of selectional rules in this respect, with its reference to the irrelevant items *Aux* and *Det*; it is atypical only in the simplicity of these elements. That this may be more than a purely notational matter is illustrated by (57xv) of Chapter 2, which assigns features of the Subject to a modifying Adjective of the Predicate. As these rules are formulated, the Adjective would actually be assigned different features in these sentences:

(7)   the boy is sad

(8)   the boy grew sad

In the case of (7), the Adjective would be assigned the feature $[[+\text{Human}]\ \text{Aux}^\frown be\ -\ ]$ by rule (57xv) of Chapter 2, whereas in the case of (8) it would be assigned the feature $[[+\text{Human}]\ \text{Aux}\ [+V]\ -\ ]$, or something of this sort.[6] These features have nothing in common, in our terms, though they actually identify the same set of lexical items. This is as serious a deficiency as the one noted in the case of a grammar that specifically distinguishes Animate Subject from Animate Object, etc. (see pp. 114–115). We may remedy it and, at the same time, eliminate the reference to irrelevant intervening contexts in selectional rules by establishing the following convention for these rules. Suppose that we have the rule schema

(9) $A \rightarrow CS/[\alpha] \cdots - \cdots [\beta]$

where $[\alpha]$ and $[\beta]$ are specified features or are null (but either one or the other is nonnull).[7] We take (9) to be *applicable* to any string

(10) $XWAVY$

where $X = [\alpha, \cdots], Y = [\beta, \cdots],$[8] $W \neq W_1[\alpha, \cdots]W_2$ (or is null) and $V \neq V_1[\beta, \cdots]V_2$ (or is null). The result of applying (9) to (10) is the string

(11) *XWBVY*

where B is the complex symbol containing the features of A (or [+A], if A is a category symbol) in addition to each contextual feature [+φ — ψ], where X = [φ, $\cdots$] and Y = [ψ, $\cdots$]. (The reader will observe that except for the condition on W, V, the notion of "applicability" and the conventions for complex symbols are as before, though stated somewhat differently.) What this means is that the rule (9) assigns to A all contextual features [+φ — ψ], where [φ] is a lexical feature of the nearest complex symbol containing [α] to the left of A, and [ψ] is a lexical feature of the nearest complex symbol containing [β] to the right of A. Thus, in particular, we should now give the rules (57xiv) and (57xv) in the form (12) and (13), respectively:

(12) [+V] → CS/[+N] $\cdots$ — ($\cdots$ [+N])

(13) Adjective → CS/[+N] $\cdots$ —

These rules would now have the effect of assigning to *frighten* the feature [+[+Abstract] — [+Animate]], in particular, and to *sad* the feature [+[+Human] —] in the case of both (7) and (8). In this way we can avoid mention of irrelevant intervening symbols in the statement of contexts and, more importantly, can avoid the deficiency of dual-feature assignment noted in the case of (7) and (8).

Within the alternative framework involving substitution transformations, the analogous convention must be established. In this case, it is necessary only to state the condition on W, V of (10). This condition, however, is not statable directly in the form of a Boolean structure index for a transformation. This fact, though of no great importance, might be taken as suggesting that the system involving rewriting rules is preferable.[9]

More important are certain questions of interpretation that have some bearing on the form of selectional rules and their placement in the grammar.[10] Consider such a typical case of violation of selectional rules as

(14) John frightened sincerity

This is a deviant sentence, formed by relaxing the restriction of *frighten* to Animate Direct-Objects. Nevertheless, there are frames in which this restriction can be violated with no consequent unnaturalness, as, for example, in

(15) (i) it is nonsense to speak of (there is no such activity as) frightening sincerity
   (ii) sincerity is not the sort of thing that can be frightened
   (iii) one can(not) frighten sincerity

Clearly, a descriptively adequate grammar must indicate that (14) is deviant (as in the case of the examples of (2)) and that the examples of (15) are not. There are various ways to approach this problem.

Suppose that the selectional rules are included in the syntax. Then (14) and (15) are only derivatively generated by the grammar (in the sense of note 2); they are generated with Phrase-markers indicating that they depart in a particular respect from grammaticalness. Since (14) nevertheless differs from (15) in "deviance" from the intuitive point of view, this intuitive notion does not correspond to grammaticalness. Rather, it is presumably a property determined by the joint operation of both the syntactic and the semantic components. Thus the projection rules of the semantic component and the lexical entries for such words as *nonsense* and *speak* must be designed in such a way that, although the constituent *frighten sincerity* of the generalized Phrase-markers of (15i–iii) is marked as semantically incongruous, the incongruity is removed by the readings assigned to constituents dominating it, and consequently the sentences (15) (but not (14)) are finally given a nondeviant interpretation.[11] This seems to me not at all an unnatural or intolerable consequence. Surely it is not surprising to find that an intuitive concept such as "deviance" can be explicated only in terms of theoretical constructs of various sorts, which have in themselves no direct and uniform intuitive interpretation. In further support of this conclusion, one might cite the fact that even strict subcategorization rules can apparently be violated without leading necessarily to semantic incongruity, as, for example, in

(16) (i) it is nonsense to speak of (there is no such activity as) elapsing a book
  (ii) elapsing a book is not an activity that can be performed
  (iii) one cannot elapse a book

Here, too, one might plausibly maintain that base strings that deviate significantly from grammaticalness are nevertheless constituents of sentences that receive nondeviant interpretations, by virtue of the semantic properties of certain lexical items and certain constructions. In further support of the argument that grammaticalness cannot, in any event, coincide with the intuitive notion of "deviance," one can cite cases of perfectly grammatical strings that are incongruous on nonsyntactic grounds (cf., for example, p. 77).

Thus it seems to me that examples such as (15) do not present a particularly strong argument for removing selectional rules from the syntactic component and assigning their function to the interpretive semantic rules. Nevertheless, if the latter course is taken, then (14) and (15) will be directly generated by the syntactic rules, and at least in such cases as these the relation of grammaticalness to intuitive deviance will therefore be much closer. This might be cited as a slight consideration in favor of the decision to eliminate the selectional rules from the syntactic component, and to modify the theory of the semantic component in some way so as to allow it to accommodate these phenomena.

We have been considering the possibility of assigning the function of selectional rules to the semantic component. Alternatively, one might raise the question whether the functions of the semantic component as described earlier should not be taken over, *in toto*, by the generative syntactic rules. More specifically, we may ask whether the cycle of interpretive rules that assign readings to higher nodes (larger constituents) of the underlying generalized Phrase-marker should not be made to apply before some of the syntactic rules, so that the distinction between the two components is, in effect, obliterated. This notion, which is by no means to be ruled out a priori, is explored by Bever and Rosenbaum (forthcoming), who show that if it is adopted, the internal organization of the syntactic component must be revised in several essential ways.

It is clear from this fragmentary and inconclusive discussion that the interrelation of semantic and syntactic rules is by no means a settled issue, and that there is quite a range of possibilities that deserve serious exploration. The approach I have adopted in Chapter 2, § 3, is a conservative compromise between the attempt to incorporate the semantic rules strictly within the syntactic component and the attempt to elaborate the semantic component so that it takes over the function of the selectional rules. Evidently, further insight into these questions will await a much more intensive study of semantic interpretive rules than it has yet been possible to undertake. The work of the last few years, I believe, has laid the groundwork for empirical investigation of this sort. There is a general theoretical framework parts of which have received empirical support. Within this framework it is possible to formulate certain reasonably clear questions, and it is also fairly clear what kind of empirical evidence would be relevant to deciding them. Alternative positions can be formulated, but for the present any one that is adopted must be extremely tentative.

In general, one should not expect to be able to delimit a large and complex domain before it has been thoroughly explored. A decision as to the boundary separating syntax and semantics (if there is one) is not a prerequisite for theoretical and descriptive study of syntactic and semantic rules. On the contrary, the problem of delimitation will clearly remain open until these fields are much better understood than they are today. Exactly the same can be said about the boundary separating semantic systems from systems of knowledge and belief. That these seem to interpenetrate in obscure ways has long been noted. One can hardly achieve significant understanding of this matter in advance of a deep analysis of systems of semantic rules, on the one hand, and systems of belief, on the other. Short of this, one can discuss only isolated examples within a theoretical vacuum. It is not surprising that nothing conclusive results from this.

§ *1.3. Some additional problems of semantic theory*

One major qualification must be added to this discussion of the relation of syntax to semantics. I have described the semantic component as a system of rules that assign readings to constituents of Phrase-markers — a system that has no intrinsic structure beyond this. But such a description is hardly sufficient. In particular, there is little doubt that the system of "dictionary definitions" is not as atomistic as implied by this account.

Concerning dictionary definitions, two major problems are open to investigation. First, it is important to determine the universal, language-independent constraints on semantic features — in traditional terms, the system of possible concepts. The very notion "lexical entry" presupposes some sort of fixed, universal vocabulary in terms of which these objects are characterized, just as the notion "phonetic representation" presupposes some sort of universal phonetic theory. It is surely our ignorance of the relevant psychological and physiological facts that makes possible the widely held belief that there is little or no a priori structure to the system of "attainable concepts."

Furthermore, quite apart from the question of universal constraints, it seems obvious that in any given linguistic system lexical entries enter into intrinsic semantic relations of a much more systematic sort than is suggested by what has been said so far. We might use the term "field properties" to refer to these undoubtedly significant though poorly understood aspects of a descriptive semantic theory.[12] Thus, for example, consider Adjectives that are mutually exclusive in some referential domain, for example, color words. Such "antonymy sets" (cf. Katz, 1964*b*) provide a simple example of a field property that cannot be described naturally in terms of separate lexical entries, though it obviously plays a role in semantic interpretation. Or consider the "have a" relation, discussed in Bever and Rosenbaum (forthcoming). We have

(17) (i)   the man has an arm
     (ii) the arm has a finger
     (iii) the finger has a cut

but not

(18) (i)   the arm has a man
     (ii) the finger has an arm
     (iii) the cut has a finger

(except, irrelevantly to this point, as possible elliptic variants of entirely different constructions, as in "the finger has an arm attached to it," "the arm has a man on it," etc.). These examples, furthermore, illustrate relations of meaning rather than relations of fact. Thus there is no grammatical objection to "the ant has a kidney," where "the kidney has an ant" is not false or impossible but senseless, with the irrelevant exception just noted. In this case, we have a hierarchy of terms with systematic relations that, once again, cannot in any natural way be described within the framework of independent lexical entries. Other systems of this sort can easily be found, and, in fact, they suggest that part of the semantic component of a grammar must be a characterization of field properties that is outside the lexicon. This matter is crucial but has been relatively unexplored within any general framework, though there have been several valuable studies of certain of its aspects. (See note 12.) Suppose, furthermore, that an attempt is made to relate "deviance" in the intuitive sense to "degree of grammaticalness" in the technical sense by excluding such examples as (18i–iii) from direct generation (cf. note 1). The consequences of such a decision are not easy to determine.

Once again, we can do no more here than indicate problems and stress the fact that there are many unanswered questions of principle that might very well affect the formulation of even those parts of the theory of grammar that seem reasonably well established.

Finally, it is important to be aware of the many other problems that face a theory of semantic interpretation of the kind referred to in the preceding discussion. It is clear, as Katz and Fodor have emphasized, that the meaning of a sentence is based on the meaning of its elementary parts and the manner of their combination. It is also clear that the manner of combination provided by the surface (immediate constituent) structure is in general almost totally irrelevant to semantic interpretation, whereas the grammatical relations expressed in the abstract deep structure are, in many cases, just those that determine the meaning of the sentence. Cf., for example, Chapter 1, § 4, and Chapter 2, § 2.2. However, there are cases that suggest the need for an even more abstract notion of grammatical function and grammatical relation than any that has been developed so far, in any systematic way. Consider, for example, these sentence pairs:

(19) (i) John strikes me as pompous — I regard John as pompous
     (ii) I liked the play — the play pleased me
     (iii) John bought the book from Bill — Bill sold the book to John
     (iv) John struck Bill — Bill received a blow at the hands of John

Clearly, there is a meaning relation, approaching a variety of paraphrase, in these cases. It is not expressible in transformational terms, as is possible, for example, in these cases:

(20) (i) John is easy for us to please — it is easy for us to please John
     (ii) it was yesterday that he came — he came yesterday

In the case of (20), the deep structures of the paired sentences are identical in all respects relevant to semantic interpretation of the sort we are considering here, so that the transformational analysis accounts for the (cognitive) synonymy. This does not seem to be true in the case of (19), however. For example, in the case of (19i), although the deep structures would show that "pompous" modifies "John" in both sentences of the pair, they would not express the relations of the two Nouns to the Verb that are (in some unclear sense) the semantically significant ones. Thus in some sense the relation of "John" to "strike" is the same as that of "John" to "regard," and the relation of "strike" to "me" is the same as that of "regard" to "I." We have no mechanism for expressing this fact, hence of accounting for the meaning relation, in terms of lexical features or grammatical relations of the deep structure.[18] Consequently, it seems that beyond the notions of surface structure (such as "grammatical subject") and deep structure (such as "logical subject"), there is some still more abstract notion of "semantic function" still unexplained. Various formal devices for expressing these facts suggest themselves, but the general problem seems to me nontrivial.

Many related problems have been raised in the extensive discussion of the distinction between the "grammatical" Subject and Predicate of a sentence and its "logical" or "psychological" Subject and Predicate (see, for example, Paul, 1886; Jespersen, 1924; Wilson, 1926). To mention just one, Cook Wilson maintains (1926, pp. 119 f.) that "in the statement 'glass is elastic,' if the matter of inquiry was elasticity and the question was what substances possessed the property of elasticity, 'glass' . . . would no longer be subject, and the kind of stress which fell upon 'elastic' when 'glass' was the subject, would now be transferred to 'glass.' " Thus in the statement *"glass* is elastic," " 'glass,' which has the stress, is the only word which refers to the supposed new fact in the nature of elasticity, that it is found in glass . . . [and therefore] . . . 'glass' would have to be the predicate. . . . Thus the same form of words should be analyzed differently according as the words are the answer to one question or another," and, in general, "the subject and predicate are not necessarily *words* in the sentence, nor even something denoted by words in the sentence." Whatever the force of such observations may be, it seems that they lie beyond the scope of any existing theory of language structure or language use.

To conclude this highly inconclusive discussion, I shall simply point out that the syntactic and semantic structure of natural languages evidently offers many mysteries, both of fact and of principle, and that any attempt to delimit the boundaries of these domains must certainly be quite tentative.

§ 2. *THE STRUCTURE OF THE LEXICON*

§ *2.1. Redundancy*

The lexicon was described earlier simply as a set of lexical entries, each consisting of a distinctive feature matrix D and a complex symbol C, the latter being a set of features of various sorts (syntactic and semantic features, features that specify which morphological or transformational processes apply to strings containing the items in question, features that exempt items from certain phonological rules, and so on).[14] We have just seen that this account is oversimplified in the case of semantic features, further structure being necessary in the lexicon to account for field properties. Furthermore, in Chapter 2, § 3, we pointed out that various general conventions can be given that permit significant simplification of such lexical entries.

To explore the question of simplification of lexical entries somewhat further, let us, for concreteness, make a specific choice at each point where, in the discussion, we listed alternative possibilities that seemed to deserve consideration. In particular, let us assume that the proper method for inserting lexical items is by a general rule that inserts the lexical entry (D,C) in a position $\cdots Q \cdots$ in a Phrase-marker (Q being a complex symbol developed by rewriting rules), where C is not distinct from Q in the technical sense of feature theory. Thus we tentatively accept the method of § 3 of Chapter 2, rather than that suggested in Chapter 2, § 4.3. Furthermore, let us make the empirical assumption that a grammar is more highly valued if the lexical entries contain few positively specified strict subcategorization features and many positively specified selectional features. Thus we tentatively accept alternative (iv) of p. 111.[15] These choices do affect the following discussion, but analogous problems arise no matter which of the proposed alternatives is selected.

We have, in effect, now adopted the following conventions:

(21) (i) only positively specified strict subcategorization features and only negatively specified selectional features appear explicitly in lexical entries, the others being introduced by the auxiliary convention (ii)

(ii)   if the lexical entry (D,C) is not explicitly provided with the feature specification $[\alpha\varphi - \psi]$ for the contextual feature $[\varphi - \psi]$ (where $\alpha = +$ in the case of a strict subcategorization feature and $\alpha = -$ in the case of a selectional feature), then assign it the specified feature $[-\alpha\varphi - \psi]$

We also pointed out (in Chapter 2, § 3) that a convention analogous to (21ii) can be established in the case of features corresponding to lexical categories.

In accordance with these conventions, we might give the lexical entry for *frighten* (cf. (58) of Chapter 2) simply as:

(22) (*frighten*, [+V, + — NP, −[+N] — [−Animate], ⋯])

The conventions will introduce: the category features $[-N]$, $[-\text{Adjective}]$, $[-M]$; the strict subcategorization features $[- -]$, $[- - \text{NP}^\frown\#^\frown\text{S}^\frown\#]$, ⋯ ; the selectional features $[+[+N] - [+\text{Animate}]]$, $[+[+N] - [+\text{Human}]]$, ⋯. Thus *frighten* will be specified (by (22) plus conventions) as a Verb, but not a Noun, Adjective, or Modal; as insertable in the context *sincerity — John* but not *sincerity —*[16] or *sincerity — justice.*[17]

We can proceed to develop an appropriate convention to simplify lexical representation of items with inherent features in the case where these are hierarchic rather than cross-classifying. Let us say that the sequence of specified features $([\alpha_1 F_1], \cdots, [\alpha_n F_n])$ $(\alpha_i = +$ or $-)$ is a *hierarchic sequence with respect to the grammar G* if $[\alpha_i F_i]$ is the only specified feature directly dominating $[\alpha_{i+1} F_{i+1}]$, for each $i < n$, in G. Thus, for example, with respect to the illustrative grammar (57) of Chapter 2 we have the hierarchic sequences

(23) (i)   ([+Animate], [±Human])
   (ii) ([+N], [+Common], [−Count], [±Abstract])
   (iii) ([+N], [±Common])[18]

Where such relationships obtain, we can utilize them to simplify lexical entries by the following rather natural convention:[19]

(24) suppose that $([\alpha_1 F_1], \cdots, [\alpha_n F_n])$ is a maximal hierarchic

sequence with respect to the grammar G, and that (D,C) is a lexical entry of G, where C contains $[\alpha_n F_n]$. Then C is extended automatically to C' containing C along with all of the specified features $[\alpha_i F_i]$, for each i, $1 \leqslant i < n$.

Using this convention, we can simplify the lexical entry in (58) of Chapter 2 for *boy* to the following:

(25)   (*boy*, [+Common, +Human, +Count, $\cdots$])

the features [+N], [+Animate] now being predictable.[20]

Let us say that the feature $[\alpha F]$ is *lexically determined* in the grammar G if there is a hierarchic sequence $([+K], \cdots , [\alpha F])$ with respect to G, where K is a lexical category ($\alpha = +$ or $-$). This is to say that if (D,C) is a lexical entry and C contains $[\alpha F]$, then (D,C) is necessarily a member of the lexical category K, with respect to this entry, and it is unnecessary (by virtue of convention (24)) to list [+K] in C. In the sample grammar (57), (58) of § 3, Chapter 2, each lexical item contains lexically determined features. Hence, it is unnecessary, in the lexicon of (58), to designate the lexical category for any item. If every lexical entry contains lexically determined features, as seems plausible, then the features [+C] and [−C], where C is a lexical category, need never receive explicit mention in the lexicon.

We have thus far considered only universal notational conventions underlying lexical representation. However, there are also many language-specific redundancies. Thus, for example, every Verb in English that can occur with a Direct-Object and a following Manner Adverbial can occur as well with just a Direct-Object, though not conversely.[21] The strict subcategorization rules of the grammatical sketch of § 3, Chapter 2, introduced the features [— NP] and [— NP⌢Manner] for Verbs, among others. In accordance with the observation just made, we see that if a lexical item is specified in the lexicon as [+ — NP⌢Manner], then it must also be specified as [+ — NP], though not necessarily conversely. For example, *read* will be specified positively for both features, but *resemble, cost* will be specified positively for [— NP] and negatively for [— NP⌢Manner], since we can have "he read the book (carefully, with great enthusiasm)," "John resembled his father," but not "John resembled his father carefully (with great enthusiasm)," etc. Here again we have a redundancy in the lexicon and a significant generalization still not expressed in the grammar. Clearly, what is needed is the following rule:

(26) $[+ - \text{NP}^\frown\text{Manner}] \rightarrow [+ - \text{NP}]$

to be interpreted in the following manner: if (D,C) is a lexical entry with distinctive feature matrix D and complex symbol C containing $[+ - \text{NP}^\frown\text{Manner}]$, then C is replaced by C', which contains each specified feature $[\alpha F]$ of C, where $F \neq [- \text{NP}]$, and also the specified feature $[+ - \text{NP}]$.

Actually, the rule (26) can be further generalized. It is also true of Intransitive Verbs that if they can take a Manner Adverbial, then they can occur without one. What is needed is a convention permitting a variable over strings to appear in the rule generalizing (26), thus, in effect, allowing us to use part of the internal structure of the notations for lexical features. Using φ as a string variable, we can give the rule in this form:

(27) $[+ - \varphi^\frown\text{Manner}] \rightarrow [+ - \varphi]$

This is to be interpreted as follows: first, select any constant string as φ; second, interpret the result in the manner described in connection with (26). It might also be expedient to develop the obvious convention that allows (27) to be stated as a context-sensitive rule, or to allow a condition on φ to be added, where this is well defined in terms of base rules.

Let us suppose that the rule (27) applies before the conventions (21), (24). Then such words as *walk, hit* will be entered in the lexicon in this form:

(28) (i) (*walk*, $[+ - \text{Manner}, \cdots]$)
     (ii) (*hit*, $[+ - \text{NP}^\frown\text{Manner}, \cdots]$)

By the rule (27) followed by the convention (21), these will be automatically extended to

(29) (i) (*walk*, $[+ - \text{Manner}, + -, - - \text{NP}^\frown\text{Manner},$
         $- - \text{NP}, \cdots]$)

(ii) (*hit*, [+ — NP⌢Manner, + — NP, – — Manner, – —,
···])

Thus *walk* can appear with or without a Manner Adverbial,
but with no Direct-Object, and *hit* can appear with or without a
Manner Adverbial, but only with a Direct-Object.

Rules such as (27), (28) are closely analogous to the phonological rules that Halle has called "morpheme structure rules"
(Halle, 1959*a*, 1959*b*), and that I have been referring to here
(following a suggestion of his) as *phonological redundancy rules*.
These rules are designed to deal with the fact that certain
phonological feature specifications are predictable, given others.
Thus in an initial sequence #CC in English, if the second C is
a true consonant (that is, not a liquid or a glide), the first must
be [s]; if the second consonant is a liquid, the first must be an
obstruent, etc. The phonological redundancy rules that state
these facts are precisely of the form (26) and are interpreted in
the same way, except that the features in question are phonological rather than syntactic, and, consequently, the generalization
to (27) has no analogue. We shall refer to the analogous syntactic
rules (26), (27) as *syntactic redundancy rules*. The redundancy
rules, both phonological and syntactic, state general properties of
all lexical entries, and therefore make it unnecessary to provide
feature specifications in lexical entries where these are not
idiosyncratic.

Observe that a distinction must be made between the *conventions* (21), (24) and the *syntactic redundancy rules* (26), (27),
though both play the role of eliminating redundant specifications
from the lexicon. The former are universal, and therefore need
no specific statement in the grammar. They are part of the
procedure for interpreting grammars (the function *f* of (12iv)–
(14iv), Chapter 1, § 6). The latter, on the other hand, are particular to a given language, and therefore must be given in the
grammar.[22] I have tried to emphasize this by calling the former
"conventions," and the latter, "rules."

Given a lexical entry (*D,C*), the phonological redundancy
rules give a fuller specification to *D*, and the syntactic redundancy

rules give a fuller specification to C. To this extent, the two systems are analogous. However, there is still an important difference between them, so far as the role that they play is concerned. To see this, it is necessary to consider an aspect of the system of phonological redundancy rules that has not always been fully appreciated. The fact that there are rules for predicting certain phonological feature specifications in terms of others has long been known, and there are many descriptive studies that give charts or rules of one sort or another to specify the set of "phonologically admissible sequences," "possible syllables," and so on. Halle's achievement was not merely to reiterate the fact that such constraints exist but to present a principled basis for selection of one set of rules rather than another to determine them. He showed that a very general and independently motivated evaluation procedure for phonology (namely, minimization of feature specification) seems to provide such a basis. That is, application of this criterion selects a system of phonological redundancy rules that defines the notion "phonologically admissible" in a way that, in many crucial cases, conforms to the known facts.[23] He thus was able to propose an explanation for the facts of phonological admissibility, in place of a mere description — in other words, to give a general, language-independent definition of the notions "accidental gap" (such as, in English, /blik/) and "systematic gap" (such as, in English, /bnik/), in place of an *ad hoc* chart or list. The real function of the phonological redundancy rules is to determine the class of phonologically admissible (though perhaps nonoccurring) sequences in a principled way. To the extent that they succeed in doing this, they provide empirical support for the linguistic theory that contains the evaluation procedure that Halle proposes, as well as the system of constraints on phonological rules that this procedure presupposes. But there is no really convincing analogue to the notion of "phonological admissibility" in the case of the syntactic redundancy rules. Consequently, it is an open question whether these have the significance of the phonological redundancy rules.

This observation suggests that we seek an analogue to the

distinction between accidental and systematic gaps, on the syntactic level. In fact, from a purely formal point of view, the syntactic redundancy rules do make a distinction between "possible, but nonoccurring lexical entry" and "impossible lexical entry," precisely as the phonological redundancy rules do. In both cases, the redundancy rules provide general constraints on all lexical entries, thus distinguishing possible from impossible lexical entries (possibility with respect to a particular language, that is, insofar as the redundancy rules are not universal conventions). But in general not all of the possibilities will be actually realized in the lexicon. What must be shown is that this formal tripartite distinction of occurring, possible but nonoccurring, and impossible has the significance in the syntactic case that it clearly does in the phonological case. Thus what must be shown is that the possible but nonoccurring lexical entries have the status of "accidental semantic gaps" in the sense that they correspond to lexical items that the language does not provide for specifically but could in principle incorporate with no alteration of the general semantic system within which it functions. I have no very satisfying examples at present.[24] The problem is reasonably clear, however, and merits investigation.

The study of syntactic redundancy rules is a large topic in itself, but instead of continuing with additional examples, I should like to consider briefly some of the problems that arise in the attempt to deal with morphological processes within a framework of the sort that has been outlined earlier.

§ 2.2. *Inflectional processes*

It is useful to compare two ways of dealing with questions of inflectional morphology, namely the traditional method of paradigms and the descriptivist method of morphemic analysis. Since English is too poor in inflection to illustrate this difference, we shall turn to German for examples. In a traditional grammar, a particular occurrence of a Noun would be described in terms of its place in a system of paradigms defined by certain inflectional categories, namely the categories of gender, number, case, and declensional type. Each of these categories constitutes an independent "dimension" of the paradigm, and each word has a particular "value" along each of these independent dimensions.[25] Thus the word *Brüder* in the phrase *der Brüder* would be characterized as Masculine, Plural, Genitive, and belonging to a certain declensional class along with *Vater*, *Mutter*, etc.

In fact, we can restate the paradigmatic description directly in terms of syntactic features. Regarding each of the dimensions of the system of paradigms as a multivalued feature, with the specifications being not $+$ and $-$ but, let us say, integers conventionally associated with the traditional designations,[26] we can represent the Phrase-marker of the sentence $\cdots$ *der Brüder* $\cdots$ as containing the subconfiguration (30). Thus, associated with this

(30)

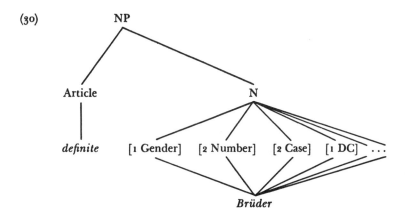

occurrence of *Brüder*, there will be a feature matrix indicating that this formative is assigned to the categories [1 Gender], [2 Number], [2 Case], and [1 DC] (as well as to many others represented in (30) simply by $\cdots$). Notice that the specified features [1 Gender] and [1 DC] are *inherent* to this formative (that is, they are part of the complex symbol C of the lexical entry $(Bruder, C)$) and that [2 Number] and [2 Case] are introduced by grammatical rules. Presumably, the specified feature

[2 Number] is introduced by a context-free rule of the base applying to Nouns,[27] and specified feature [2 Case] is introduced by
a rule that does not belong to the base subcomponent of the
syntax at all but rather to its transformational part (cf. note 35,
Chapter 2). If so, then of these features only [2 Number] will be
a feature of the preterminal symbol for which *Bruder* is substituted by the lexical rule, and all but [2 Case] will appear in the
terminal string generated by the base rules. Notice, incidentally,
that the specification [1 DC] might be introduced by a redundancy rule that, in this case, takes into account both phonological and other lexical features. A rule of the (interpretive)
phonological component will operate on (30), giving the form
Brüder. This rule will assert that a Vowel is fronted in a
formative that is simultaneously of the categories [2 Number],
[1 DC]. (A separate rule that is quite general would specify that
/(V)n/ is suffixed if, furthermore, it belongs to the category
[3 Case].)

In short, the theory of syntactic features developed earlier
can incorporate the traditional paradigmatic treatment directly.
The system of paradigms is simply described as a system of
features, one (or perhaps some hierarchic configuration) corresponding to each of the dimensions that define the system of
paradigms. Interpretive phonological rules, some quite specific,
some of considerable generality, then operate on the phonological
matrix of the lexical entry, giving, finally, a phonetic matrix.
Where these features are not completely independent (as, for
example, if declensional type depends on Gender), or where they
are partially determined by other aspects of a formative, redundancy rules of the kind discussed earlier will apply.

The characteristic method of analysis of modern linguistics
is rather different from the traditional approach that we have
just restated in our terms. In place of the traditional categories
(our features), this approach would substitute morphemes. Thus
Brüder in (30) would perhaps be represented in the manner of
(31), in a completely consistent "item-and-arrangement" grammar:

case of (31), the rule for fronting of the Vowel must refer to the morpheme *Masculine*, and this is the usual situation in the case of agreement rules. But in the paradigmatic representation, these elements, not being part of the terminal string, need not be referred to at all in the rules to which they are not relevant. Finally, notice that the order of morphemes is often quite arbitrary, whereas this arbitrariness is avoided in the paradigmatic treatment, the features being unordered.

I know of no compensating advantage for the modern descriptivist reanalysis of traditional paradigmatic formulations in terms of morpheme sequences. This seems, therefore, to be an ill-advised theoretical innovation.

Within our framework, either paradigmatic analysis in terms of features or sequential morphemic analysis is available, whichever permits the optimal and most general statement of some aspect of the syntactic or phonological system. It seems that in inflectional systems, the paradigmatic analysis has many advantages and is to be preferred, though there may be cases where some compromise should be made.[30] It is difficult to say anything more definite, since there have been so few attempts to give precise and principled descriptions of inflectional systems in a way that would have some bearing on the theoretical issues involved here.[31]

If we assume now that the paradigmatic solution is the correct one, it follows that we must allow the transformational component to contain rules that alter and expand the matrix of features constituting a lexical item. For example, the feature (or features) of Case must in general be specified by rules that apply after many transformational rules have already taken effect. (See note 35 of Chapter 2.) Similarly, rules of agreement clearly belong to the transformational component (cf. in this connection, Postal, 1964a, pp. 43f.), and these rules add to Phrasemarkers specified features that enter into particular formatives dominating their phonological matrices. In the case of (30), for example, the grammar must contain agreement rules that assi to the Article all of the feature specifications for [Gen

(31)   *Bruder⌢DC₁⌢Masculine⌢Plural⌢Genitive*

where each of these elements is regarded as a single morpheme, DC_1 being a kind of "class marker."[28] Rules would then be given that would convert (31) into a sequence of phonemes.

Respresentations such as (31) are clumsy for a grammar based on rewriting rules or transformations. There are several reasons for this. For one thing, many of these "morphemes" are not phonetically realized and must therefore be regarded, in particular contexts, as zero elements. In each such case a specific context-sensitive rule must be given stating that the morpheme in question is phonetically null. But this extensive set of rules is entirely superfluous and can simply be omitted under the alternative paradigmatic analysis. Thus compare the rules that must be provided for the paradigmatic analysis (30) and for the morphemic analysis (31). In the case of (31), we first apply a rule stating that the Vowel is fronted in the context: — DC_1 ⋯ *Plural* ⋯ , where the item in question is a Noun. In the case of (30), we have the corresponding rule that the Vowel is fronted when the item in question has the features [1 DC] and [2 Number]. But in the case of the morphemic analysis we now have the additional rules stating that in such contexts as (31), all four inflectional morphemes are phonetically null. With the feature analysis (30), we simply give no rule at all expressing the fact that certain features are phonetically unrealized, just as we give no rule expressing the fact that [+N], or, for that matter, NP, is phonetically unrealized.[29]

More generally, the often suppletive character of inflectional systems, as well as the fact that (as in the example) the effect of the inflectional categories may be partially or even totally internal, causes cumbersome and inelegant formulation of rules when the representations to which they apply are in the form (31). However, suppletion and internal modification cause no special difficulty at all in the paradigmatic formulation. Similarly, with morphemic representations, it is necessary to refer to irrelevant morphemes in many of the grammatical rules. For example, in the

[Number], and [Case] of the Noun it modifies. Thus we must have a rule that might be given in the form:

$$(32) \quad \text{Article} \rightarrow \begin{bmatrix} \alpha \text{Gender} \\ \beta \text{ Number} \\ \gamma \text{ Case} \end{bmatrix} / \text{---} \cdots \begin{bmatrix} +\text{N} \\ \alpha \text{ Gender} \\ \beta \text{ Number} \\ \gamma \text{ Case} \end{bmatrix},$$

where Article $\cdots$ N is an NP.

This rule is interpreted as asserting that in a string analyzable as $(X, \text{Article}, Y, N, Z)$, where the second plus third plus fourth elements constitute an NP, the second element is to be assigned to the categories [α Gender], [β Number], and [γ Case] if the fourth element is of these categories, α, β, and γ being variables that range over integers. This rule thus asserts that the Article agrees with its Noun in Gender, Number, and Case. In particular, rule (32) assigns to the formative *definite*[32] in (30) the features [1 Gender], [2 Number], [2 Case]. This formative, so categorized, would be converted to /der/ by rules of the phonology.

The rule (32) is a transformational rule of the usual kind except that it introduces specified features instead of only non-lexical formatives. Thus the features play a role which is intermediate between that of formatives and that of true categories with respect to the operation of transformational rules, as is quite natural. There is no particular difficulty in extending the theory of transformations to allow for the formulation of rules such as (32), which provide an appropriate formalization for traditional rules of agreement. Regarding features as constituent elements of formatives, these transformational rules will, in effect, rewrite terminal symbols in certain restricted ways.

Formally, rules of agreement such as (32) are quite analogous to the rules of assimilation of the phonological component. For example, in English, as in many other languages, nasals are neutralized before stops, so that the words *limp*, *lint*, *link*, *send*, *ring* would be represented /liNp/, /liNt/, /liNk/, /seNd/, /riNg/ in lexical entries, where /N/ = [+nasal] and the other symbols are also abbreviations for certain sets of phonological features. The nasal assimilates to the following consonant with respect to the features of gravity and compactness, so that we have the rule

$$(33) \qquad [+ \text{nasal}] \rightarrow \begin{bmatrix} \alpha \text{ grave} \\ \\ \beta \text{ compact} \end{bmatrix} / - \begin{bmatrix} + \text{ consonantal} \\ \alpha \text{ grave} \\ \beta \text{ compact} \end{bmatrix}$$

interpreted in the manner of rule (32).[33] Thus (33) asserts that the features [α grave] and [β compact] are added to a [+ nasal] that precedes an [α grave], [β compact] consonant, where α, β range over $\{+, -\}$. It asserts, in other words, that the nasal is /m/ before labials, /n/ before dentals, and /ŋ/ before velars (where the voiced velar then drops in certain positions, giving /siŋ#/, etc. — I have not given the full statement of required context in (33)).

In the case of rule (32), the features added are, apparently, the only features associated with the nonlexical item *definite* (but cf. note 32). Other agreement rules expand an already present matrix of features — for example, the rule assigning features of a Noun to a modifying Adjective. The latter, being a lexical item, will have an independent feature matrix of its own, which is expanded by the agreement rule. The Adjective, in this case, is introduced into the prenominal position by a transformational rule, and its features will include its inherent features (those given in its lexical entry) and those associated with the complex symbol that it replaces by the lexical rule.

It seems, then, that the traditional approach to the description of inflectional systems can be formalized quite readily within the framework that we have established. Furthermore, this appears to be the most natural way to deal with inflectional systems.

Before turning to the much more perplexing problems of derivational morphology, I should like to mention a few additional problems that arise when inflectional features are considered in further detail. We have been regarding a lexical item as a set of phonological, semantic, and syntactic features. When inserted into a Phrase-marker, a lexical item may acquire other features beyond those inherent to it in the lexicon. Thus if we adopt the method of lexical insertion described in § 3 of Chapter 2, then contextual features may be added to the lexical entry beyond those that it already contains; and, quite apart from this, such features as [α Number] are inherent to the Phrase-marker rather than the lexical item, as we have just observed, and become part of the formative only after it is inserted into a Phrase-marker. Furthermore, the features involved in the case dimension are certainly added to a formative by rather late transformations (since case often depends on aspects of surface rather than deep structure — but see note 35, Chapter 2), and certain features that are inherent to Nouns (such as Gender) are assigned to Verbs and Adjectives only by transformations. We have been assuming that these various operations simply extend the set of features constituting the formative. But various problems arise if we follow this assumption consistently.

We have mentioned in several places (Chapter 3, notes 1 and 13, and pp. 144f.) that deletions must be recoverable, and have suggested that this condition can be formalized by the following convention relating to what we called "erasure transformations": an erasure transformation can use a term X of its proper analysis to erase a term Y of the proper analysis only if X and Y are identical. In the case of lexical items, "identity" might be taken to mean strict identity of feature composition.

In some cases this decision has just the right consequences. Consider, for example, the case of the relativization transformation discussed previously (p. 145). Just as the generalized Phrase-marker for the string "I saw the [# the man was clever #] boy" is not the deep structure underlying any well-formed surface structure and hence does not provide the semantic interpretation for any sentence (cf. pp. 137–138), so the generalized Phrase-marker for "I saw the [# the boys were clever #] boy" does not underlie a sentence. This is so because the element *boys* (containing the feature [+Plural]) is not identical with the element *boy* (containing the feature [−Plural]) just as the element *man* is not identical with *boy*. Hence, in neither case is relativization permitted.

But matters do not always work out quite this smoothly.

Consider the rules that provide for comparative constructions of various sorts, in particular, for such sentences as

(34)   John is more clever than Bill

In this case, the sentence is formed from the underlying deep structure given as (35), following previous conventions. The fea-

(35)

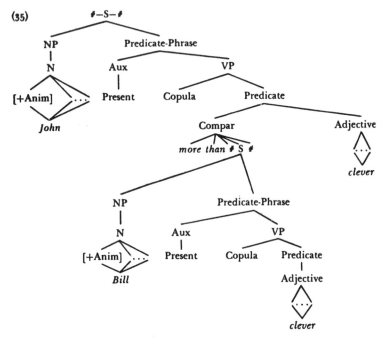

tures constituting the lexical formatives of (35) are not given explicitly, but, rather, indicated by $\cdots$. To derive (34) from (35) in the manner described earlier, the transformational rules first apply to the most deeply embedded base Phrase-marker, namely that of "Bill is clever." Next, they reapply to the full configuration (35), which has, at this point (omitting various refinements), this terminal string:

(36)   John is more than [# Bill is clever #] clever

The comparative transformation, which applies next, can be

formulated as an erasure operation that uses the Adjective of the matrix sentence to delete the corresponding Adjective of the embedded sentence.[34] Thus it applies to a string of this form:

(37)

$$\underbrace{NP}_{1} - \underbrace{is}_{2} - \underbrace{\cdots}_{3} - \underbrace{\cdots \# NP \text{ is}}_{4} - \underbrace{\text{Adjective} \#}_{5} - \underbrace{\text{Adjective}}_{6}$$

(where $\cdots - \cdots$ is *as-as*, *more-than*, etc.), deleting 5 and #. Finally, it permutes 4 and 6 (technically, it places 4 to the right of 6, deleting 4). This gives

(38) John is more clever than Bill is

A final option is to delete the repeated copula, giving (34).

But recall that the deletion of the Adjective in the fifth position of (37) by the comparative transformation is possible only when the two Adjectives are identical. Similarly, the deletion of the final copula in (38) requires identity of the two copulas. In the case of (34), derived from (35), this causes no difficulty. But consider the example (39), or the perfectly analogous French example (40):

(39) these men are more clever than Mary

(40) ces hommes sont plus intelligents que Marie

In the case of (39), deletion of the Adjective is straightforward, but our deletion conventions should prevent the deletion of the copula, since it has the feature [−Plural] in the embedded sentence and [+Plural] in the matrix sentence. Furthermore, in the case of (40), the deletion of the Adjective of the embedded sentence should be blocked, since it differs from the Adjective of the matrix sentence in gender and number.

These observations suggest that it may not be correct to regard a formative simply as a set of features, some inherent and some added by transformation and as a consequence of insertion into a Phrase-marker. In particular, it seems from such examples as these that the features added to a formative by agreement transformations are not part of the formative in the same sense as those which are inherent to it or as those which it assumes as it enters a Phrase-marker. Thus in the case of the relative transformation, plurality of the Noun (which is a feature that the Noun assumes as it enters a Phrase-marker) is a feature that must be considered in determining whether it is identical to another Noun, as we have just seen. However, in the case of Adjectives and the copula (also Verbs, which take part in similar rules) the inflectional features that are added by agreement transformations are apparently not considered in determining whether the item in question is strictly identical with some other item.[35]

Some further support for this conclusion is given by such examples as the following:

(41) (i) John is a more clever man than Bill
  (ii) *The Golden Notebook* is as intricate a novel as *Tristram Shandy*
  (iii) I know several more successful lawyers than Bill

It is clear that the deep structures for these three sentences must contain the base Phrase-markers underlying "Bill is a man," "*Tristram Shandy* is a novel," "Bill is a lawyer," respectively. Thus (41iii) implies that Bill is a lawyer; similarly, one cannot replace "Bill" by "Mary" in (41).[36] Sentences (41i) and (41ii) pose no problems. But consider (41iii). However the transformational rules are actually formulated, it is clear that we are deleting "successful" and "a lawyer" as Predicates of "Bill" in the underlying structure. But the deletion of "a lawyer," in particular, is permitted only under the identity condition discussed earlier, and the string with which it is compared is not "a lawyer" but rather its pluralized form, "lawyers,"[37] from the base string "I know several [# S #] lawyers." Here, then, is a case where plurality is not considered a distinguishing property of Nouns, for the purposes of a deletion operation, as contrasted with the case of relativization, discussed earlier, where a distinction in the feature of plurality was sufficient to block deletion. The crucial difference apparently is that in this case, the Noun Phrase in question is in Predicate position and therefore receives its number not inherently (as in the example discussed in connection with relativization) but rather by an agreement transformation. Thus we cannot have "They are a lawyer," "Bill is several lawyers," etc., and such facts as these show that Predicate-Nominals must be neutral with regard to number. Hence, the conflict in number between the italicized Noun Phrases of "I know *several lawyers*" and "Bill is *a lawyer*" is on a par with the conflict in number and gender between the italicized Adjectives of "ces hommes sont *intelligents*" and "Marie est *intelligente*" (cf. (40)). In both cases, the conflicting features are introduced by agreement transformations.

These examples suggest two conclusions. First, features introduced by transformation into lexical formatives are not to be considered in determining when deletion is permitted; a formative, in other words, is to be regarded as a pair of sets of features, one member of the pair consisting of features that are inherent to the lexical entry or the position of lexical insertion, the second member of the pair consisting of features added by transformation. Only the first set is considered in determining legitimacy of deletion in the manner previously described. Second, what is involved in determining legitimacy of deletion is not identity but rather nondistinctness in the sense of distinctive feature theory (cf. Chapter 2, § 2.3.2). Thus consider once again the case of "I know several lawyers" — "Bill is a lawyer." The Predicate-Nominal of the latter is not singular, in the base structure; rather, it is unspecified with respect to number exactly as the nasal is unspecified with respect to point of articulation in the lexical representations of the formatives *king, find, lamp*, etc. Hence, it is not *identical with* the corresponding nominal element of "I know several lawyers"; it is, rather, nondistinct from it, and the example suggests that this is sufficient to permit deletion.[38]

Notice that this analysis of a formative as a pair of sets of features need not actually be described or mentioned in any way in the rules of the grammar, since it is, apparently, determined by a general convention regarding the form of grammar. In other words, we are tentatively proposing it for consideration as a linguistic universal, admittedly, on rather slender evidence (but see note 2 of Chapter 2). If this proposal is a correct one, then the analysis of formatives that we have suggested is a general condition on the functioning of erasure transformations. The only apparent alternative to the proposal just advanced is a revision of the general conditions suggested earlier on the order of application of transformational rules. Whether this may be feasible, I do not know; but in any event, the proposal just discussed seems clearly preferable.

Summarizing, we seem to be led to the conclusion that non-distinctness rather than strict identity is what is involved in deletion, and that only those features of a formative that are inherent either to its lexical entry or to the position in the sentence where it is inserted are to be considered in determining nondistinctness. Formally, we can say that a formative must be regarded as a pair of sets of features, one member consisting of the "inherent" features of the lexical entry or the sentence position, the other member consisting of the "noninherent" features introduced by transformation. The general principle for erasure operations, then, is this: *a term* X *of the proper analysis can be used to erase a term* Y *of the proper analysis just in case the inherent part of the formative* X *is not distinct from the inherent part of the formative* Y. But notice that this is an entirely natural decision to reach. The original intuition motivating this condition was that deletions should, in some sense, be recoverable; and the noninherent features of the formative are precisely those that are determined by the context, hence that are recoverable even if deleted. Similarly, it is natural to base the operation on nondistinctness rather than identity, because the features unspecified in underlying structures (such as number, in predicate position) also make no independent contribution to sentence interpretation, being added by what are, in essence, redundancy rules, and are, in fact, simply a reflection of context. Thus they are recoverable in the sense that the context that determined them is still present in the string after deletion of the item in question. Hence, the italicized condition formalizes a very reasonable sense of "recoverability of deletion."

Consider now one last set of questions relating to the comparative transformations. Suppose that we adopt the method of lexical insertion proposed in § 3 of Chapter 2 and based on non-distinctness, rather than that proposed in § 4.3 of Chapter 2. In the Phrase-marker (35), then, each occurrence of the Adjective *clever* will have such features as [post-Animate] (that is, [+[+Animate] —]) added to it by selectional rules of the base component (in this case, (57xv) of Chapter 2, now revised as (13) of this chapter). But we clearly must allow such sentences as "John is heavier than this rock"; and in this case, *heavy* will have the feature [post-Animate] in the matrix sentence and the feature [post-Inanimate] in the embedded sentence of the Phrase-marker corresponding to (35) (this Phrase-marker will be identical with (35) except that each occurrence of *clever* in (35) will be replaced by *heavy*; and *Bill*, with the features [+Animate], ···, is replaced by *the rock*, with the features [—Animate], ···, associated with *rock*). Hence, the two occurrences of *heavy* that are compared when we attempt to apply the comparative transformation differ in feature composition, one containing the feature [post-Animate] and the other the feature [post-Inanimate]. As matters now stand, this difference of feature composition does not make the two items distinct from one another, in the technical sense of feature theory (that is, it is not the case that one of them is marked $[+F]$ and the other $[-F]$, for some feature $[F]$. Furthermore, it would be natural to regard these contextual features of the Adjective as noninherent, in the sense of the preceding paragraph; therefore deletion is permitted.

There is, however, one class of examples that suggests that in certain cases a difference in the composition of two formatives with respect to such features as [post-Animate] should suffice to block deletion. Consider such sentences as

(42) (i) John is as sad as the book he read yesterday
    (ii) he exploits his employees more than the opportunity to please
    (iii) is Brazil as independent as the continuum hypothesis?

Clearly, these are deviant and must be marked as such in a descriptively adequate grammar. In each case, the deleted items differ in selectional features from the items with which they are compared. Thus *sad* is [post-Animate] in the matrix sentence of (42i) and [post-Inanimate] in the embedded sentence, and possibly this might be regarded as the factor that blocks the transformation and prevents deletion. The only alternative, in these cases, would be to assume that two homonymous lexical entries are involved, in each of the examples of (42).[39] In introducing examples of this sort, however, we touch on problems of homonymity and range of meaning that are cloaked in such obscurity, for the moment, that no conclusions at all can be drawn from them.

§ 2.3. *Derivational processes*

Derivational processes create much more of a problem for any sort of generative (that is, explicit) grammar than do inflectional systems. This results from the fact that they are typically sporadic and only quasi-productive. We shall consider several examples briefly, without, however, arriving at any very satisfactory way of dealing with the problems that arise.

Where derivational processes are productive, they in fact raise no serious difficulties. Consider, for example, nominalization transformations of the sort that form the sentences "their destruction of the property . . . ," "their refusal to participate . . . ," etc. Clearly, the words *destruction, refusal*, etc., will not be entered in the lexicon as such. Rather, *destroy* and *refuse* will be entered in the lexicon with a feature specification that determines the phonetic form they will assume (by later phonological rules) when they appear in nominalized sentences. A nominalization transformation will apply at the appropriate stage of derivation to the generalized Phrase-marker containing the configuration "they destroy the property" dominated by S,[40] forming ultimately the Phrase-marker (43), where irrelevant details are omitted,[41] and where $F_1, \cdots, F_m, G_1, \cdots, G_n$ stand for specified features. It is not at all clear that *destruction* or *refusal* should be regarded as Nouns in "their destruction of the property . . . ," "their refusal to come . . ." (although *refusal* happens

(43)

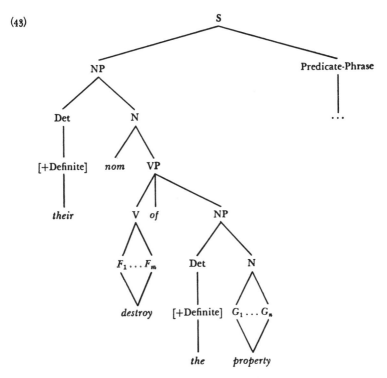

to be a Noun in "their refusal surprised me," which derives in part from the string underlying "they refuse"). Alternatively, the nominalized Predicate-Phrase as a whole might be said to occupy the Noun position. In any event, phonological rules will determine that $nom \frown destroy$ becomes *destruction* and that $nom \frown$ *refuse* becomes *refusal*, and so on.[42] To have the proper effect, these rules must, of course, take account of inherent features associated with items in lexical entries, namely the features that determine which form of *nom* these items take. In such cases as these, the proposed framework is quite adequate for formulating the syntactic generative rules as well as the rules of semantic and phonological interpretation.

Notice, incidentally, that in the light of these remarks we must revise the description of the example (1) of Chapter 2

(="sincerity may frighten John"), which served as a basis for discussion throughout that Chapter. In fact, *sincerity* would surely not be entered into the lexicon, though *sincere* would. *Sincerity* is formed by a transformation, and is a "defective Predicate" in just the same way as *refusal* is a defective Predicate in "their refusal surprised me" or "the refusal surprised me." That is to say, there is a transformational rule that operates on "NP-is-Adjective" constructions such as "John is sincere (of manner)" and gives such nominalizations as "John's sincerity (of manner)," where "sincerity (of manner)," like "refusal (to come)," can be regarded as a Noun. The phrase *sincerity* appears as a full NP, in a manner which we shall not describe in detail here, when the underlying sentence "NP-is-sincere" has an Unspecified Subject and the matrix sentence in which it is embedded has a non-Definite Article. Details aside, it is clear that, contrary to what we assumed earlier, *sincerity* is not introduced in (1) of Chapter 2 by the lexical rule, so that actually even this very simple sentence is the result of a transformational development from a complex basis.

But consider now the case of quasi-productive processes, such as those that are involved in the formation of such words as *horror, horrid, horrify; terror, (*terrid), terrify; candor, candid, (*candify);* or *telegram, phonograph, gramophone,* etc., or, for that matter, such words as *frighten,* in the example (1) of Chapter 2). In these cases, there are no rules of any generality that produce the derived items, as there are in the case of *sincerity, destruction,* and so on. Hence, it seems that these items must be entered in the lexicon directly. This, however, is a very unfortunate conclusion, since it is clear that from the point of view of both the semantic and the phonological interpretation it is important to have internal structure represented in these words. Their meaning is clearly to some extent predictable (or at least limited) by the inherent semantic properties of the morphemes that they contain, and it is easy to show that internal structure must be assigned to these items if the phonological rules are to apply properly in forming their phonetic representations (cf. the discussion of the transformational cycle for English in

Halle and Chomsky, 1960; Chomsky, 1962*b*; Chomsky and Miller, 1963; and, for a detailed statement, Halle and Chomsky, forthcoming).

This dilemma is typical of a wide class of examples with varying degrees of productivity, and it is not at all clear how it is to be resolved, or, in fact, whether there is any non–*ad hoc* solution that can be achieved at all.[48] Perhaps one must regard the gaps as accidental, at least in some such cases, and incorporate in the grammar overly general rules that allow for nonoccurring as well as actual cases. Alternatively, it may be necessary to extend the theory of the lexicon to permit some "internal computation," in place of simple application of the general lexical rule in the manner already described. Thus *telegraph, horrify, frighten,* might be entered in the lexicon as

(44) (i) (*tele*⌢Stem$_1$, [F_1, ···])
   (ii) (Stem$_2$⌢*ify*, [G_1, ···])
   (iii) (Stem$_3$⌢*en*, [H_1, ···])

these items being entered into strings by means of the general lexical rule. Furthermore, the lexicon would also contain the entries

(45) (i) (*graph*, [+Stem$_1$, ···])
   (ii) (*horr*, [+Stem$_2$···])
   (iii) (*fright*, [+N, +Stem$_3$, ···])

these now being inserted in strings formed by prior insertion in preterminal strings of items selected from (44). There may be several layers of such extension of base derivations within the lexicon, in the case of morphologically complex forms.

However, the rule that replaces categories such as Stem$_i$ by items of (45) must be formulated with some care. There are contextual restrictions on these replacements that must be specified because these processes are only marginally productive. Thus Stem$_1$ can be replaced by *graph, scope, phone* in the context *tele* —, but not by *scope* or *phone* in the context *phono* —. The same is true in the other cases. More seriously, these extensions of base derivations within the lexicon must in general depend also on the feature composition of the item being analyzed. Thus Stem$_3$ can be rewritten *fright* in the context — *en* only when the features H_1, H_2, $\cdots$ of (44iii) indicate that it is a pure transitive, takes only Animate Object, etc. In other words, provision must be made for the fact that *frighten* is not a Verb of the same type as *redden* or *soften*, and this can only be done by taking into account the feature composition of the only partially specified lexical entries of (44) as well as the feature composition of the items of (45) that substitute for the categories appearing in the entries of (44). Precisely how such rules should be formulated is not at all clear to me. It may be possible to determine the restrictions completely by feature specifications in (44), (45), relying on a reapplication of the lexical rule to insert the items appropriately. Alternatively, it may be better to allow the lexicon to contain context-sensitive rewriting rules to effect these extensions of base derivations. The former alternative is of course preferable, since it does not affect the structure of the lexicon. The lexicon would, under this alternative, be simply a list of entries, and the lexical rule (now reapplicable) would be the only rule involving lexical entries. However, I do not know whether this approach will prove feasible when it is attempted in detail.

In the examples just discussed, whichever method is chosen for extending base derivations, we shall have a complex symbol dominating a sequence of symbols. There is apparently no empirical motivation for allowing complex symbols to appear above the level of lexical categories, with the substantial enrichment of linguistic theory and corresponding reduction in its interest and importance that this elaboration entails. Limitation of complex symbols to lexical categories implies that no complex symbol will dominate a branching configuration, within the categorial component. Now, however, we have some evidence that within a word, branching must be permitted in a configuration dominated by a complex symbol.[44]

In the light of such examples, we may have to relax the requirement (pp. 112–113) that branching is not tolerated within the dominance scope of a complex symbol. This restriction seems to hold only above the level of the word. With this modification, we still retain the earlier restriction of complex symbols to lexical categories.

Alternative analyses suggest themselves for several of these examples. In the case of such words as *frighten*, one might seek syntactic justification for a transformational analysis from an underlying causative construction so that "it frightens John" would derive from the structure underlying "it makes John afraid," this in turn deriving from the abstract structure "it makes S" where S dominates "John is afraid." Adjectives would then have to be divided in the lexicon into two classes depending on whether or not they undergo this transformation. Thus, *afraid, red, soft* would be in one category; whereas *happy, green, tender* would be in the other. Conceivably, we might go on to analyze such words as *wizen, chasten* as based on a similar analysis, with the underlying Adjective designated lexically as one that must undergo this transformational process (in the case of *chasten*, the underlying form would have to be lexically distinguished from the homonymous Adjective that belongs to the class of those that cannot undergo the transformational process in question). Such an analysis could be extended to many other forms — for example, such Verbs as *enrage, clarify*. It might even be extended to account for such words as *drop, grow,* discussed in note 15 of Chapter 2, where it was observed that the Intransitive occurrences cannot be derived from underlying Transitives. A general "causative" transformation might permit a derivation of "he dropped the ball," "he grows corn," etc., from an underlying structure of the form "he caused S," where S is the structure underlying "the ball drops," "corn grows," and so on. A number of syntactic arguments might be given in favor of a general "causative" operation to accommodate these and other cases. There is no doubt that items must be specified lexically in terms of the operations that apply to them; this is particularly clear from a consideration of phonological rules, but is no less true of syntactic processes. Much of lexical structure is, in fact, simply a classification induced by the system of phonological and syntactic rules. Postal has suggested, furthermore, that there should be a general analysis of lexical items with respect to each rule R, into those which must, those which may, and those which cannot be subject to R, and has investigated some of the consequences of this assumption. I mention these possibilities simply to indicate that there remain numerous relatively unexplored ways to deal with the problems that arise when the structure of a lexicon is considered seriously.

Problems similar to those of derivational morphology are not lacking beyond the word level as well. Consider, for example, such phrases as "take for granted," which abound in English. From a semantic and distributional point of view, this phrase seems to be a single lexical item, and it therefore must be entered in the lexicon as such, with its unique set of syntactic and semantic features. On the other hand, its behavior with respect to transformations and morphological processes obviously shows that it is some sort of Verb-with-Complement construction. Once again, then, we have a lexical item with a rich internal structure. In such a phrase as "take offense at" the problem is more acute. Again, distributional as well as semantic considerations suggest that this is a lexical item, but certain transformations apply to this phrase as if "offense" were a normal Noun Phrase (cf. "I didn't think that any offense would be taken at that remark"). Verb⌒Particle constructions also provide a variety of related problems. To some extent, the Particle is a fairly free "Adverbial" element, as in "I brought the book (in, out, up, down)." Often, however, the Verb⌒Particle construction is (distributionally as well as semantically) a unique lexical item (such as "look up," "bring off," "look over"). In all cases, however, the syntactic structure is apparently the same, with respect to the possibility of applying familiar transformational rules. I see no way, for the present, to give a thoroughly satisfactory treatment of this general question.[45]

The Verb⌒Particle constructions "look up (the record)," "bring in (the book)," and so on, are of course not to be confused with the very different constructions discussed in Chapter 2, § 2.3.4. There we noted that certain Verbs were in close construction with certain Adverbials (for example, "decide on the boat," in the sense of "choose the boat"), and that these Verb⌢Adverbial constructions are very different from others (such as "decide (while) on the boat") that involve a much looser association of Verb and Adverbial. In these close constructions, the choice of Particle is often narrowly or even uniquely constrained by the choice of Verb (for example, "argue with X about Y"). We must therefore indicate in the lexical entry for such words as *decide, argue,* that they take certain particles and not others, as, in fact, is commonly done in dictionaries. This information can be presented in various ways. One possibility is to develop the Adverbial freely and to assign a contextual feature to the Verb (for example, to *decide,* the contextual feature $[-on⌢NP]$, to *argue,* the feature $[-with⌢NP⌢about⌢NP]$). If either of the methods of lexical insertion described in Chapter 2, § 4.3 is used, the Verbs in question will now be inserted only in the permitted positions, and the resulting Phrase-marker will now have the structure required for further rules. A second possibility is to develop the Adverbial freely but to give the lexical entry as a sequence of formatives, much as in the case of *telescope, take for granted,* and so on. Thus we would have the entries *decide # on, argue(# about)(# with),* etc. Associated with these lexical entries, then, will be an erasure transformation that will use the freely generated Particles of the Prepositional-Phrases to delete the Particles of the lexical entries. Under this alternative, we rely on the filtering effect of transformations to guarantee correct insertion in well-formed deep structures, and, once again, we derive the correctly formed Phrase-markers when successful lexical insertion takes place. Still a third possibility would be to enter the lexical items in the manner just proposed, and to derive the Adverbials with a dummy element in the Preposition-position, then distributing the Particles of the lexical entry by substitution transformations. Again, the same Phrase-markers result. There are still further possibilities.

The same choices, incidentally, are also available in Verb⌢Particle constructions. In this case, however, the Phrase-marker that results from lexical insertion and associated operations must be different from that of the Verb⌢Adverbial constructions, since later rules apply very differently in the two cases.

I see little basis for choosing among these alternatives at the moment; until sharper criteria are discovered, these can only be regarded as essentially notational variants.

Obviously, this discussion by no means exhausts the complexity or variety of topics that, so far, resist systematic and revealing grammatical description. It is possible that we are approaching here the fringe of marginal cases, to be expected in a system as complex as a natural language, where significant systematization is just not possible. Still, it is much too early to draw this conclusion with any confidence and, even if it is eventually justified, we still must face the problem of extracting whatever subregularities exist in this domain. In any event, the questions we have touched on here have not yet been illuminated in any serious way by approaching them within the framework of any explicit grammatical theory. For the present, one can barely go beyond mere taxonomic arrangement of data. Whether these limitations are intrinsic, or whether a deeper analysis can succeed in unraveling some of these difficulties, remains an open question.

Notes

NOTES TO CHAPTER *1*

1. To accept traditional mentalism, in this way, is not to accept Bloomfield's dichotomy of "mentalism" versus "mechanism." Mentalistic linguistics is simply theoretical linguistics that uses performance as data (along with other data, for example, the data provided by introspection) for the determination of competence, the latter being taken as the primary object of its investigation. The mentalist, in this traditional sense, need make no assumptions about the possible physiological basis for the mental reality that he studies. In particular, he need not deny that there is such a basis. One would guess, rather, that it is the mentalistic studies that will ultimately be of greatest value for the investigation of neurophysiological mechanisms, since they alone are concerned with determining abstractly the properties that such mechanisms must exhibit and the functions they must perform.

In fact, the issue of mentalism versus antimentalism in linguistics apparently has to do only with goals and interests, and not with questions of truth or falsity, sense or nonsense. At least three issues are involved in this rather idle controversy: (*a*) dualism — are the rules that underlie performance represented in a nonmaterial medium?; (*b*) behaviorism — do the data of performance exhaust the domain of interest to the linguist, or is he also concerned with other facts, in particular those pertaining to the deeper systems that underlie behavior?; (*c*) introspectionism — should one make use of introspective data in the attempt to ascertain the properties of these underlying systems? It is the dualistic position against which Bloomfield irrelevantly inveighed. The behaviorist position is not an arguable matter. It is simply an expression of lack of interest in theory and explanation. This is clear, for example, in Twaddell's critique (1935) of Sapir's mentalistic phonology, which used informant responses and comments as evidence bearing on the psychological reality of some abstract system of phonological elements. For Twaddell, the enterprise has no point because all that interests him is the behavior itself, "which is already available for the student of language, though in less concentrated form." Characteristically, this lack of interest in linguistic theory expresses itself in the proposal to limit the term "theory" to "summary of data" (as in Twaddell's paper, or, to take a more recent example, in Dixon, 1963, although the discussion of "theories" in the latter is sufficiently vague as to allow other interpretations of what he may have in mind). Perhaps this loss of interest in theory, in the usual sense, was fostered by certain ideas (e.g., strict operationalism or strong verificationism) that were considered briefly in positivist philosophy of science, but rejected forthwith, in the early nineteen-thirties. In any event, question (*b*) poses no substantive issue. Question (*c*) arises only if one rejects the behaviorist limitations of (*b*). To maintain, on grounds of methodological purity, that introspective judgments of the informant (often, the linguist himself) should be disregarded is, for the present, to condemn the study of language to utter sterility. It is difficult to imagine what possible reason might be given for this. We return to this matter later. For further discussion, see Katz (1964*c*).

2. This has been denied recently by several European linguists (e.g., Dixon, 1963; Uhlenbeck, 1963, 1964). They offer no reasons for their skepticism concerning traditional grammar, however. Whatever evidence is available today seems to me to show that by and large the traditional views are basically correct, so far as they go, and that the suggested innovations are totally unjustifiable. For example, consider Uhlenbeck's proposal that the constituent analysis of "the man saw the boy" is [*the man saw*] [*the boy*], a proposal which presumably also implies that in the sentences [*the man put*] [*it into the box*], [*the man aimed*] [*it at John*], [*the man persuaded*] [*Bill that it was unlikely*], etc., the constituents are as indicated. There are many considerations relevant to the determination of constituent structure (cf. note 7); to my knowledge, they support the traditional analysis without exception against this proposal, for which the only argument offered is that it is the result of a "pure linguistic analysis." Cf. Uhlenbeck (1964), and the discussion there. As to Dixon's objections to traditional grammars, since he offers neither any alternative nor any argument (beyond the correct but irrelevant observation that they have been "long condemned by professional linguists"), there is nothing further to discuss, in this case.

3. Furthermore, it seems to me that speech perception is also best studied in this framework. See, for example, Halle and Stevens (1962).

4. Tests that seem to determine a useful notion of this sort have been described in various places — for example, Miller and Isard (1963).

5. These characterizations are equally vague, and the concepts involved are equally obscure. The notion "likely to be produced" or "probable" is sometimes thought to be more "objective" and antecedently better defined than the others, on the assumption that there is some clear meaning to the notion "probability of a sentence" or "probability of a sentence type." Actually, the latter notions are objective and antecedently clear only if probability is based on an estimate of relative frequency and if sentence type means something like "sequence of word or morpheme classes." (Furthermore, if the notion is to be at all significant, these classes must be extremely small and of mutually substitutable elements, or else unacceptable and ungrammatical sentences will be as "likely" and acceptable as grammatical ones.) But in this case, though "probability of a sentence (type)" is clear and well defined, it is an utterly useless notion, since almost all highly acceptable sentences (in the intuitive sense) will have probabilities empirically indistinguishable from zero and will belong to sentence types with probabilities empirically indistinguishable from zero. Thus the acceptable or grammatical sentences (or sentence types) are no more likely, in any objective sense of this word, than the others. This remains true if we consider, not "likelihood," but "likelihood relative to a given situation," as long as "situations" are specified in terms of observable physical properties and are not mentalistic constructs. It is noteworthy that linguists who talk of hardheaded objective study of use of sentences in real situations, when they actually come to citing examples, invariably describe the "situations" in completely mentalistic terms. Cf., e.g., Dixon (1963, p. 101), where, in the only illustrative example in the book, a sentence is described as gaining its meaning from the situation "British Culture." To describe British culture as "a situation" is, in the first place, a category mistake; furthermore, to regard it as a pattern abstracted from observed behavior, and hence objectively describable in purely physical terms, betrays a complete misunderstanding of what might be expected from anthropological research.

For further discussion, see Katz and Fodor (1964).

6. That it may be true is suggested by several (for the moment, quite untested) observations. For example, in Chomsky and Miller (1963, p. 286) the following example is cited: "anyone who feels that if so many more students whom we haven't actually admitted are sitting in on the course than ones we have that the room had

to be changed, then probably auditors will have to be excluded, is likely to agree that the curriculum needs revision." This contains six nested dependencies (along with other dependencies that go beyond nesting) with no self-embedding. Though hardly a model of felicitous style, it seems fairly comprehensible, and not extremely low on the scale of acceptability. In comparison, self-embedding of degree two or three seems to disturb acceptability much more severely. The matter is worth studying, since a positive result concerning (4ii) would, as noted, support a conclusion about organization of memory which is not entirely obvious.

7. It has sometimes been claimed that the traditional coordinated structures are necessarily right-recursive (Yngve, 1960) or left-recursive (Harman, 1963, p. 613, rule 3i). These conclusions seem to me equally unacceptable. Thus to assume (with Harman) that the phrase "a tall, young, handsome, intelligent man" has the structure [[[[*tall young*] *handsome*] *intelligent*] *man*] seems to me no more justifiable than to assume that it has the structure [*tall* [*young* [*handsome* [*intelligent man*]]]]. In fact, there is no grammatical motivation for any internal structure, and, as I have just noted, the assumption that there is no structure is also supported on grounds of acceptability, with extremely weak and plausible assumptions about organization of memory. Notice that there are cases where further structure might be justified (e.g., [*intelligent* [*young man*]] or, perhaps [*YOUNG* [*intelligent man*]], with contrastive stress on "young"), but the issue is rather whether it is always necessary.

The same is true if we consider the very different type of Adjective-Noun construction that we find in such phrases as "all the young, old, and middle-aged voters" (for an interesting discussion of these various kinds of modification relations, see Ornan, 1964). Here, too, neither the structure [[*young, old*] *and middle-aged*] nor [*young* [*old and middle-aged*]] has any justification.

Similarly, it is surely impossible to assume, with Yngve, that in the phrase "John, Mary, and their two children" the structure is [*John*] [[*Mary*] [*and their two children*]], so that "John" is coordinated with "Mary and their two children," the latter being analyzed into the coordinated items "Mary" and "their two children." This is entirely counter to the sense. Notice, again, that conjunction *can* have this structure (e.g., "John, as well as Mary and her child"), but surely it is false to claim that it *must* have this structure.

In these cases all known syntactic, semantic, phonetic, and perceptual considerations converge in support of the traditional view that these constructions are typically coordinating (multiple-branching). Notice also that this is the weakest assumption. The burden of proof rests on one who claims additional structure beyond this. There are various ways of justifying assignment of constituent structure. For example, in such a phrase as "all (none) of the blue, green, red, and (or) yellow pennants," if one wanted to argue that "blue, green, red" is a constituent (i.e., that the structure is left-branching), or that "green, red, and (or) yellow" is a constituent (that the structure is right-branching), then he would have to show that these analyses are required for some grammatical rule, that the postulated intermediate phrases must receive a semantic interpretation, that they define a phonetic contour, that there are perceptual grounds for the analysis, or something of this sort. All of these claims are patently false in this case, and the other cases mentioned here. Thus no semantic interpretation can be assigned to "old and middle-aged" in "young, old, and middle-aged voters" or to "green, red, or yellow" in "none of the blue, green, red, or yellow pennants" or to "Mary and their two children" in "John, Mary, and their two children"; the phonetic rules explicitly preclude such constituent analysis; there are no grammatical rules that require these analyses; there are no perceptual or other arguments to support them. It seems difficult, then, to see any grounds for objecting to the traditional analysis and insisting on additional intermediate categorization, in such cases as these.

8. Yngve (1960, and several other papers) has proposed a different theory to account for certain observations such as those of (4). Beyond the obvious condition of finiteness of memory, his theory assumes also that order of generation is identical with order of production — that the speaker and hearer produce sentences "from top-to-bottom" (they first decide on the major structures, then the substructures of these, etc., leaving to the very end of the process the choice of lexical items). Under this highly restrictive additional assumption, the optimal perceptual device mentioned earlier is no longer constructible, and left-branching and multiple-branching, as well as nesting and self-embedding, contribute to "depth" in Yngve's sense, hence to unacceptability. To support this hypothesis, it would be necessary to show (a) that it has some initial plausibility, and (b) that left-branching and multiple-branching in fact contribute to unacceptability exactly as do nesting and self-embedding. As to (a), I see no plausibility at all to the assumption that the speaker must uniformly select sentence type, then determine subcategories, etc., finally, at the last stage, deciding what he is going to talk about; or that the hearer should invariably make all higher-level decisions before doing any lower-level analysis. As

to (b), the hypothesis is supported by no evidence at all. The examples given by Yngve all involve nesting and self-embedding and hence are irrelevant to the hypothesis, since the unacceptability in this case follows from the assumption of finiteness alone without the additional assumption of "top-to-bottom" production for speaker and hearer. Furthermore, the hypothesis is contradicted by the observation (4iii) that multiply coordinated structures (cf. note 7) are the most acceptable (rather than the least acceptable, as predicted) and that left-branching structures are far more acceptable than nested structures of equal "depth," in Yngve's sense. It also fails to explain why examples of type (4iv), such as (2i), though very low in "depth," are still unacceptable.

However, Yngve makes one important point in these papers, namely, that some transformations can be used to decrease nesting, hence to reduce the perceptual load. This suggests an interesting argument as to why grammars should contain transformational rules. Some additional weight to this argument is given by the discussion of performance models involving transformational grammars in Miller and Chomsky (1963, Part 2).

9. It is astonishing to find that even this truism has recently been challenged. See Dixon (1963). However, it seems that when Dixon denies that a language has infinitely many sentences, he is using the term "infinite" in some special and rather obscure sense. Thus on the same page (p. 83) on which he objects to the assertion "that there are an infinite number of sentences in a language" he states that "we are clearly unable to say that there is any definite number, N, such that no sentence contains more than N clauses" (that is, he states that the language is infinite). Either this is a blatant self-contradiction, or else he has some new sense of the word "infinite" in mind. For further discussion of his remarks in this connection, see Chomsky (in press).

10. Aside from terminology, I follow here the exposition in Katz and Postal (1964). In particular, I shall assume throughout that the semantic component is essentially as they describe it and that the phonological component is essentially as described in Chomsky, Halle, and Lukoff (1956); Halle (1959a, 1959b, 1962a); Chomsky (1962b); Chomsky and Miller (1963); Halle and Chomsky (1960; forthcoming).

11. I assume throughout that the syntactic component contains a lexicon, and that each lexical item is specified in the lexicon in terms of its intrinsic semantic features, whatever these may be. I shall return to this matter in the next chapter.

12. In place of the terms "deep structure" and "surface structure," one might use the corresponding Humboldtian notions "inner form"

of a sentence and "outer form" of a sentence. However, though it seems to me that "deep structure" and "surface structure," in the sense in which these terms will be used here, do correspond quite closely to Humboldtian "inner form" and "outer form," respectively (as used of a sentence), I have adopted the more neutral terminology to avoid the question, here, of textual interpretation. The terms "depth grammar" and "surface grammar" are familiar in modern philosophy in something roughly like the sense here intended (cf. Wittgenstein's distinction of *"Tiefengrammatik"* and *"Oberflächengrammatik,"* 1953, p. 168); Hockett uses similar terminology in his discussion of the inadequacy of taxonomic linguistics (Hockett, 1958, Chapter 29). Postal has used the terms "underlying structure" and "superficial structure" (Postal, 1964*b*) for the same notions.

The distinction between deep and surface structure, in the sense in which these terms are used here, is drawn quite clearly in the Port-Royal *Grammar* (Lancelot *et al.*, 1660). See Chomsky (1964, pp. 15–16; forthcoming) for some discussion and references. In philosophical discussion, it is often introduced in an attempt to show how certain philosophical positions arise from false grammatical analogies, the surface structure of certain expressions being mistakenly considered to be semantically interpretable by means appropriate only to other, superficially similar sentences. Thus Thomas Reid (1785) holds a common source of philosophical error to lie in the fact that

> in all languages, there are phrases which have a distinct meaning; while at the same time, there may be something in the structure of them that disagrees with the analogy of grammar or with the principles of philosophy. . . . Thus, we speak of feeling pain as if pain was something distinct from the feeling of it. We speak of pain coming and going, and removing from one place to another. Such phrases are meant by those who use them in a sense that is neither obscure nor false. But the philosopher puts them into his alembic, reduces them to their first principles, draws out of them a sense that was never meant, and so imagines that he has discovered an error of the vulgar [pp. 167–168].

More generally, he criticizes the theory of ideas as based on a deviation from the "popular meaning," in which "to have an idea of anything signifies nothing more than to think of it" (p. 105). But philosophers take an idea to be "the object that the mind contemplates" (p. 105); to have an idea, then, is to possess in the mind such an image, picture, or representation as the immediate object of thought. It follows that there are two objects of thought:

the idea, which is in the mind, and the thing represented by it. From this conclusion follow the absurdities, as Reid regards them, of the traditional theory of ideas. One of the sources of these absurdities is the failure of the philosopher to attend "to the distinction between the operations of the mind and the objects of these operations . . . although this distinction be familiar to the vulgar, and found in the structure of all languages . . ." (p. 110). Notice that these two senses of "having an idea" are distinguished by Descartes in the Preface to the *Meditations* (1641, p. 138). Reid's linguistic observation is made considerably earlier by Du Marsais, in a work published posthumously in 1769, in the following passage (pp. 179-180):

> Ainsi, comme nous avons dit *j'ai un livre, j'ai un diamant, j'ai une montre,* nous disons par imitation, *j'ai la fièvre, j'ai envie, j'ai peur, j'ai un doute, j'ai pitié, j'ai une idée,* etc. Mais *livre, diamant, montre* sont autant de noms d'objects réels qui existent indépendamment de notre manière de penser; au lieu que *santé, fièvre, peur, doute, envie,* ne sont que des termes métaphysiques qui ne désignent que des manières d'êtres considérés par des points de vue particuliers de l'esprit.
>
> Dans cet exemple, *j'ai une montre,* j'ai est une expression qui doit être prise dans le sens propre: mais dans *j'ai une idée,* j'ai n'est dit que par une imitation. C'est une expression empruntée. *J'ai une idée,* c'est-à-dire, *je pense, je conçois de telle ou telle manière. J'ai envie,* c'est-à-dire, *je désire; j'ai la volonté,* c'est-à-dire, *je veux,* etc.
>
> Ainsi, *idée, concept, imagination,* ne marquent point d'objets réels, et encore moins des êtres sensibles que l'on puisse unir l'un avec l'autre.

In more recent years, it has been widely held that the aims of philosophy should, in fact, be strictly limited to "the detection of the sources in linguistic idioms of recurrent misconstructions and absurd theories" (Ryle, 1931).

13. These descriptions are not fully accurate. In fact, the sentential complement in (10) should, more properly, be regarded as embedded in a Prepositional-Phrase (cf. Chapter 3); and, as Peter Rosenbaum has pointed out, the sentential complement of (11) should be regarded as embedded in the Noun-Phrase Object of "expect." Furthermore, the treatment of the Verbal Auxiliaries in (10) and (11) is incorrect, and there are other modifications relating to the marking of the passive transformation, to which we shall return in the next chapter.

14. It seems clear that many children acquire first or second languages

quite successfully even though no special care is taken to teach them and no special attention is given to their progress. It also seems apparent that much of the actual speech observed consists of fragments and deviant expressions of a variety of sorts. Thus it seems that a child must have the ability to "invent" a generative grammar that defines well-formedness and assigns interpretations to sentences even though the primary linguistic data that he uses as a basis for this act of theory construction may, from the point of view of the theory he constructs, be deficient in various respects. In general, there is an important element of truth in the traditional view that "the pains which everyone finds in conversation . . . is not to comprehend what another thinketh, but to extricate his thought from the signs or words which often agree not with it" (Cordemoy, 1667), and the problem this poses for speech perception is magnified many times for the language learner.

15. For example, Russell (1940, p. 33: "from a logical point of view, a proper name may be assigned to any continuous portion of space-time"), if we interpret his notion of "logically proper name" as embodying an empirical hypothesis. Interpreted in this way, Russell is stating what is, no doubt, a psychological truth. Interpreted otherwise, he is giving an unmotivated definition of "proper name." There is no logical necessity for names or other "object words" to meet any condition of spatiotemporal contiguity or to have other Gestalt qualities, and it is a nontrivial fact that they apparently do, insofar as the designated objects are of the type that can actually be perceived (for example, it is not true of "United States" — similarly, it need not be true of somewhat more abstract and functionally defined notions such as "barrier"). Thus there are no logical grounds for the apparent nonexistence in natural languages of words such as "LIMB," similar to "limb" except that it designates the single object consisting of a dog's four legs, so that "its LIMB is brown" (like "its head is brown") would mean that the object consisting of the four legs is brown. Similarly, there is no a priori reason why a natural language could not contain a word "HERD," like the collective "herd" except that it denotes a single scattered object with cows as parts, so that "a cow lost a leg" implies "the HERD lost a leg," etc.

16. Thus for Aristotle (*De Anima*, 403b), the "essence of a house is assigned in such a formula as 'a shelter against destruction by wind, rain, and heat,'" though "the physicist would describe it as 'stones, bricks, and timbers.'" For interesting comments on such definitions, see Foot (1961), Katz (1964d).

17. By a "reasonable procedure" I mean one that does not involve

extralinguistic information — that is, one that does not incorporate an "encyclopedia." See Bar-Hillel (1960) for discussion. The possibility of a reasonable procedure for translation between arbitrary languages depends on the sufficiency of substantive universals. In fact, although there is much reason to believe that languages are to a significant extent cast in the same mold, there is little reason to suppose that reasonable procedures of translation are in general possible.

18. Actually, a set of structural descriptions should be assigned by f to each s_i (and each structural description must be assigned to exactly one s_i), given G_j, one for each way of interpreting the sentence s_i with respect to G_j. Thus an unambiguous sentence should receive one structural description, a doubly ambiguous sentence two structural descriptions, etc. We assume that mappings are effective — that there is an algorithm for enumerating sentences, structural descriptions, and grammars and (throughout this is less obvious) for determining the values of f and m in all cases.

19. Obviously, to construct an actual theory of language learning, it would be necessary to face several other very serious questions involving, for example, the gradual development of an appropriate hypothesis, simplification of the technique for finding a compatible hypothesis, and the continual accretion of linguistic skill and knowledge and the deepening of the analysis of language structure that may continue long after the basic form of the language has been mastered. What I am describing is an idealization in which only the moment of acquisition of the correct grammar is considered. Introduction of these additional considerations might affect the general discussion in many ways. For example, in some limited but nevertheless real way, the preconditions (i)–(v) themselves might possibly be developed on the basis of deeper innate structure, in ways that depend in part on primary linguistic data and the order and manner in which they are presented. Furthermore, it might very well be true that a series of successively more detailed and highly structured schemata (corresponding to maturational stages, but perhaps in part themselves determined in form by earlier steps of language acquisition) are applied to the data at successive stages of language acquisition. There are, a priori, many possibilities that can be considered here.

20. It is instructive to see how modern structural linguistics has attempted to meet these conditions. It assumes that the technique for discovering the correct hypothesis (grammar) must be based on procedures of successive segmentation and classification of the items in the corpus (which constitutes the primary linguistic data, when supplemented, perhaps, by certain kinds of semantic in-

formation the exact relevance of which to the problem at hand has never been clarified). To compensate for this extremely strong demand on the procedure of grammar discovery, it was necessary to sacrifice descriptive adequacy, over a wide range of cases. In fact, the methodological discussions of modern linguistics pay very little attention to considerations (ii)–(iv) (though they do imply certain conclusions about them) and concentrate almost solely on development of constructive, step-by-step procedures of classification and segmentation. For discussion, see Lees (1957), Chomsky (1964).

21. This point has some historical interest. In fact, as has generally been noted by commentators, Locke's attempt to refute the doctrine of innate ideas is largely vitiated by his failure to observe the distinction we have just been discussing, although this was clear to Descartes (and was later re-emphasized by Leibniz, in his critique of Locke's *Essay*). Cf. § 8.

22. See note 19. An actual acquisition model must have a strategy for finding hypotheses. Suppose, for example, that the strategy is to consider only grammars that have better than a certain value (in terms of the evaluation measure (v)), at each stage in the process of language learning. What is required of a significant linguistic theory, then, is that given primary linguistic data D, the class of grammars compatible with D be sufficiently scattered, in terms of value, so that the intersection of the class of grammars compatible with D and the class of grammars which are highly valued be reasonably small. Only then can language learning actually take place.

23. See references of note 10.

24. Failure of attempts to justify an explanatory theory may be interpreted in various ways, of course. It may indicate that the theory is wrong, or that its consequences were incorrectly determined — in particular, that the grammar tested for descriptive adequacy was not the most highly valued one. Since any reasonable evaluation measure must be a systematic measure, and since language is a tightly interconnected system, the latter possibility is not to be discounted. In short, justification of linguistic theory does not avoid the problems faced by justification of any substantive and nontrivial empirical hypothesis.

25. Actually, it is not clear that Quine's position should be taken as in any real sense an empiricist one. Thus he goes on to propose that in the innate quality space a red ball might be less distant from a green ball than from a red kerchief, so that we have not just a pre-experiential characterization of distance but also an innate analysis of this into distance in various respects. On the

basis of these few comments, one might interpret him as proposing that such concepts as "ball" are innate ideas, hence as adopting an extreme form of nativism; at least, it is difficult to see wherein the cited proposal differs from this. In further support of such an antiempiricist interpretation, one may point to Quine's virtual renunciation of reinforcement theory (cf. my note 26).

Unfortunately, what are intended as empiricist views have generally been formulated in such an indefinite way that it is next to impossible to interpret them with any certainty, or to analyze or evaluate them. An extreme example, perhaps, is Skinner's account of how language is learned and used (Skinner, 1957). There seem to be only two coherent interpretations that one can give to this account. If we interpret the terms "stimulus," "reinforcement," "conditioning," etc., which appear in it, as having the meanings given to them in experimental psychology, then this account is so grossly and obviously counter to fact that discussion is quite beside the point. Alternatively, we may interpret these terms as metaphoric extensions of the (essentially homonymous) terms used in experimental psychology, in which case what is proposed is a mentalist account differing from traditional ones only in that many distinctions are necessarily obscured because of the poverty of the terminological apparatus available for paraphrase of the traditional mentalistic notions. What is particularly puzzling, then, is the insistent claim that this paraphrase is somehow "scientific" in a way in which traditional mentalism is not.

26. This application is perhaps mediated by "reinforcement," though many contemporary behaviorists use this term in such a loose way that reference to reinforcement adds nothing to the account of acquisition of knowledge that they propose. For example, Quine suggests (1960, pp. 82–83) that "some basic predilection for conformity" may take the place of "ulterior values," and that society's reinforcement of the response may consist "in no more than corroborative usage, whose resemblance to the child's effort is the sole reward." As Quine correctly notes, "this again is congenial enough to Skinner's scheme, for he does not enumerate the rewards" (this being one of the contributory factors to the near vacuity of Skinner's scheme). What this proposal comes to is that the only function of "reinforcement" may be to provide the child with information about correct usage; thus the empirical claim of "reinforcement theory" will be that learning of language cannot proceed in the absence of data. Actually, Skinner's concept of "reinforcement" is apparently still weaker than this, for he does not even require that the "reinforcing stimulus" impinge on the responding organism; it is sufficient that it be hoped for

or imagined (for a collection of examples bearing on this matter, see Chomsky, 1959*b*).

27. These mechanisms, as is now known, need not be at all elementary. Cf., for example, Lettvin *et al.* (1959), Hubel and Wiesel (1962), Frishkopf and Goldstein (1963). This work has demonstrated that peripheral processing in the receptor system or in lower cortical centers may provide a complex analysis of stimuli that, furthermore, seems to be rather specific to the animal's life-space and well correlated with behavior patterns. Thus it seems that not even peripheral processing can be described within the unstructured and atomistic framework that has been presupposed in empiricist thinking.

28. I depart here from the Langley translation, which renders this passage inaccurately. The French original is as follows: ". . . je demeure d'accord que nous apprenons les idées et les véritées innées, soit en prenant garde à leur source, soit en les vérifiant par l'expérience. Ainsi je ne saurois admettre cette proposition, *tout ce qu'on apprend n'est pas inné.* Les vérités des nombres sont en nous, et on ne laisse pas de les apprendre, soit en les tirant de leur source lorsqu'on les apprend par raison démonstrative (ce qui fait voir qu'elles sont innées) soit en les éprouvant dans les exemples comme font les arithméticiens vulgaires. . . ."

29. Cf. Chomsky (1964) for additional discussion and quotations illustrating Humboldt's views on these questions.

30. That this is a fair interpretation of taxonomic linguistics is not at all clear. For one thing, structural linguistics has rarely been concerned with the "creative" aspect of language use, which was a dominant theme in rationalistic linguistic theory. It has, in other words, given little attention to the production and interpretation of new, previously unheard sentences — that is, to the normal use of language. Thus the suggestion that the various theories of immediate constituent analysis might be interpreted as generative, phrase structure grammars (as in Chomsky, 1956, 1962*a*, or Postal, 1964*a*) certainly goes beyond what is explicitly stated by linguists who have developed these theories, and very likely beyond their intentions as well. Hence, the central problem of descriptive adequacy is not really raised within structural linguistics. Secondly, many "neo-Bloomfieldian" linguists, accepting Bloomfield's behaviorism under interpretation (*b*) of note 1 (as well as Firthians and "neo-Firthians" and many others), have thereby explicitly rejected any concern for descriptive adequacy, limiting the task of grammatical description, at least in theory, to organization of the primary linguistic data. Others have held that a grammar should at least describe the "habits" or "disposi-

tions" of the speaker, though the sense in which language use might be regarded as a matter of habit or disposition has never been satisfactorily clarified. To be more precise, there is no clear sense of the term "habit" or "disposition" in accordance with which it would be correct to describe language as a "habit structure" or a "system of dispositions."

In general, it is not clear that most behaviorist tendencies should be regarded as varieties of empiricism at all, since, as distinct from classical empiricism, they renounce any interest in mental processes or faculties (that is, in the problems of descriptive or explanatory adequacy).

31. This is the only respect in which a comparison of such alternatives is relevant, apart from their relative success in accounting for the given facts of language acquisition. But this consideration apparently offers no information that has any bearing on the choice among alternative theories.

In general, it is important to bear in mind that an extremely specialized input-output relation does not necessarily presuppose a complex and highly structured device. Whether our assumption about the mind is that it contains the schema for transformational grammar or that it contains mechanisms for making arbitrary associations or for carrying out certain kinds of inductive or taxonomic operations, there is apparently little knowledge about the brain and little engineering insight into plausible physical systems that can be used to support these hypotheses. Similarly, there is no justification for the common assumption that there is an asymmetry between rationalist and empiricist views in that the former somehow beg the question, not showing how the postulated internal structure arises. Empiricist views leave open precisely the same question. For the moment, there is no better account of how the empiricist data-processing operations might have been developed, as innate structure, in a species, than there is of how the rationalist schema may arise through evolutionary processes or other determinants of the structure of organisms. Nor does comparison with species other than man help the empiricist argument. On the contrary, every known species has highly specialized cognitive capacities. It is important to observe that comparative psychology has not characteristically proceeded on empiricist assumptions about knowledge and behavior, and lends no support to these assumptions.

32. There is reason to believe that the language-acquisition system may be fully functional only during a "critical period" of mental development or, more specifically, that its various maturational stages (see note 19) have critical periods. See Lenneberg (forth-

coming) for an important and informative review of data bearing on this question. Many other aspects of the problem of biologically given constraints on the nature of human language are discussed here and in Lenneberg (1960).

Notice that we do not, of course, imply that the functions of language acquisition are carried out by entirely separate components of the abstract mind or the physical brain, just as when one studies analyzing mechanisms in perception (cf. Sutherland, 1959, 1964), it is not implied that these are distinct and separate components of the full perceptual system. In fact, it is an important problem for psychology to determine to what extent other aspects of cognition share properties of language acquisition and language use, and to attempt, in this way, to develop a richer and more comprehensive theory of mind.

33. It is a curious fact that empiricism is commonly regarded as somehow a "scientific" philosophy. Actually, the empiricist approach to acquisition of knowledge has a certain dogmatic and aprioristic character that is largely lacking in its rationalist counterpart. In the particular case of language acquisition, the empiricist approach begins its investigation with the stipulation that certain arbitrarily selected data-processing mechanisms (e.g., principles of association, taxonomic procedures) are the only ones available to the language-acquisition device. It then investigates the application of these procedures to data, without, however, attempting to show that the result of this application corresponds to grammars that can be shown, independently, to be descriptively adequate. A nondogmatic alternative to empiricism would begin by observing that in studying language acquisition, what we are given is certain information about the primary data that are presented and the grammar that is the resulting product, and the problem we face is that of determining the structure of the device that mediates this input-output relation (the same is true of the more general problem of which language acquisition is a special case). There are no grounds for any specific assumptions, empiricist or otherwise, about the internal structure of this device. Continuing with no preconceptions, we would naturally turn to the study of uniformities in the output (formal and substantive universals), which we then must attribute to the structure of the device (or, if this can be shown, to uniformities in the input, this alternative rarely being a serious one in the cases that are of interest). This, in effect, has been the rationalist approach, and it is difficult to see what alternative there can be to it if dogmatic presuppositions as to the nature of mental processes are eliminated.

34. That is, a theory that meets conditions (i)–(iv) of p. 31. I shall

henceforth assume, with no further comment, that any linguistic theory under discussion attempts to meet at least these conditions.

35.   There has, during the past few years, been a fair amount of investigation into the formal properties of very simple theories of grammar. For the most part, it has been restricted to weak generative capacity, though there are a few results involving strong generative capacity as well (in particular, those referred to in § 2). The latter is, obviously, by far the more interesting notion, but it is much more difficult to study. For surveys of this work, see Chomsky (1963), Chomsky and Schützenberger (1963).

36.   See Postal (1962b, 1964a, 1964c). Neither the theory of context-free grammar nor the theory of finite-state grammar is an artifact invented for mathematical investigation. Each is well motivated formally and has independent interest, apart from linguistics, and each has in fact been proposed by linguists as a comprehensive theory of language. In fact, as Postal shows (1964a), almost every linguistic theory that has received any substantial attention in recent years, insofar as it is clear, falls within the framework of context-free grammar. As we shall see later, a special form of the theory of context-free grammar apparently plays a crucial role within the general theory of transformational grammar.

37.   This possibility cannot be ruled out a priori, but, in fact, it seems definitely not to be the case. In particular, it seems that, when the theory of transformational grammar is properly formulated, any such grammar must meet formal conditions that restrict it to the enumeration of recursive sets. Cf. the conditions on base rules; also note 1, Chapter 3, and further discussion in Chapter 3 and Chapter 4, § 2.2, of conditions on deletion transformations.

NOTES TO CHAPTER 2

1.   In detail, there is some room for discussion about both terminology and substance throughout (2), and, particularly in the case of (2ii), alternative conventions and decisions have been applied. However, I think that the central facts are clear enough, and there has, in fact, been overwhelming accord about most of them. For present purposes, I shall raise no further question (except of detail) about the adequacy of these observations, taking them simply as facts to be accounted for by a grammatical theory.

2.   A theory of language must state the principles interrelating its theoretical terms (e.g., "phoneme," "morpheme," "transformation," "Noun Phrase," "Subject") and ultimately must relate this system of concepts to potential empirical phenomena (to primary linguistic data). For reasons discussed in Chomsky (1957) and

elsewhere, it seems to me that all significant structural notions will have to be characterized in terms of the previously defined notion "generative grammar" (whereas structural linguistics has assumed, in general, that the notion "grammar" must be developed and explained in terms of previously defined notions such as "phoneme," and "morpheme"). That is, I am assuming that the basic notion to be defined is "G is a most highly valued grammar of the language of which primary linguistic data D constitutes a sample," where D is represented in terms of primitive notions of the theory; the phonemes, morphemes, transformations, etc., of the language are, then, the elements that play a specified role in the derivations and representations determined by G. If so, partial generative grammars will provide the only empirical data critical for evaluating a theory of the form of language. For the present, then, such evidence must be drawn from grammatical descriptions of relatively few languages. This is not particularly disturbing. What is important is that such assumptions be supported by available evidence and formulated with enough clarity so that new or improved generative grammars will have bearing on their correctness, as the depth and range of linguistic study increases. We must, in short, accept Humboldt's conclusion, expressed in a letter of 1822 to Schlegel (Leitzmann, 1908, p. 84): "dass jede grammatische Discussion nur dann wahrhaften wissenschaftlichen Gewinn bringt, wenn sie so durchgeführt wird, als läge in ihr allein der ganze Zweck, und wenn man jede, noch so rohe Sprache selbst, gerade mit derselben Sorgfalt behandelt als Griechisch und Lateinisch."

Study of a wide range of languages is only one of the ways to evaluate the hypothesis that some formal condition is a linguistic universal. Paradoxical as this may seem at first glance, considerations internal to a single language may provide significant support for the conclusion that some formal property should be attributed not to the theory of the particular language in question (its grammar) but rather to the general linguistic theory on which the particular grammar is based.' Study of descriptive or explanatory adequacy may lead to such a conclusion; furthermore, the difficulty or impossibility of formulating certain conditions within the framework of an otherwise well-supported theory of grammar provides some evidence that these are, in reality, general conditions on the applicability of grammatical rules rather than aspects of the particular language, to be expressed within the system of grammatical rules itself. Several cases of this sort will be mentioned later.

In general, it should be expected that only descriptions concerned with deep structure will have serious import for proposals concerning linguistic universals. Since descriptions of this sort are few, any such proposals are hazardous, but are clearly no less interesting or important for being hazardous.

3. A weak though sufficient condition is given in Chomsky (1955, Chapter 6). A stronger but rather well-motivated condition is proposed by Postal (1964a). Some aspects of this question are discussed in Chomsky and Miller (1963, § 4); Chomsky (1963, § 3).

4. For some discussion, see the references cited on p. 16, and many others. These demonstrations of the inadequacies of phrase structure grammar have not been challenged, although some confusions have been introduced by terminological equivocations. The most extreme example of this can be found in Harman (1963), where many of the standard arguments against phrase structure grammar are repeated, with approval, in an article with the subtitle "a defense of phrase structure." This curious situation results simply from the author's redefinition of the term "phrase structure" to refer to a system far richer than that to which the term "phrase structure grammar" has been universally applied in the rather ample literature on this subject (in particular, to a system in which in place of category symbols, in the sense of phrase structure grammar, we have pairs (α, φ), where α is a category symbol and φ is a set of indices used to code transformations, contextual restrictions, etc.). That is, Harman in effect restates the arguments against phrase structure grammar as arguments against limiting the term "phrase structure grammar" to the particular systems that have previously been defined as "phrase structure grammar." This terminological proposal does not touch on the substantive issue as to the adequacy of the taxonomic theory of grammar for which phrase structure grammar (in the usual sense) is a model. The essential adequacy of phrase structure grammar as a model for taxonomic grammatical theory (with the possible but irrelevant exception of problems involving discontinuous constituents — see Chomsky, 1957, Postal, 1964a) is demonstrated quite convincingly by Postal, and is not challenged by Harman, or anyone else, to my knowledge. The only issue that Harman raises, in this connection, is whether the term "phrase structure grammar" should be restricted to taxonomic models or whether the term should be used in some far richer sense as well, and this terminological question is of no conceivable importance. The terminological equivocation has only the effect of suggesting to the casual reader, quite erroneously, that there is some issue about the linguistic adequacy of the theory of phrase structure grammar (in the usual sense).

A further source of possible confusion, in connection with this paper, is that there is a way of interpreting the grammar presented there as a phrase structure grammar, namely by regarding each complex element (α, φ) as a single, unanalyzable category symbol. Under this interpretation, what we have here is a new proposal as to the proper evaluation procedure for a phrase structure grammar, a proposal which is immediately refuted by the fact that under this interpretation, the structural description provided by the Phrase-marker of the now highest-valued grammar is invariably incorrect. For example, in *John saw Bill, did Tom see you?*, the three elements *John, Bill, Tom* would belong to three distinct and entirely unrelated categories, and would have no categorial assignment in common. Thus we have the following alternatives: we may interpret the paper as proposing a new evaluation measure for phrase structure grammars, in which case it is immediately refuted on grounds of descriptive inadequacy; or we may interpret it as proposing that the term "phrase structure grammar" be used in some entirely new sense, in which case it has no bearing on the issue of the adequacy of phrase structure grammar. For some further discussion see Chomsky (in press), where this and other criticisms of transformational grammar, some real, some only apparent, are taken up.

5. This assumption is made explicitly in Chomsky (1955), in the discussion of the base of a transformational grammar (Chapter 7), and, to my knowledge, in all subsequent empirical studies of transformational grammar. An analogous assumption with respect to transformational rules is made in Matthews (1964, Appendix A, § 2). Formal properties of *sequential grammars* have been studied by Ginsburg and Rice (1962) and Shamir (1961), these being context-free grammars where the sequential property is, furthermore, intrinsic (in the sense of note 6, Chapter 3), rather than extrinsic, as presupposed here (for the context-sensitive case, at least).

6. As noted earlier, there are rather different conventions, and some substantive disagreements about the usage of these terms. Thus if we were to change the rules of (5), and, correspondingly, the Phrase-marker (3), to provide a binary analysis of the major category S into *sincerity* (NP) and *may frighten the boy* (VP), then the latter would be the Predicate-of the sentence in the sense defined in (11). See the final paragraph of § 2.3.4 for an emendation of these suggested definitions of functional notions.

7. Let us assume, furthermore, that Y, Z are unique, in this case — in other words, that there is only one occurrence of B in X. The definition can be generalized to accommodate the case where this

condition is violated, but it seems to me reasonable to impose this condition of uniqueness on the system of base rules.

8. Notice that accurate definitions require a precise specification of the notions "occurrence," "dominate," etc. This raises no difficulty of principle, and throughout the informal discussion here I shall simply avoid these questions. Precise definitions for most of the notions that will be used here, taking occurrences into account, may be found in Chomsky (1955).

9. One might question whether M should be regarded as a lexical category, or whether, alternatively, the rules M → *may, can,* · · · should not be included in the set (5I). The significance of this distinction will be discussed later. This is by no means merely a terminological issue. Thus, for example, we might hope to establish general conventions involving the distinction between lexical and nonlexical categories. To illustrate the range of possibilities that may be relevant, I mention just two considerations. The general rule for conjunction seems to be roughly this: if XZY and $XZ'Y$ are two strings such that for some category A, Z is an A and Z' is an A, then we may form the string $X\frown Z\frown and\frown Z'\frown Y$, where $Z\frown and\frown Z'$ is an A (see Chomsky 1957, § 5.2, and for a much more far-reaching study, Gleitman, 1961). But, clearly, A must be a category of a special type; in fact, we come much closer to characterizing the actual range of possibilities if we limit A to major categories. By this criterion, M should be a lexical category.

Second, consider the phonological rules that assign stress in English by a transformational cycle (see Chomsky, Halle, and Lukoff, 1956; Halle and Chomsky, 1960, forthcoming; Chomsky and Miller, 1963). These rules assign stress in a fixed way in strings belonging to certain categories. By and large, the categories in question seem to be the major categories, in the sense just described. In particular, elements of nonlexical formative categories (e.g., Articles) are unstressed. By this criterion, one might want M to be a nonlexical category, though even here the situation is unclear; cf. the well-known contrast of *máy-mày*, as in *John mày try* (it is permitted) and *John máy try* (it is possible).

10. Some have argued that the distinction in question has nothing to do with rules of English, but only with statistics of usage. What seem to be insuperable difficulties for any such analysis have been raised and frequently reiterated, and I see no point in considering this possibility any further as long as proponents of this most implausible view make no attempt to deal with these objections. Cf. Chapter 1, § 2.

11. For some discussion of a possible syntactic basis for such subcategorization, with a small amount of supporting evidence, see

Chomsky (1955, Chapter 4), summarized in part in Chomsky (1961) and Miller and Chomsky (1963). A critique of these and other discussions is given in Katz (1964a). I think that Katz's major criticisms are correct, but that they can perhaps be met by narrowing the scope of the proposals to just what is being discussed here, namely the question of subcategorization of lexical categories within the framework of an independently justified generative grammar.

12. In the syntactic component of this (pretransformational) grammar, indices on category symbols were used to express agreement (and, in general, what Harris, 1951, calls long components) but not subcategorization and selectional restrictions. These devices become unnecessary once grammatical transformations are introduced. See, in this connection, the discussion in Postal (1964a).

13. Matthews devised a technique of indexing category symbols to meet the difficulties that he found, and he later incorporated this technique as one of the main devices of the COMIT programming system that he developed with the collaboration of V. Yngve. Similar difficulties were noted independently by R. Stockwell, T. Anderson, and P. Schachter, and they have suggested a somewhat different way of handling them (see Stockwell and Schachter, 1962; Schachter, 1962). E. Bach has also dealt with this question, in a somewhat different way (Bach, 1964). The method that I shall elaborate later incorporates various features of these proposals, but differs from them in certain respects. The problem of remedying this defect in phrase structure grammar is clearly very much open, and deserves much further study. Although this defect was pointed out quite early, there was no attempt to deal with it in most of the published work of the last several years.

14. Thus [s] is an abbreviation for the set of features [+ consonantal, − vocalic, − voiced, + continuant, + strident, − grave] and [m] for the set of features [+ consonantal, − vocalic, + nasal, + voiced, + grave]. Rule (18) applies to any segment specified as [+ continuant] (hence to [s]) in a context which is specified as − [+ voiced] (hence to the context [− m]), converting the segment to which it applies to a voiced segment with, otherwise, the same features as before (hence converting [s] to [z] = [+ consonantal, − vocalic, + voiced, + continuant, + strident, − grave]).

I shall henceforth use the convention, customary on the phonological level, of enclosing sets of features by square brackets.

15. But notice that a phonological matrix can be regarded simply as a set of specified phonological features, if we index each specified feature by an integer indicating the column it occupies in the matrix. Thus the two-column matrix representing the formative

bee can be regarded as consisting of the features [+ consonantal$_1$, − vocalic$_1$, − continuant$_1$, · · · , − consonantal$_2$, + vocalic$_2$, − grave$_2$, · · ·]. A lexical entry can now be regarded simply as a set of features, some phonological, some syntactic. Of course, a lexical entry must also contain a definition, in a complete grammar, and it can be plausibly argued (see Katz and Fodor, 1963) that this too consists simply of a set of features. (Actually the Katz-Fodor definitions are not simply sets, but it does not seem that the further structure they impose plays any role in their theory.) We might, then, take a lexical entry to be simply a set of features, some syntactic, some phonological, some semantic.

However, largely for ease of exposition, we shall not follow this course but shall, rather, regard a lexical entry as a matrix-complex symbol pair, as in the text.

If we regard a lexical entry as a set of features, then items that are similar in sound, meaning, or syntactic function will not be related to one another in the lexicon. For example, the Intransitive "grow" of "the boy grew" or "corn grows," and the Transitive "grow" of "he grows corn" would have to constitute two separate lexical entries, despite the meaning relation that holds between them, since there is apparently no way to derive the Intransitive structures from the Transitive ones, as can be done in the case of "the window broke," "someone broke the window." Cf. p. 189. The same would be true of "drop" in "the price dropped," "he dropped the ball," "he dropped that silly pretense"; or of "command" in the example discussed on p. 119, and in innumerable other cases of many different kinds. Alternatively, such relationships can be expressed by taking a lexical entry to be a Boolean function of features. Although it is likely that such a modification of the theory of lexical structure is necessary, it raises many problems of fact and principle to which I have no answer, and I therefore continue the exposition without developing it.

16. Recall Bloomfield's characterization of a lexicon as the list of basic irregularities of a language (1933, p. 274). The same point is made by Sweet (1913, p. 31), who holds that "grammar deals with the general facts of language, lexicology with the special facts."

17. More generally, the *phonological redundancy rules*, which determine such features as voicing of vowels or unrounding of high front vowels in English, can be supplemented by analogous syntactic and semantic redundancy rules. Furthermore, redundancy rules may relate features of these various types. For example, if the traditional view that syntactic categorization is in part de-

termined semantically can be substantiated in any serious way, it can be expressed by a redundancy rule determining syntatic features in terms of semantic ones. We shall return to the question of redundancy rules in § 6.

Notice, incidentally, that the rules (20) (and, in fact, all rules that establish a partial hierarchy among syntactic features) might be regarded as redundancy rules rather than as rules of the base. Such a decision would have various consequences, to which we shall return in § 4.3.

18. By a *local transformation (with respect to A)* I mean one that affects only a substring dominated by the single category symbol *A*. Thus all rules of the transformational cycle in phonology are local, in this sense. There is some reason to suspect that it might be appropriate to intersperse certain local transformations among the rewriting rules of the base. Thus Adverbial Phrases consisting of Preposition⌢Determiner⌢Noun are in general restricted as to the choice of these elements, and these restrictions could be stated by local transformations to the effect that Preposition and Noun can be rewritten in certain restricted ways when dominated by such category symbols as Place Adverbial and Time Adverbial. In fact, one might consider a new extension of the theory of context-free grammar, permitting rules that restrict rewriting by local transformations (i.e., in terms of the dominating category symbol), alongside of the fairly widely studied extension of context-free grammar to context-sensitive grammars that permit rules that restrict rewriting in terms of contiguous symbols.

The example of the preceding paragraph involves a transformation that is local with respect to a category *A* (*A*, in this case, being some type of Adverbial), and, furthermore, that introduces a string into a position dominated by the lexical category *B* which is immediately dominated by *A*. Let us call such a transformation *strictly local*. The only motivation for this highly special definition is that many of the examples of local transformations that come to mind meet this restrictive condition as well (for example, quite generally, nominalization transformations that give such forms as "I persuaded John of my seriousness" from an underlying form "I persuaded John of N S," where S dominates the string underlying "I am serious" and the transformation substitutes a transform of this string for the dummy symbol occupying the position of the lexical category N, which is immediately dominated by the category symbol NP with respect to which the transformation is local).

19. Notice that an important question is begged when we assume that Noun subcategorization is independent of context and that the

selectional restrictions on Subject-Verb-Object are given completely by rules determining the subcategorization of Verbs in terms of previously chosen Noun subcategories. We shall return to this matter in § 4.2.

20. This decision, as several of the others, will be slightly modified later in the text.

21. The status of the symbol S′ in this rule is unexplained at the present state of the exposition. It will indicate the position of a transform of a sentence, as the theory of the syntactic component is extended later on.

22. Observe that in (36) such an expression as " — like⌢Predicate-Nominal" is a *single symbol*, standing for a particular syntactic feature.

The careful reader will notice that as these rules are formulated, lexical items can be inserted in the wrong position by the lexical rule. We shall return to this question in § 3, avoiding it now only so as not to overburden the exposition. Actually, a more careful analysis would revise (40) and (41) in detail.

23. An apparent exception to the last remark is the subcategorization of Verbs in terms of choice of the Progressive form *be + Ing*. To maintain the suggested generalization concerning strict subcategorization, we should have to claim that such Verbs as *own*, *understand*, and *know* occur freely with or without Progressive (along with all other Verbs), but that the Progressive form is deleted by an obligatory transformation when it precedes these Verbs (this peculiarity would be marked by a feature that constitutes part of the lexical entries for these forms). But, in fact, there is good reason to assume this, as has been pointed out to me by Barbara Hall. Thus each element of the Auxiliary has associated with it certain characteristic Adverbials that may (or, in the case of Present tense, must) cooccur with this Auxiliary element, and the characteristic Adverbials of Progressive do occur with the Verbs *own*, *understand*, *know*, etc. (cf. "I know the answer right now," alongside of "I know the answer"), although such forms as "I eat the apple right now," "I eat the apple," are ruled out (except, in the latter case, as "generic," which can, in fact, be treated as involving deletion of a "dummy" Adverbial).

24. Strictly speaking, this is not the case, as we have defined "syntactic feature" (cf. pp. 82f.). Actually, it is only the features involved in the set of rules of which (20)–(21) constitute a sample that determine selectional classification. Idiosyncratic syntactic features of particular lexical items, not introduced by such general rules as (20)–(21) but simply listed in the lexical entries, play no role in Verb subclassification.

25. Notice that these alternatives are not strictly equivalent. Thus, for example, of the three mentioned only the one we are using permits also the free use of variables, as in the case of schema (44). On the other hand, the use of labeled brackets is appropriate for the formulation of the transformational rules of the phonological component. Use of complex symbols at arbitrary nodes (as in Harman, 1963 — cf. note 4) gives a form of transformational grammar that is richer in some respects and poorer in others than the formulation in terms of Boolean conditions on Analyzability, as in most current work on generative grammar. Cf. Chomsky (in press) for some discussion.

26. Proper Nouns of course can have nonrestrictive relatives (and, marginally, Adjective modifiers derived from nonrestrictive relatives — e.g., "clever Hans" or "old Tom"). But although restrictive relatives belong to the Determiner system, there are several reasons for supposing that nonrestrictive relatives are, rather, Complements of the full NP (and in some cases, of a full sentence — e.g., "I found John likable, which surprised me very much"). Notice that Adjective modifiers can derive from either restrictive or nonrestrictive relatives (consider, for example, the ambiguity of the sentence "the industrious Chinese dominate the economy of Southeast Asia"). This matter is discussed in the Port-Royal *Logic* (Arnauld *et al.*, 1662), and, in more recent times, by Jespersen (1924, Chapter 8).

Notice also that Proper Nouns can also be used as Common Nouns, in restricted ways (e.g., "this cannot be the England that I know and love," "I once read a novel by a different John Smith"). Some such expressions may be derived from Proper Nouns with nonrestrictive relatives by transformation; others suggest that a redundancy rule may be needed, in the lexicon, assigning certain of the features of Common Nouns to Proper Nouns.

27. Once again, this is not to deny that an interpretation can sometimes be imposed on such phrases as those of (54). See the discussion of the problem of justification at the outset of § 2.3.1, and the references of footnote 11.

Notice, in particular, that the relation of the Verb to the Place Adverbial in "John died in England" (= "in England, John died") is very different from that in "John stayed in England" ("John lived in England" is, in fact, an ambiguous representative of both constructions, being interpretable as either "John resided in England," analogous structurally to "John stayed in England" with a Verbal Complement introduced by rule (52iii), or roughly as "in England, John really lived" or "in England,

John remained alive," with a Place Adverbial that is a Verb Phrase Complement introduced by (52ii) — cf. "John will surely die on the Continent, but he may live in England"). This difference of structure between "live in England" and "die in England" accounts for the fact (noted by Ralph Long) that "England is lived in by many people" is much more natural than "England is died in by many people" — in fact, this remark is true only when "live in" has the sense of "reside in" or "inhabit." Cf. p. 104 for further discussion of such "pseudopassives."

28.   There are well-known marginal exceptions to this remark (e.g., "a good time was had by all" or "recourse was had to a new plan"), and it is also clear that the locution "take Manner Adverbials freely" requires considerable further analysis and clarification (see Lees, 1960a, p. 26), as does the distinction between Adverbials that qualify the Verb and those which might more properly be said to qualify the Subject. (As an example of the latter, consider the Adverbial of "John married Mary with no great enthusiasm," which means, roughly, "John was not very enthusiastic about marrying Mary," and therefore seems to play a role more like that of the Adverbial modifier of the Subject in "John, cleverly, stayed away yesterday" than like that of the Adverbial modifier of the Verb in "John laid his plans cleverly." See Austin (1956) for some discussion of such cases.) Nevertheless, the essential correctness of the comments in the text does not seem to me in doubt.

It must be borne in mind that the general rules of a grammar are not invalidated by the existence of exceptions. Thus one does not eliminate the rule for forming the past tense of Verbs from the grammar on the grounds that many Verbs are irregular; nor is the generalization that relates Manner Adverbials to passivization invalidated by the fact that certain items must be listed, in the lexicon, as conflicting with this generalization, if this turns out to be the case. In either the case of past tense or that of passivization, the generalization is invalidated (in the sense of "internal justification" — cf. Chapter 1, § 4) only if a more highly valued grammar can be constructed that does not contain it. It is for this reason that the discovery of peculiarities and exceptions (which are rarely lacking, in a system of the complexity of a natural language) is generally so unrewarding and, in itself, has so little importance for the study of the grammatical structure of the language in question, unless, of course, it leads to the discovery of deeper generalizations.

It is also worth noting that many of the Manner Adverbials, like many other Adverbials, are Sentence transforms with deleted

Subjects. Thus underlying the sentence "John gave the lecture with great enthusiasm," with the Adverbial "with great enthusiasm," is the base string "John has great enthusiasm" (note that "with" is quite generally a transform of "have"), with the repeated NP "John" deleted, as is usual (cf. Chapter 3 and Chapter 4, § 2.2). Similarly, Place Adverbials (at least those which are VP complements) must sometimes, or perhaps always, be regarded as Sentence transforms (so that, for example, "I read the book in England" derives from an underlying structure very much like the one that underlies "I read the book while (I was) in England"). Adverbials are a rich and as yet relatively unexplored system, and therefore anything we say about them must be regarded as quite tentative.

29. Alternatively, we may drop this condition and extend the first convention so that the complex symbol introduced in the analysis of a lexical category A contains not only the feature $[+ A]$, but also the feature $[- B]$ for any lexical category B other than A. This convention entails that a word specified as belonging to two lexical categories must have two separate lexical entries, and it raises unanswered questions about the structure of the lexicon. It would have the advantage of overcoming a defect in our notation for features introduced by context-sensitive subcategorization rules. Thus, in the grammar (57), the feature $[-]$ designates both Proper Nouns and Intransitive Verbs. (This is why the feature $[+ N]$ had to be mentioned in rule (57xi).) This might lead to difficulty if a certain lexical item were both a Noun and a Verb, since it might be non-Proper as a Noun but Transitive as a Verb, or Transitive as a Verb and Proper as a Noun. If the proposal of this note is adopted, the problem cannot arise. Alternatively, it will be necessary to designate such features by a more complex notation indicating not only the frame in question but also the symbol that dominates it.

There may be some point to allowing a lexical item to appear in several categorial positions (either by specifying it positively with respect to several lexical categories, or by leaving it totally unspecified with respect to these categories) — for example, in the case of such words as "proof," "desire," "belief." Suppose that these are specified as taking Sentential Complements of various forms, but are permitted to enter either the Noun or Verb position. Then the lexical insertion rule will place them in either the frame ". . . N that S . . ." or the frame ". . . V that S . . . ," in the positions of the Noun and Verb, respectively. Hence it will not be necessary to derive the former by transformation from the latter, as is necessary, for example, in the case of ". . . proving that S . . .".

Under such an analysis, "John's proof that S" would derive from
the structure underlying "John has a proof that S" by the
sequence of transformations that derives "John's book" from the
structure underlying "John has a book." One might go on to
relate "John has a proof that S" to "John proves that S" (perhaps,
ultimately, as "John takes a walk" is related to "John walks"), but
this is another matter.

In connection with this discussion, it is also necessary to establish a general distinctness condition regarding the idiosyncratic,
purely lexical features (e.g., the feature [Object-deletion] in (58),
(59)). For discussion of this question, which becomes critical in
case these features relate to the phonological component, see Halle
and Chomsky (forthcoming).

30. It has been maintained that these relations can be defined in
terms of some notion of cooccurrence, but this seems to me du-
bious, for reasons presented in various places (e.g., in Bar-Hillel,
1954; and Chomsky, 1964). Observe that the definitions of grammatical relation or grammatical function that have been suggested
here refer only to the base of the syntax and not to surface
structures of actual sentences in other than the simplest cases. The
significant grammatical relations of an actual sentence (e.g. (7),
p. 70), are those which are defined in the basis (deep structure)
of this sentence.

31. I give these informally, instead of using the notation developed
earlier, to simplify the reading. There is nothing essential involved in this change of notation.

32. For example, if we were to adapt the definitions of universal
categories and functions so that they apply to such sentences as
"in England is where I met him," which are often cited to show
that phrases other than NP's can occur as Subjects, these proposals
would fail completely. This sentence, however, is obviously trans-
formationally derived. It would be perfectly correct to say that
"in England" is the Subject of "in England is where I met him,"
extending the grammatical relation *Subject-of*, that is, [NP, S],
to the *derived* Phrase-marker (the surface structure). In the basis,
however, "in England" is an Adverbial of Place, associated with
the VP *meet him* in the Predicate-Phrase "met him in England,"
and the sentence is interpreted in accordance with the grammatical relations defined in this underlying deep structure.

This extension to surface structures of such functional notions
as Subject-of is not an entirely straightforward matter. Thus in
base structures, there is apparently never more than a single
occurrence of a category such as NP in any structure immediately
dominated by a single category (cf. note 7), and our definitions

of these notions relied on this fact. But this is not true of surface structures. In the sentence "this book I really enjoyed," both "this book" and "I" are NP's immediately dominated by S. Apparently, then, order is significant in determining the grammatical relations defined by surface structures (not surprisingly), though it seems to play no role in the determination of grammatical relations in deep structures. Consequently, somewhat different definitions are needed for the surface notions.

It might be suggested that Topic-Comment is the basic grammatical relation of surface structure corresponding (roughly) to the fundamental Subject-Predicate relation of deep structure. Thus we might define the Topic-of the Sentence as the leftmost NP immediately dominated by S in the surface structure, and the Comment-of the Sentence as the rest of the string. Often, of course, Topic and Subject will coincide, but not in the examples discussed. This proposal, which seems plausible, was suggested to me by Paul Kiparsky. One might refine it in various ways, for example, by defining the Topic-of the Sentence as the leftmost NP that is immediately dominated by S in the surface structure and that is, furthermore, a major category (cf. p. 74 — this will make *John* the Topic in the cleft sentence "it was John who I saw"). Other elaborations also come to mind, but I shall not go into the question any more fully here.

33. This very fruitful and important insight is as old as syntactic theory itself; it is developed quite clearly in the *Grammaire générale et raisonnée* of Port-Royal (cf. Chomsky, 1964, § 1.0; forthcoming, for discussion). What is, in essence, the same idea was reintroduced into modern linguistics by Harris, though he has not discussed it in quite these terms (cf. Harris, 1952, 1954, 1957). For further discussion of this notion, within the framework of transformational generative grammar, see Chomsky (1957), and for steps toward a substantive theory of semantic interpretation based on this assumption, see Katz and Fodor (1963) and Katz and Postal (1964).

34. Curry's proposals are so sketchy that it is impossible to extract from them more than a general point of view. The position of Saumjan and Soboleva is much more explicitly worked out, but it is defective in crucial respects. Cf. Hall (1965), for an analysis of this approach. It is possible that "stratificational grammar" also adopts a similar position, but the published references to this theory (e.g., Gleason, 1964) are much too vague for any conclusion to be drawn.

35. Notice, for example, that Case is usually determined by the position of the Noun in surface structure rather than in deep struc-

ture, although the surface structures given by stylistic inversions do not affect Case. Even in English, poor as it is in inflection, this can be observed. For example, the Pronoun in the sentences "he was struck by a bullet," "he is easy to please," "he frightens easily" is, in each case, the "logical Object," that is, the Direct-Object of Verbs *strike, please, frighten*, respectively, in the underlying deep structures. Nevertheless, the form is *he* rather than *him*. But stylistic inversion of the type we have just been discussing gives such forms as "him I really like," "him I would definitely try not to antagonize." Where inflections are richer, this phenomenon, which illustrates the peripheral character of these processes of inversion, is much more apparent.

The relation between inflection, ambiguity, and word order was discussed at some length in traditional linguistic theory. See Chomsky, forthcoming, for some references.

NOTES TO CHAPTER 3

1. Some details irrelevant to the problem under discussion are omitted in these examples. We here regard each lexical item as standing for a complex of features, namely those that constitute its lexical entry in addition to those entered by redundancy rules. The use of the dummy symbol Δ has been extended here to the case of various unspecified elements that will be deleted by obligatory transformations. There is, in fact, good reason to require that only "recoverable deletions" be permitted in the grammar. For discussion of this very important question, see Chomsky, 1964, § 2.2. We shall return to it at the end of this chapter and in Chapter 4, § 2.2.

The formative *nom* in (3) is one of several that might be assigned to the Tense⌢Modal position of the Auxiliary, and that determine the form of the Nominalization (*for-to, possessive-ing*, etc.).

2. The details of this, both for Transformation-markers and Phrase-markers, are worked out in Chomsky (1955), within the following general framework. Linguistic theory provides a (universal) system of *levels of representation*. Each level L is a system based on a set of primes (minimal elements — i.e., an alphabet); the operation of concatenation, which forms strings of primes of arbitrary finite length (the terms and notions all being borrowed from the theory of concatenation algebras — cf. e.g., Rosenbloom, 1950); various relations; a designated class of strings (or sets of strings) of primes called L-markers; a mapping of L-markers onto L'-markers, where L' is the next "lower" level (thus levels are arranged in a hierarchy). In particular, on the level P of phrase structure and the

level T of transformations we have P-markers and T-markers in the sense just described informally. A hierarchy of linguistic levels (phonetic, phonological, word, morphological, phrase structure, transformational structure) can be developed within a uniform framework in this way. For details, see Chomsky (1955). For a discussion of T-markers, see Katz and Postal (1964).

3. For discussion of negation, see Klima (1964), Katz (1964b). The formation of questions and imperatives and the semantic interpretation of the question and imperative markers are discussed in Katz and Postal (1964). In Hockett (1961) the proposal is made that the passive transformation be conditional on a marker in the underlying form, but no supporting argument is given for what, in the context of that paper, is no more than a notational innovation.

Notice that the reformulation of the passive transformation as obligatory, relative to choice of an optional marker in the underlying string, is independent of the principle that we have just cited, since the passive marker, as distinct from the question, negation, and imperative markers, has no independent semantic interpretation. Furthermore, we have noted in § 4.4 of Chapter 2 that there are good reasons to distinguish such transformations as passive from purely stylistic inversion operations. These observations suggest that we attempt to formulate a more general condition of which the principle just cited is itself a consequence, namely that "nonstylistic transformations" are all signaled by optional markers drawn from a fixed, universal, language-independent set. This attempt presupposes a deeper analysis of the notion "nonstylistic transformation" than we have been able to provide here, however.

4. For illuminating discussion of this question, and several others that we are considering here, see Fillmore (1963) and Fraser (1963).

5. Both of these observations are due to Fillmore (1963).

6. In connection with ordering of rules, it is necessary to distinguish *extrinsic order*, imposed by the explicit ordering of rules, from *intrinsic order*, which is simply a consequence of how rules are formulated. Thus if the rule R_1 introduces the symbol A and R_2 analyzes A, there is an intrinsic order relating R_1 and R_2, but not necessarily any extrinsic order. Similarly, if a certain transformation T_1 applies to a certain structure that is formed only by application of T_2, there is an intrinsic order T_1, T_2. Taxonomic linguistics disallows extrinsic ordering, but has not been clear about the status of intrinsic ordering. Generative grammars have ordinarily required both. For some discussion of this matter, see Chomsky (1964).

7. We are discussing only embedding transformations here, but should extend the discussion to various generalized transformations that form coordinate constructions (e.g., conjunction). There are certain problems concerning these, but I believe that they can be incorporated quite readily in the present scheme by permitting rule schemata (in the sense of Chomsky and Miller, 1963, p. 298; Chomsky and Schützenberger, 1963, p. 133) introducing coordinated elements that are then modified, rearranged, and appropriately interrelated by singulary transformations. If the suggestion of note 9, Chapter 2, is workable, then such rule schemata need not be stated in the grammar at all. Rather, by a general convention we can associate such a schema with each major category. This approach to coordination relies heavily on the filtering effect of transformations, discussed later. Thus wherever we have coordination, some category is coordinated n times in the matrix sentence, and n occurrences of matched sentences are independently generated by the base rules.

8. Notice, incidentally, that we can now eliminate *Complement* from the set of category symbols. We could go on, at this point, to define "Complement" as a functional notion (to be more precise, as a cover term for several functional notions), in the manner of pp. 70–71.

9. As it stands, this claim seems to me somewhat too strong, though it is true in one important sense of semantic interpretation. For example, it seems clear that the order of "quantifiers" in surface structures sometimes plays a role in semantic interpretation. Thus for many speakers — in particular, for me — the sentences "everyone in the room knows at least two languages" and "at least two languages are known by everyone in the room" are not synonymous. Still, we might maintain that in such examples both interpretations are latent (as would be indicated by the identity of the deep structures of the two sentences in all respects relevant to semantic interpretation), and that the reason for the opposing interpretations is an extraneous factor — an overriding consideration involving order of quantifiers in surface structures — that filters out certain latent interpretations provided by the deep structures. In support of this view, it may be pointed out that other sentences that derive from these (e.g., "there are two languages that everyone in the room knows") may switch interpretations, indicating that these interpretations must have been latent all along. There are other examples that suggest something similar. For example, Grice has suggested that the temporal order implied in conjunction may be regarded as a feature of discourse rather than as part of the meaning of "and," and Jakobson has

also discussed "iconic" features of discourse involving relations between temporal order in surface structure and order of importance, etc. Also relevant in this connection is the notion of Topic-Comment mentioned in note 32, Chapter 2. For some references to remarks in the Port-Royal Logic on the effect of grammatical transformations on meaning, see Chomsky (forthcoming).

10. The other function of the transformational component is to express restrictions on distribution for lexical items and for sentence structures.

11. Formally speaking, what we are suggesting is this. Suppose that the symbol A immediately dominates XBY (where B is a symbol) in the Phrase-marker K; that is, $A \rightarrow XBY$ was one of the categorial rules used in generating this Phrase-marker. Then (A,B) constitutes a branch of K. Furthermore, if this occurrence of B immediately dominates ZCW (where C is a symbol), so that (B,C) is a branch, then (A,B,C) is a branch, etc. Suppose now that $(A_1, \cdots, A_n)$ is a branch of the generalized Phrase-marker K formed by base rules, and that $A_1 = A_n$. Then it must be that for some i, $1 \leqslant i \leqslant n$, $A_i = S$. In other words, the only way to form new deep structures is to insert elementary "propositions" — technically, base Phrase-markers — in other Phrase-markers. This is by no means a logically necessary feature of phrase structure grammars.

Notice that the schemata that underlie coordination (cf. note 7) also provide infinite generative capacity, but here too the true recursive property can apparently be limited to the schema $S \rightarrow S\#S\# \cdots \#S$, hence to rules introducing "propositions."

This formulation leaves unexplained some rather marginal phenomena (e.g., the source of such expressions as "very, very, . . . , very Adjective" and some more significant ones (e.g., the possibility of iterating Adverbials and various kinds of parenthetic elements, the status of which in general is unclear). For some discussion of Adverbial sequences, see Matthews (1961).

12. Cf. pp. 117–118. For some discussion, see Chomsky (1964, § 1.0, and forthcoming).

13. Notice, incidentally, that this identity condition need never be stated in the grammar, since it is a general condition on the functioning of grammars. This is important, since (as was pointed out by Lees, 1960a), the condition is not really identity of strings but rather total identity of structures, in all cases in which identity conditions appear in transformations. But to define identity of structures in terms of Analyzability it is necessary to use quantifiers; in fact, this may be the only case in which quantifiers must

appear in the structural analyses that define transformations. Extracting the identity condition from grammars, we are therefore able to formulate the structural analyses that define transformations strictly as Boolean conditions on Analyzability, thus greatly restricting the power of the theory of transformational grammar.

14. For discussion see Miller and Chomsky (1963); Schlesinger (1964); Miller and Isard (1964); and the résumé in Chapter 1, § 2.

15. See § 2.3.1 of Chapter 2, and § 1 of Chapter 4. A serious discussion of this question, as well as the question of dependency of syntax on semantics, awaits a development of the theory of universal semantics, that is, an account of the nature of semantic representation. Although various positions about these questions have been stated with great confidence and authority, the only serious work that I know of on the relation of these domains is that of Katz, Fodor, and Postal (see bibliography; for discussion of other claims that have been made, see Chomsky, 1957, and many other publications). For the moment, I see no reason to modify the view, expressed in Chomsky (1957) and elsewhere, that although, obviously, semantic considerations are relevant to the construction of general linguistic theory (that is, obviously the theory of syntax should be designed so that the syntactic structures exhibited for particular languages will support semantic interpretation), there is, at present, no way to show that semantic considerations play a role in the choice of the syntactic or phonological component of a grammar or that semantic features (in any significant sense of this term) play a role in the functioning of the syntactic or phonological rules. Thus no serious proposal has been advanced to show how semantic considerations can contribute to an evaluation procedure for such systems or provide some of the primary linguistic data on the basis of which they are selected. See Chapter 1, § 6, and Chapter 4, § 1, for some additional related discussion.

16. Some of the details of this modification are worked out in Fraser (forthcoming). The extent to which the complexity of the theory of derived constituent structure depends on the presence of permutations is quite clear, for example, from the analysis of these notions in Chomsky (1955, Chapter 8).

17. Notice that in this case the third term of the proper analysis is not strictly deleted. Rather, this term is deleted except for the feature [± Human], which then assumes its phonological shape (giving *who*, *which*, or *that*) by later rules. This is often true of what we are here calling erasure operations.

18. A natural notational decision would be to restrict the integers one and two to first and second person, respectively.

NOTES TO CHAPTER 4

1. Whether the rule is a rewriting rule or a substitution transformation — cf. Chapter 2, § 4.3 — does not concern us here; for convenience of exposition, we shall assume the latter.

2. To avoid what has been a persistent misunderstanding, it must be emphasized again that "grammaticalness" is being used here as a technical term, with no implication that deviant sentences are being "legislated against" as "without a function" or "illegitimate." Quite the contrary is true, as has repeatedly been stressed and illustrated, in discussions of generative grammar. For discussion, see Chomsky (1961) and many other references. The question as to whether the grammar should generate deviant sentences is purely terminological, having to do with nothing more than the technical sense of "generate." A descriptively adequate grammar must assign to each string a structural description that indicates the manner of its deviation from strict well-formedness (if any). A natural terminological decision would be to say that the grammar *directly generates the language* consisting of just the sentences that do not deviate at all (such as (3)), with their structural descriptions. The grammar *derivatively generates* all other strings (such as (1) and (2)), with their structural descriptions. These structural descriptions will indicate the manner and degree of deviance of the derivatively generated sentences. The principles that determine how interpretations can be imposed on deviant sentences may be universal (as suggested in Chomsky, 1955, 1961; Miller and Chomsky, 1963; and again here) or specific to a given language (as suggested in Katz, 1964a). This is a substantive issue, but many of the other questions that have been debated concerning these notions seem to me quite empty, having to do only with terminological decisions.

3. Recall that selectional rules, as illustrated earlier, are rules that insert Verbs and Adjectives into generalized Phrase-markers on the basis of the intrinsic syntactic features of the Nouns that appear in various positions. But not all of the rules referring to intrinsic syntactic features of Nouns are selectional rules; in particular, the rules violated in the formation of (4) involve such features but are not selectional rules.

4. Many of the Verbs of the category $[+[+ \text{Abstract}] \cdots - \cdots [+ \text{Animate}]]$ do not have Adjectival forms with *ing*, but these seem invariably to have other affixes as variants of *ing* (*bothersome* for *bothering*, *scary* for *scaring*, *impressive* for *impressing*, etc.).

5. These examples do not begin to exhaust the range of possibilities that must be considered in a full study of interpretation of deviant sentences. For one thing, they do not illustrate the use of order-

inversion as a stylistic device (cf. Chapter 2, § 4.4, for some discussion). The discussion of deviation from grammaticalness that has been carried on here offers no insight into this phenomenon. For example, consider the following line: "Me up at does/out of the floor/quietly Stare/a poisoned mouse/still who alive/is asking What/have i done that/You wouldn't have" (E. E. Cummings). This poses not the slightest difficulty or ambiguity of interpretation, and it would surely be quite beside the point to try to assign it a degree of deviation in terms of the number or kind of rules of the grammar that are violated in generating it.

6. Notice that the formulation given previously left an ambiguity in the latter case, which is resolved only by the convention that we now state.

7. We are, in effect, assuming the convention $e = [e, \cdots]$, where e is the null element. Notice that features are unordered in a complex symbol. As elsewhere in this discussion, I make no attempt here to present an absolutely precise account or to give these definitions in their simplest and most general forms.

8. Thus X is null if $[\alpha]$ is null; Y is null if $[\beta]$ is null.

9. This difficulty would, in fact, not arise if we were to give a somewhat different analysis of post-Verbal Adjectives in English, deriving them from underlying strings with Sentence-Complements to the Verbs. In some cases, this is surely correct (e.g., "John seems sad" from an underlying structure containing the base string "John is sad," which becomes "John seems to be sad," and then "John seems sad" by further transformations — similarly, in the case of "become" this analysis is well motivated, in particular, because it can provide a basis for excluding "become" from passivization), and it may be correct to extend it to many or all such cases. For some other proposals for derivation of certain of these forms, see Zierer (1964).

    It is worth noting that a condition like that imposed on W and V in the discussion of the schema (9) is probably necessary in the theory of transformations, although this problem has never been discussed explicitly.

10. I am indebted to Thomas Bever and Peter Rosenbaum for many interesting and suggestive comments relating to this question.

11. In many or all such cases, some notion of "generic" seems to be involved critically (I owe this observation to Barbara Hall). One might therefore try to show that part of the semantic effect of "generic" is to cancel semantic conflicts of certain sorts. Notice, incidentally, that the deep structure of each of the sentences of (15) will contain a string with *sincerity* as the Direct-Object of the Main Verb *frighten* (and with an unspecified Subject).

12. Interest in these questions can be traced to Humboldt (1836); for representative statements of his, see Chomsky (1964). See Ullmann (1959) for discussion of much related descriptive work. Also relevant are some psychological studies that have attempted to place a linguistic item in a context of somehow related items, such as Luria and Vinogradova (1959), and much current work in "componential analysis."

13. Although the sentences of (19i) are near-paraphrases, still it is by no means true that a "cooccurrence relation" of the sort that has been discussed by Harris (1957), Hiż (1961), and others holds between them. Thus *pompous* can be replaced quite naturally by *a friend* in "I regard John as ——————," but hardly in "John strikes me as —————— " (I owe this observation to J. Katz). It is clear, then, that the close meaning relation between *regard* and *strike* (involving, in particular, inversion of the Subject-Verb-Object relations) does not determine a corresponding similarity of distributional restrictions. The rules involving contextual features, in other words, may be partially independent of semantic properties. Such examples must be borne in mind if any attempt is made to give some substance to the widely voiced (but, for the moment, totally empty) claim that semantic considerations somehow determine syntactic structure or distributional properties.

I have been assuming, in discussing (19i) that the Subject-of *strikes* in the deep structure is *John*, but it should be noted that this is not at all obvious. One alternative would be to take the underlying structure to be *it⌒S — strikes me*, where *it⌒S* is an NP and S dominates the structure underlying "John is pompous." An obligatory transformation would give the structure underlying "it strikes me that John is pompous," and a further optional transformation would give "John strikes me as pompous." The lexical item *strike* of (19i) would then have very different strict subcategorization features from the phonetically identical item of "it struck me blind," while both would differ in strict subcategorization from *strike* in "he struck me," "he struck an outlandish pose," etc. (cf. note 15, Chapter 2). If this analysis can be justified on syntactic grounds, then the deep structures will be somewhat more appropriate for the semantic interpretation than assumed in the text. As several people have observed, there are other relevant syntactic differences between the paired examples of (19i). For example, such sentences as "John strikes me as pompous," "his remarks impress me as unintelligible" do not passivize, although the sentences "I regard John as pompous," "it struck me blind," and so on, are freely subject to passivization.

In connection with (19iii), Harris has suggested (1952, pp. 24–25) that it may be possible to express the meaning relation on distributional grounds, but his suggestions as to how this might be possible have not yet been developed to the point where their merits can be evaluated.

Notice that the problems mentioned here admit of no merely terminological solution. Thus we could perfectly well state the facts relating to (19) in terms of such new notions as "semantic subject," "semantic object," various kinds of "sememes," etc., but such proliferation of terminology contributes nothing toward clarifying the serious issues raised by such examples.

14. As pointed out in note 15, Chapter 2, a distinctive-feature matrix is simply a way of representing a set of abstract phonological features, so that a lexical entry (a formative) may be regarded simply as a set of features, with further structure defined on them in the manner suggested informally in this discussion.

15. With respect to selectional features, alternative (iv) is well motivated. See note 20.

To say that a feature is positively (negatively) specified is to say that it is marked + (respectively, −). Notice that these or any analogous conventions make a distinction amounting to the marked/ unmarked distinction that has often been discussed, though quite inconclusively, in connection with features and categories.

16. Such examples as "sincerity frightens" can be found, of course, but only as (rather mannered) transforms of "sincerity frightens Unspecified-Object," and so on. The possibilities for this are, in fact, quite limited — for example, no one would interpret "his sincerity was frightening" as ambiguous. Notice that words of the category of "frighten" do appear quite naturally as Intransitives in surface structures, as in "John frightens easily" (this in fact is much more general — cf. "the book reads easily," etc.). But this is irrelevant here. In such a case, the "grammatical Subject" is the "logical Object" — that is, the Direct Object of the deep structure "Unspecified-Subject frightens John easily." The often obligatory Adverbial of Manner, in these cases, suggests that one might seek a generalization involving also the passive transformation.

17. The latter would be interpretable only as a deviant sentence.

18. One might question the factual correctness of this, particularly in the case of {[− Count], [± Abstract]}. I have been assuming that the features {[− Count], [+ Abstract]} characterize the true Abstract Nouns such as *virtue, justice,* while the features {[− Count], [− Abstract]} characterize the Mass Nouns such as *water, dirt.* But there is a subdivision of Inanimate Count Nouns that seems to correspond to this, namely the distinction into [+ Concrete], such

as *table, mountain,* and [− Concrete], such as *problem, effort.* If it turns out that the features [± Concrete] and [± Abstract] (as subfeatures of [− Animate] and [− Count], respectively) should be identified, then the feature [Abstract] would be cross-classifying rather than hierarchic with respect to [+ Count]. This question is not easy to resolve without much more empirical study, however.

19. The desirability of such a convention was pointed out by Paul Postal.

20. Notice that if we were explicitly to list positively specified rather than negatively specified selectional features in the lexicon, then this convention would have to be extended to selectional features as well. Thus we should not want to have to list both the features corresponding to "takes Human Subject" and "takes Animate Subject" for "run," for example. Such a convention would, in effect, treat a selectional feature as itself being a kind of complex symbol.

21. As always, there are a few exceptions that require separate statement. Recall that we have presented some reasons for regarding the phrase *by⌒passive* (where *passive* is a dummy terminal symbol, replaceable, in fact, by the universal dummy symbol Δ) as a Manner Adverbial. A Verb that can appear only in the passive would therefore be an exception to this rule (e.g., "he is said to be a rather decent fellow," or, perhaps, such forms as "he was shorn of all dignity").

22. The phonological redundancy rules are also subject to certain universal constraints, and there is no doubt that, for all features, these constraints go well beyond what has been illustrated here. As these are formulated, they will also play the role of general conventions (i.e., aspects of the general definition of "human language") that can be relied on to reduce the specificity of particular grammars.

See Halle 1959a, 1959b, 1961, 1962a, 1964. Cf. also the discussion of evaluation procedures and explanatory adequacy in Chapter 1, §§ 6, 7, and in the references given there. Notice that Halle's definition of the notion "phonologically admissible" (i.e., "accidental" versus "systematic gap") suggests what in Chapter 1 was called a "formal" rather than a "substantive" linguistic universal, though there are, no doubt, also substantive constraints to be discovered here.

24. As possible examples of "accidental gaps" we might point to the nonexistence of a Verb X taking as Direct-Object expressions designating animals and having otherwise the same meaning as the transitive "grow," so that "he X's dogs" is parallel in meaning

to "he grows corn" ("raise" appears to cover both senses); or the
absence of a word that bears to plants the relation that "corpse"
bears to animals (this example was suggested by T. G. Bever).

25. Thus we can regard the category of case in German as a four-
valued, gender as a three-valued, and number as a two-valued
dimension, and we can consider all Nouns as being arrayed in a
single multivalued dimension of declensional classes. Presumably,
this is not the optimal analysis, and further structure must be
imposed along these "dimensions." It is also possible to try to give
a language-independent characterization of these categories. These
are important matters and have been the subject of much study
that, however, goes well beyond the scope of this discussion. I
shall therefore consider only an unstructured description in these
illustrative examples.

26. Simply for expository purposes, let us take the integers in the
order of conventional presentations, so that [1 Gender] is Masculine, [2 Number] is Plural, [2 Case] is Genitive, and *Bruder* is
assigned to Class 1 along the "dimension" of declensional class.
Notice that we have assumed all along that features are "binary"
— that they simply partition their domain of applicability into
two disjoint classes. There was no logical necessity for this. In
phonology, it seems clear that the distinctive features are, in fact,
best regarded as binary in their phonological function (cf., e.g.,
Halle, 1957), though obviously not always in their phonetic function. Thus in the case of the feature Stress, we can easily find five
or more degrees that must be marked in English, and other
phonetic features would also have to be regarded as multivalued
in a detailed grammar. It has been maintained (cf. Jakobson,
1936) that such "dimensions" as Case should also be analyzed into
a hierarchy of binary features (like phonological distinctive features), but we shall not consider this question here.

27. That is, the categorial rule that develops Nouns will not be $N \to \Delta$
(cf. p. 122), but rather $N \to [\Delta, \alpha \text{ Number}]$ ($\alpha = +$ or $-$ for English
or German, though it may have more values or a different organiza-
tion of values — cf. note 25 — for other systems).

28. Actually, in descriptivist grammars of the item-and-arrangement
type the latter might be omitted, since its only function is to permit some generality to be introduced into the "morphophonemic"
rules and since these grammars are, in fact, designed in such a way
as to exclude the possibility of all but the most elementary general
rules. See Chomsky (1964, pp. 31f.) for discussion.

29. This defect of morphemic analysis of inflectional systems, which
is quite serious, in practice, was pointed out to me by Morris
Halle.

30. Thus an alternative to the analysis presented in (30) would be to regard a lexical item such as *Bruder* as consisting of a Stem followed by an Ending, and to regard the Ending as belonging to the paradigmatic categories.

31. In the last few years, there has been very intensive and fruitful study of the transformational cycle of Russian and Latvian phonology (for references, see Chomsky, 1964, note 6, p. 14). The rules that constitute this system apply to Phrase-markers, and consequently their formulation depends very heavily on answers to the questions being considered here. There has, so far, been no serious investigation of how a transformational cycle applies to a feature system and to Phrase-markers such as (30). When this is clarified, it will be possible to bring phonological evidence to bear on the question of morphemic versus paradigmatic representation of inflectional systems. For the moment, the empirical evidence suggests that the ordering of the transformational cycle in phonology is determined completely by categories, not features (though of course certain rules may be restricted in application in terms of syntactic features). This is, furthermore, the most natural assumption, if we regard the features as actually constituting the terminal symbol (the formative).

32. This formative might, in fact, be regarded as consisting of the feature [+ Definite], hence as a degenerate complex symbol that is expanded by the rule into the full complex symbol [+ Definite, α Gender, β Number, γ Case]. See note 38 for some support for this assumption.

33. Variables over feature specifications were used in Chomsky, Halle, and Lukoff (1956) and Halle and Chomsky (1960), in developing the transformational stress cycle. The idea of using them to deal with assimilation is due to Halle (1962b). T. G. Bever has pointed out that the same device can be applied to a description of various kinds of alternations that involve feature shift (e.g., Ablaut). Cf. Bever (1963), Bever and Langendoen (1963).

34. See Lees (1961) and Smith (1961). When the two Adjectives are paired in a rather special way that is for the present poorly understood, the transformation is not blocked even when they are distinct. Thus we have such forms as "this is taller than that is wide." Cf. Harris (1957), p. 314.

35. Notice that the distinction that is emerging in this discussion is not coincident with that suggested in note 30.

It is interesting to note that the correctness of such examples as (40) has been questioned. In one of the earliest descriptive studies of French, Vaugelas (1647, pp. 461–462) maintains that such a *façon de parler* cannot be considered either "absolument mauvaise" or "fort bonne," and suggests that it be avoided when masculine and feminine forms of the Adjective differ. Thus, a man speaking to a woman should not say *je suis plus beau que vous*, but should rather ("pour parler regulièrement") resort to the paraphrase *je suis plus beau que vous n'êtes belle*, although it would be perfectly all right for him to say *je suis plus riche que vous*.

36. This fact, pointed out to me by Brandon Qualls, raises various difficulties for the analysis of comparatives. In particular, if such sentences as (41iii) are regarded as derived from "I know several lawyers (who are) more successful than Bill" by Noun-Adjective inversion following deletion of "who are," as seems quite plausible, we must somehow account for such facts as the following: the impossibility of "I know a more clever man than Mary" or "I have never seen a heavier book than this rock," although the presumed sources of these (namely, "I know a man (who is) more clever than Mary" and "I have never seen a book (which is) heavier than this rock") are perfectly all right; the fact that the sentence "I have never read a more intricate poem than *Tristram Shandy*" implies that the latter is a poem, whereas the sentence "I have never read a poem (which is) more intricate than *Tristram Shandy*," which, in this view, is taken to be its source, does not imply that *Tristram Shandy* is a poem; etc.

   Again, as throughout this discussion, I should like to emphasize that there is no particular difficulty in formulating an *ad hoc* system of transformational rules that will have the desired properties. The problem, rather, is to provide some explanation for such phenomena as those of the preceding paragraph.

37. The deletion of the pluralized non-Definite Article is automatic, in this position.

38. Similar considerations may account for another apparent violation of the general condition on recoverability of deletions. As has frequently been observed, the identity condition for relativization involves only the Noun, and not the Determiner of the deleted Noun Phrase. Thus from "I have a [# the friend is from England #] friend" we can form, by relativization, "I have a friend (who is) from England" in the usual way. The deleted Noun Phrase is "the friend," and the problem is the deletion of the Article, which differs from the Article that is used to erase it by the relative transformation. The embedded sentence could not be "a friend is from England," in which case the problem would not arise, since definiteness of the Article is automatic in this position. But the fact that definiteness is obligatory suggests that in the underlying Phrase-

marker the Article be left unspecified for definiteness, this being added by a "redundancy rule" (in this case, an obligatory transformation). If this is the correct analysis, then by the principle just established, deletion of the Article will be permissible, since in its underlying form it is nondistinct from the Article of the Noun Phrase of the matrix sentence.

Note that this decision requires a feature analysis for Articles, with [± Definite] taken as a syntactic feature.

39. Notice that although *sad*, for example, need not be marked in the lexicon for post-Animateness (if we decide that what is involved here is not a matter of homonymity), it may very well be assigned contextual features corresponding to various subfeatures of [− Animate], so as to characterize as deviant such sentences as "the pencil is sad," which cannot receive an interpretation analogous to that of "the book was sad." This matter has no relevance to the point at issue, though it raises nontrivial problems of a different sort.

40. We oversimplify somewhat. Thus the constituent base Phrasemarker, in this case, might contain a certain nominalization morpheme in place of the pre-Aspect part of the Auxiliary.

41. These constructions are interesting in many respects. See Lees (1960a, pp. 64f.), Chomsky (1964, pp. 47f.), and Katz and Postal (1964, pp. 120f.) for discussion.

42. Here, too, we might raise the question whether the nominalization element should be represented as a morpheme *nom* or as one of the features $F_1, \cdots, F_m$ — in this case, a feature added by the transformation.

43. A detailed study of one system of essentially this sort, namely formation of compound nouns, is presented in Lees (1960a, Chapter 4, and appendices). See now also Zimmer (1964).

44. Cf. also note 30. Perhaps it will be possible to rephrase this convention as part of a general definition of the notion "word." That is, one might try to state a general rule determining placement of word boundaries in terms of lexical categories and branching within the scope of complex symbols. This possibility was suggested by some observations of Paul Postal's, and should be further explored.

45. A related class of problems is examined briefly by Harris (1957, § 4.5), in his discussion of "quasi-transformations." Bolinger, in various articles (e.g., Bolinger, 1961), has listed many examples of poorly understood quasi-productive processes. Such lists simply indicate areas where all presently known theories of language have failed to provide any substantial insight, and they can be extended in many ways, with little difficulty. Bolinger suggests that

his examples support an alternative theory of grammar, but this seems to me an entirely unwarranted conclusion, for reasons discussed elsewhere (in particular, Chomsky, 1964, p. 54).

Bibliography

Aristotle. *De Anima*. Translated by J. A. Smith. In R. McKeon (ed.), *The Basic Works of Aristotle*. New York: Random House, 1941.

Arnauld, A., and P. Nicole (1662). *La Logique, ou l'art de penser*.

Austin, J. L. (1956). "A plea for excuses." *Proceedings of the Aristotelian Society*. Reprinted in J. O. Urmson and G. J. Warnock (eds.), *Philosophical Papers of J. L. Austin*. London: Oxford University Press, 1961.

Bach, E. (1964). "Subcategories in transformational grammars." In H. Lunt (ed.), *Proceedings of the Ninth International Congress of Linguists*. The Hague: Mouton & Co.

Bar-Hillel, Y. (1954). "Logical syntax and semantics." *Language, 30*, pp. 230–237.

—— (1960). "The present status of automatic translation of languages." In F. L. Alt (ed.), *Advances in Computers*, Vol. I, pp. 91-163. New York: Academic Press.

——, A. Kasher, and E. Shamir (1963). *Measures of Syntactic Complexity*. Report for U.S. Office of Naval Research, Information Systems Branch. Jerusalem.

Beattie, J. (1788). *Theory of Language*. London.

Bever, T. G. (1963). "The e-o Ablaut in Old English." *Quarterly Progress Report*, No. 69, Research Laboratory of Electronics, M.I.T., pp. 203–207.

——, and T. Langendoen (1963). "The reciprocating cycle of the Indo-European e-o Ablaut." *Quarterly Progress Report*, No. 69, Research Laboratory of Electronics, M.I.T., pp. 202–203.

——, and P. Rosenbaum (forthcoming). *Two Studies on Syntax and Semantics*. Bedford, Mass.: Mitre Corporation Technical Reports.

Bloch, B. (1950). "Studies in colloquial Japanese IV: Phonemics." *Language, 26*, pp. 86–125. Reprinted in M. Joos (ed.), *Readings in Linguistics*. Washington, 1957.

Bloomfield, L. (1933). *Language*. New York: Holt.

Bloomfield, M. (1963). "A grammatical approach to personification allegory." *Modern Philology, 60*, pp. 161–171.

Bolinger, D. L. (1961). "Syntactic blends and other matters." *Language, 37*, pp. 366–381.

Breland, K., and M. Breland (1961). "The misbehavior of organisms." *American Psychologist, 16*, pp. 681–684.

Chomsky, N. (1951). *Morphophonemics of Modern Hebrew.* Unpublished Master's thesis, University of Pennsylvania.

—— (1955). *The Logical Structure of Linguistic Theory.* Mimeographed, M.I.T. Library, Cambridge, Mass.

—— (1956). "Three models for the description of language." *I.R.E. Transactions on Information Theory*, Vol. IT-2, pp. 113–124. Reprinted, with corrections, in R. D. Luce, R. Bush, and E. Galanter (eds.), *Readings in Mathematical Psychology*, Vol. II. New York: Wiley, 1965.

—— (1957). *Syntactic Structures.* The Hague: Mouton & Co.

—— (1959a). "On certain formal properties of grammars." *Information and Control, 2*, pp. 137–167. Reprinted in R. D. Luce, R. Bush, and E. Galanter (eds.), *Readings in Mathematical Psychology*, Vol. II. New York: Wiley, 1965.

—— (1959b). Review of Skinner (1957). *Language, 35*, pp. 26–58. Reprinted in Fodor and Katz (1964).

—— (1961). "Some methodological remarks on generative grammar." *Word, 17*, pp. 219–239. Reprinted in part in Fodor and Katz (1964).

—— (1962a). "A transformational approach to syntax." In A. A. Hill (ed.), *Proceedings of the 1958 Conference on Problems of Linguistic Analysis in English*, pp. 124–148. Austin, Texas. Reprinted in Fodor and Katz (1964).

—— (1962b). "Explanatory models in linguistics." In E. Nagel, P. Suppes, and A. Tarski, *Logic, Methodology and Philosophy of Science.* Stanford, California: Stanford University Press.

—— (1963). "Formal properties of grammars." In R. D. Luce, R. Bush, and E. Galanter (eds.), *Handbook of Mathematical Psychology*, Vol. II, pp. 323–418. New York: Wiley.

—— (1964). *Current Issues in Linguistic Theory.* The Hague: Mouton & Co. A slightly earlier version appears in Fodor and Katz (1964). This is a revised and expanded version of a paper presented to the session "The logical basis of linguistic theory," at the Ninth International Congress of Linguists, Cambridge, Mass., 1962. It appears under the title of the session in H. Lunt (ed.), *Proceedings* of the Congress. The Hague: Mouton & Co., 1964.

—— (in press). "Topics in the theory of generative grammar." In T. A. Sebeok (ed.), *Current Trends in Linguistics.* Vol. III. *Linguistic Theory.* The Hague: Mouton & Co.

—— (forthcoming). "Cartesian Linguistics."

——, M. Halle, and F. Lukoff (1956). "On accent and juncture in English." In M. Halle, H. Lunt, and H. MacLean (eds.), *For Roman Jakobson*, pp. 65–80. The Hague: Mouton & Co.

——, and G. A. Miller (1963). "Introduction to the formal analysis of natural languages." In R. D. Luce, R. Bush, and E. Galanter (eds.), *Handbook of Mathematical Psychology*, Vol. II, pp. 269–322. New York: Wiley.

——, and M. P. Schützenberger (1963). "The algebraic theory of context-free languages." In P. Braffort and D. Hirschberg (eds.), *Computer Programming and Formal Systems*, pp. 119–161, *Studies in Logic Series*. Amsterdam: North-Holland.

Cordemoy, G. de (1667). *A Philosophicall Discourse Concerning Speech*. The English translation is dated 1668.

Cudworth, R. (1731). *A Treatise Concerning Eternal and Immutable Morality*. Edited by E. Chandler.

Curry, H. B. (1961). "Some logical aspects of grammatical structure." In R. Jakobson (ed.), *Structure of Language and Its Mathematical Aspects, Proceedings of the Twelfth Symposium in Applied Mathematics*, pp. 56–68. Providence, R. I.: American Mathematical Society.

Descartes, R. (1641). *Meditations*.

—— (1647). "Notes directed against a certain programme." Both works by Descartes translated by E. S. Haldane and G. T. Ross in *The Philosophical Works of Descartes*, Vol. I. New York: Dover, 1955.

Diderot, D. (1751). *Lettre sur les Sourds et Muets*. Page references are to J. Assézat (ed.), *Oeuvres Complètes de Diderot*, Vol. I (1875). Paris: Garnier Frères.

Dixon, R. W. (1963). *Linguistic Science and Logic*. The Hague: Mouton & Co.

Du Marsais, C. Ch. (1729). *Les véritables principes de la grammaire*. On the dating of this manuscript, see Sahlin (1928), p. ix.

—— (1769). *Logique et principes de grammaire*.

Fillmore, C. J. (1963). "The position of embedding transformations in a grammar." *Word, 19*, pp. 208–231.

Fodor, J. A., and J. J. Katz (eds.) (1964). *The Structure of Language: Readings in the Philosophy of Language*. Englewood Cliffs, N. J.: Prentice-Hall.

Foot, P. (1961). "Goodness and choice." *Proceedings of the Aristotelian Society*, Supplementary Volume 35, pp. 45–80.

Fraser, B. (1963). "The position of conjoining transformations in a grammar." Mimeographed. Bedford, Mass.: Mitre Corporation.

—— (forthcoming) "On the notion 'derived constituent structure.'"

Proceedings of the 1964 Magdeburg Symposium, Zeichen und System der Sprache.

Frishkopf, L. S., and M. H. Goldstein (1963). "Responses to acoustic stimuli from single units in the eighth nerve of the bullfrog." *Journal of the Acoustical Society of America, 35*, pp. 1219–1228.

Ginsburg, S., and H. G. Rice (1962). "Two families of languages related to ALGOL." *Journal of the Association for Computing Machinery, 10*, pp. 350–371.

Gleason, H. A. (1961). *Introduction to Descriptive Linguistics*, second edition. New York: Holt, Rinehart & Winston.

——— (1964). "The organization of language: a stratificational view." In C. I. J. M. Stuart (ed.), *Report of the Fifteenth Annual Round Table Meeting on Linguistics and Language Studies*, pp. 75–95. Washington, D. C.: Georgetown University Press.

Greenberg, J. H. (1963). "Some universals of grammar with particular reference to the order of meaningful elements." In J. H. Greenberg (ed.), *Universals of Language*, pp. 58–90. Cambridge: M.I.T. Press.

Gleitman, L. (1961). "Conjunction with *and,*" *Transformations and Discourse Analysis Projects*, No. 40, mimeographed. Philadelphia: University of Pennsylvania.

Gross, M. (1964). "On the equivalence of models of language used in the fields of mechanical translation and information retrieval." *Information Storage and Retrieval, 2*, pp. 43–57.

Hall, B. (1964). Review of Šaumjan and Soboleva (1963). *Language 40*, pp. 397–410.

Halle, M. (1957). "In defense of the number two." In E. Pulgram (ed.), *Studies Presented to Joshua Whatmough*. The Hague: Mouton & Co.

——— (1959a). "Questions of linguistics." *Nuovo Cimento, 13*, pp. 494–517.

———(1959b). *The Sound Pattern of Russian*. The Hague: Mouton & Co.

——— (1961). "On the role of the simplicity in linguistic description." In R. Jakobson (ed.), *Structure of Language and Its Mathematical Aspects, Proceedings of the Twelfth Symposium in Applied Mathematics*, pp. 89–94. Providence, R.I.: American Mathematical Society.

——— (1962a). "Phonology in generative grammar." *Word, 18*, pp. 54–72. Reprinted in Fodor and Katz (1964).

——— (1962b). "A descriptive convention for treating assimilation and dissimilation." *Quarterly Progress Report*, No. 66, Research Laboratory of Electronics, M.I.T., pp. 295–296.

——— (1964). "On the bases of phonology." In Fodor and Katz (1964).

————, and N. Chomsky (1960). "The morphophonemics of English." *Quarterly Progress Report*, No. 58, Research Laboratory of Electronics, M.I.T., pp. 275–281.

———— (in preparation). *The Sound Pattern of English*. New York: Harper & Row.

————, and K. Stevens (1962). "Speech recognition: a model and a program for research." *I.R.E. Transactions in Information Theory*, Vol. IT-8, pp. 155–159. Reprinted in Fodor and Katz (1964).

Harman, G. H. (1963). "Generative grammars without transformational rules: a defense of phrase structure." *Language, 39*, pp. 597–616.

Harris, Z. S. (1951). *Methods in Structural Linguistics*. Chicago: University of Chicago Press.

———— (1952). "Discourse analysis." *Language, 28*, pp. 18–23.

———— (1954). "Distributional structure." *Word, 10*, pp. 146–162.

———— (1957). "Co-occurrence and transformation in linguistic structure." *Language, 33*, pp. 293–340.

Held, R., and S. J. Freedman (1963). "Plasticity in human sensorimotor control." *Science, 142*, pp. 455–462.

————, and A. Hein (1963), "Movement-produced stimulation in the development of visually guided behavior." *Journal of Comparative and Physiological Psychology, 56*, pp. 872–876.

Herbert of Cherbury (1624). *De Veritate*. Translated by M. H. Carré (1937). University of Bristol Studies, No. 6.

Hiż, H. (1961). "Congrammaticality, batteries of transformations and grammatical categories." In R. Jakobson (ed.), *Structure of Language and Its Mathematical Aspects, Proceedings of the Twelfth Symposium in Applied Mathematics*, pp. 43–50. Providence, R.I.: American Mathematical Society.

Hockett, C. F. (1958). *A Course in Modern Linguistics*. New York: Macmillan.

———— (1961). "Linguistic elements and their relations." *Language, 37*, pp. 29–53.

Hubel, D. H., and T. N. Wiesel (1962). "Receptive fields, binocular interaction and functional architecture in the cat's visual cortex." *Journal of Physiology, 160*, pp. 106–154.

Hull, C. L. (1943). *Principles of Behavior*. New York: Appleton-Century-Crofts.

Humboldt, W. von. (1836). *Über die Verschiedenheit des Menschlichen Sprachbaues*. Berlin.

Hume, D. (1748). *An Enquiry Concerning Human Understanding*.

Jakobson, R. (1936). "Beitrag zur allgemeinen Kasuslehre." *Travaux du Cercle Linguistique de Prague, 6*, pp. 240–288.

Jespersen, O. (1924). *Philosophy of Grammar*. London: Allen & Unwin.

Katz, J. J. (1964a). "Semi-sentences." In Fodor and Katz (1964).

——— (1964b). "Analyticity and contradiction in natural language." In Fodor and Katz (1964).

——— (1964c). "Mentalism in linguistics." *Language, 40*, pp. 124–137.

——— (1964d). "Semantic theory and the meaning of 'good.' " *Journal of Philosophy*.

——— (forthcoming). "Innate ideas."

———, and J. A. Fodor. "The structure of a semantic theory." *Language, 39*, pp. 170–210. Reprinted in Fodor & Katz (1964).

———, and J. A. Fodor (1964). "A reply to Dixon's 'A trend in semantics.' " *Linguistics, 3*, pp. 19–29.

———, and P. Postal (1964). *An Integrated Theory of Linguistic Descriptions*. Cambridge, Mass.: M.I.T. Press.

Klima, E. S. (1964). "Negation in English." In Fodor and Katz (1964).

Lancelot, C., A. Arnauld, *et al.* (1660). *Grammaire générale et raisonnée*.

Lees, R. B. (1957). Review of Chomsky (1957). *Language, 33*, pp. 375–407.

——— (1960a). *The Grammar of English Nominalizations*. The Hague: Mouton & Co.

——— (1960b). "A multiply ambiguous adjectival construction in English." *Language, 36*, pp. 207–221.

——— (1961). "Grammatical analysis of the English comparative construction." *Word, 17*, pp. 171–185.

———, and E. S. Klima (1963). "Rules for English pronominalization." *Language, 39*, pp. 17–28.

Leibniz, G. W. *New Essays Concerning Human Understanding*. Translated by A. G. Langley. LaSalle, Ill.: Open Court, 1949.

Leitzmann, A. (1908). *Briefwechsel zwischen W. von Humboldt und A. W. Schlegel*. Halle: Niemeyer.

Lemmon, W. B., and G. H. Patterson (1964). "Depth perception in sheep." *Science, 145*, p. 835.

Lenneberg, E. (1960). "Language, evolution, and purposive behavior." In S. Diamond (ed.), *Culture in History: Essays in Honor of Paul Radin*. New York: Columbia University Press. Reprinted in a revised and extended version under the title "The capacity for language acquisition" in Fodor and Katz (1964).

——— (in preparation). *The Biological Bases of Language*.

Lettvin, J. Y., H. R. Maturana, W. S. McCulloch, and W. H. Pitts (1959). "What the frog's eye tells the frog's brain." *Proceedings of the I.R.E., 47*, pp. 1940–1951.

Luria, A. R., and O. S. Vinogradova (1959). "An objective investigation of the dynamics of semantic systems." *British Journal of Psychology, 50*, pp. 89–105.

Matthews, G. H. (1964). *Hidatsa Syntax*. The Hague: Mouton & Co.

Matthews, P. H. (1961). "Transformational grammar." *Archivum Linguisticum, 13,* pp. 196–209.

Miller, G. A., and N. Chomsky (1963). "Finitary models of language users." In R. D. Luce, R. Bush, and E. Galanter (eds.), *Handbook of Mathematical Psychology,* Vol. II, Ch. 13, pp. 419–492. New York: Wiley.

———, E. Galanter, and K. H. Pribram (1960). *Plans and the Structure of Behavior.* New York: Henry Holt.

———, and S. Isard (1963). "Some perceptual consequences of linguistic rules." *Journal of Verbal Learning and Verbal Behavior, 2,* No. 3, pp. 217–228.

———, and S. Isard (1964). "Free recall of self-embedded English sentences." *Information and Control, 7,* pp. 292–303.

———, and D. A. Norman (1964). *Research on the Use of Formal Languages in the Behavioral Sciences.* Semi-annual Technical Report, Department of Defense, Advanced Research Projects Agency, January–June 1964, pp. 10–11. Cambridge: Harvard University, Center for Cognitive Studies.

———, and M. Stein (1963). *Grammarama.* Scientific Report No. CS-2, December. Cambridge: Harvard University, Center for Cognitive Studies.

Ornan, U. (1964). *Nominal Compounds in Modern Literary Hebrew.* Unpublished doctoral dissertation, Jerusalem, Hebrew University.

Paul, H. (1886). *Prinzipien der Sprachgeschichte,* second edition. Translated into English by H. A. Strong. London: Longmans, Green & Co., 1891.

Peshkovskii, A. M. (1956). *Russkii Sintaksis v Nauchnom Osveshchenii.* Moscow.

Postal, P. M. (1962a). *Some Syntactic Rules in Mohawk.* Unpublished doctoral dissertation, New Haven, Yale University.

——— (1962b). "On the limitations of context-free phrase-structure description." *Quarterly Progress Report* No. 64, Research Laboratory of Electronics, M.I.T., pp. 231–238.

——— (1964a). *Constituent Structure: A Study of Contemporary Models of Syntactic Description.* The Hague: Mouton & Co.

——— (1964b). "Underlying and superficial linguistic structure." *Harvard Educational Review, 34,* pp. 246–266.

——— (1964c). "Limitations of phrase structure grammars." In Fodor and Katz (1964).

Quine, W. V. (1960). *Word and Object.* Cambridge, Mass.: M.I.T. Press, and New York: Wiley.

Reichling, A. (1961). "Principles and methods of syntax: cryptanalytical formalism." *Lingua, 10,* pp. 1–17.

Reid, T. (1785). *Essays on the Intellectual Powers of Man.* Page references are to the abridged edition by A. D. Woozley, 1941. London: Macmillan and Co.

Rosenbloom, P. (1950). *The Elements of Mathematical Logic*. New York: Dover.

Russell, B. (1940). *An Inquiry into Meaning and Truth*. London: Allen & Unwin.

Ryle, G. (1931). "Systematically misleading expressions." *Proceedings of the Aristotelian Society*. Reprinted in A. G. N. Flew (ed.), *Logic and Language*, first series. Oxford: Blackwell, 1951.

——— (1953). "Ordinary language." *Philosophical Review, 62*, pp. 167–186.

Sahlin, G. (1928). *César Chesneau du Marsais et son rôle dans l'évolution de la grammaire générale*. Paris: Presses Universitaires.

Šaumjan, S. K., and P. A. Soboleva (1963). *Applikativnaja poroždajuščaja model' i isčislenie transformacij v russkom jazyke*. Moscow: Izdatel'stvo Akademii Nauk SSSR.

Schachter, P. (1962). Review: R. B. Lees, "Grammar of English nominalizations." *International Journal of American Linguistics, 28*, pp. 134–145.

Schlesinger, I. (1964). *The Influence of Sentence Structure on the Reading Process*. Unpublished doctoral dissertation, Jerusalem, Hebrew University.

Shamir, E. (1961). "On sequential grammars." Technical Report No. 7, O.N.R. Information Systems Branch, November 1961. To appear in *Zeitschrift für Phonetik, Sprachwissenschaft and Kommunikationsforschung*.

Skinner, B. F. (1957). *Verbal Behavior*. New York: Appleton-Century-Crofts.

Smith, C. S. (1961). "A class of complex modifiers in English." *Language, 37*, pp. 342–365.

Stockwell, R., and P. Schachter (1962). "Rules for a segment of English syntax." Mimeographed, Los Angeles, University of California.

Sutherland, N. S. (1959). "Stimulus analyzing mechanisms." *Mechanization of Thought Processes*, Vol. II, National Physical Laboratory Symposium No. 10, London.

——— (1964). "Visual discrimination in animals." *British Medical Bulletin, 20*, pp. 54–59.

Sweet, H. (1913). *Collected Papers*, arranged by H. C. Wyld. Oxford: Clarendon Press.

Twaddell, W. F. (1935). *On Defining the Phoneme. Language Monograph No. 16*. Reprinted in part in M. Joos (ed.), *Reading in Linguistics*. Washington: 1957.

Uhlenbeck, E. M. (1963). "An appraisal of transformation theory." *Lingua, 12*, pp. 1–18.

———— (1964). Discussion in the session "Logical basis of linguistic theory." In H. Lunt (ed.), *Proceedings of the Ninth Congress of Linguists*, pp. 981–983. The Hague: Mouton & Co.

Ullmann, S. (1959). *The Principles of Semantics*. Second edition. Glasgow: Jackson, Son & Co.

Vaugelas, C. F. de (1647). *Remarques sur la langue Française*. Facsimile edition, Paris: Librairie E. Droz, 1934.

Wilson, J. C. (1926). *Statement and Inference*, Vol. I. Oxford: Clarendon Press.

Wittgenstein, L. (1953). *Philosophical Investigations*. Oxford: Blackwell's.

Yngve, V. (1960). "A model and a hypothesis for language structure." *Proceedings of the American Philosophical Society, 104*, pp. 444–466.

Zierer, E. (1964). "Linking verbs and non-linking verbs. *Lenguaje y Ciencias, 12*, pp. 13–20.

Zimmer, K. E. (1964). *Affixal Negation in English and Other Languages*. Monograph No. 5, Supplement to *Word, 20*.

Index